WIT
WATCHM
THE BENCH

A BOOK FOR THE PRACTICAL WATCHMAKER, THE STUDENT AND ALL INTERESTED IN THE WATCH TRADE

ALSO FOR THOSE ENGAGED IN THE AIRCRAFT INSTRUMENT MAKING AND REPAIRING INDUSTRY

BY

DONALD DE CARLE, F.B.H.I.

Medal of the B.H.I.

City and Guilds Honors, Etc.

FIFTH EDITION

"(I) It is universally allowed that the most ordinary clock with a royal pendulum measures time better than any watch constructed in the manner hitherto practiced. And,

"(II) That watches are, in general, as well executed as clocks. From which it is evident,

"(III) That clocks derive their superiority from principle, and that a due attention to their natural properties may, at most, be the means of improving watch-work."

Alexander Cumming
(*The Elements of Clock and Watch-work*)

February, 1766

PREFACE TO FOURTH EDITION

Recent events have shown that watchmakers, as craftsmen, are valuable in other branches of small mechanics, such as aircraft instrument makers and repairers, etc. No doubt this is due to the peculiar training watchmakers receive, peculiar in the sense that such men are, or should be, meticulous as to detail. They are not necessarily used to working to blue prints and using the micrometer, but are particularly suited to such work and owing to the high degree of mechanical intelligence the average watchmaker possesses he is quickly adaptable.

The foregoing and many requests have prompted me to revise this book and delete some matter which can be omitted until more peaceful times, and to substitute material which should help the prospective craftsman and, I hope, act as a "refresher" to the experienced man.

It would not be desirable to describe in detail the making of all the parts of a watch; various pieces have been selected with the view that the method described should cover the procedure when making parts not mentioned.

I should like to place on record my grateful appreciation of Dr. J. Bradbury Winter's help in reading through the manuscript for the new edition of this book. Also my thanks to Mr. E. A. Ayres, the artist, who has, with considerable skill (and some patience in bearing with me), made the majority of the sketches.

DONALD DE CARLE

PREFACE TO FIFTH EDITION

The fact that a fifth edition, making the ninth impression of this book, has been called for is very gratifying to me.

It indicates the extensive demand for such a book, and my concern has been to make it as accurate as possible. Professor D. S. Torrens has kindly read through the fourth edition, and has made many suggestions, which I have adopted, and this new edition should be the better for his help.

DONALD DE CARLE

LONDON, 1945

PREFACE TO FIRST EDITION

Before placing a book such as this before my readers, the thought that arises is, "Has it been done before?" Broadly speaking, the answer is "Yes, many times," but if one is deterred by what has been done, then nothing remains to be done.

There are, however, various viewpoints, and in this book I have attempted to explain mine. Further, I have viewed the subject as if the reader were sitting with me at the bench. I have not left the matter with "and then we do this," but have explained how it is done, and here, I believe, this book is unique.

There are many books of reference on this trade, but my experience is that the majority do not tell you how to do the work. They tell you what to do, and leave it at that.

I sincerely trust, therefore, that this slight contribution will help those who have not been able to avail themselves of direct tuition in the matters this book deals with.

I should like to place on record my thanks to Messrs. A. Baume, Paul Ditisheim, J. Graham, E. H. Golay, and A. L. Fraissard, for their assistance, and also to Messrs. Grimshaw, Baxter & Elliott, Ltd., for illustrations of tools.

DONALD DE CARLE

Table of Contents

Chapter 4 – The Mainspring and Barrel 99

Chapter 5 – The Train 122

Chapter 7 – The Balance and Balance Spring 170

CHAPTER 1

THE WORKSHOP

In order to obtain a steady light, the workshop should face the north. We shall not then suffer by the glare of the sun, and consequently there will not be such a marked variation of light during the day-time as would be the case in a shop, say, facing south.

Another good position is at the top of the building, as we then benefit by the sky light, and the light which enters the shop will not be the reflected light of the buildings opposite, as would be the case if the workshop were on a lower floor.

It is obviously advisable to have the benches placed as near the windows as possible. Should the staff of the workshop be more than can be seated, at the windows, the benches should be arranged in rows facing the window. Make sure there is sufficient room to pass freely behind the men to prevent interruptions.

The Bench

Now regarding the actual bench, it should be of such a height as to allow a man to work comfortably when standing; a high stool should be provided for sitting. Such a bench has the advantage of allowing a change of position during work; for instance, after the movement under repair is completed, he can stand, push the stool under the bench, and continue quite comfortably to clean the case and fit in the movement, etc.

Such jobs as filing, using the topping tool,

mandrel, etc., can be carried out with greater ease while standing at a high bench and it obviates the necessity of stooping.

The high bench has the further advantage of keeping the feet out of all draughts, a foot rail in convenient position being provided under the bench.

Where a number of men are employed, it is much better to have each bench separate and self-contained. This prevents any disturbance to the adjoining benches. A man may be fitting a balance spring or carrying out some work where absolute steadiness of the bench is essential, while the man at the next bench may want to file or do some job which will cause the bench to vibrate. However slight the vibration may be, it will affect the man on finer work if the benches are of the running board type.

A nest of drawers fitted at the right-hand side and a shelf under the bench will be found useful for the storage of tools, etc., and the lathe box and boxes containing other large tools, on the shelf.

Avoid all superstructures which are likely to obstruct the light. A bench with a whole array of tools at the back, such as a topping tool under a glass shade, a stack of boxes containing screw head tool, poising tool, punches, etc., may be a very imposing sight, but is most impractical.

Keep the bench as clear as possible; not only does this allow the entry of all available light, but at the same time does not permit of the harboring of dust, and entails less work when cleaning the bench.

The Walls

With regard to the best color for the walls of the workshop, there seems to be a diversity of opinion.

Some favor a pale shade of green, as it is claimed to be restful, but I prefer white or cream, even for all woodwork, such as window frames, and doors, etc., the benches being left either in the natural state or stained a light color.

White and cream reflect the light, and quite a dull looking room can be made bright by the introduction of the color scheme suggested.

The Floor

The floor should be covered with a good quality linoleum, also of a light color. It is preferable, however, where possible, to cover the floor with a solid type of flooring such as a plastic jointless floor, when all corners, such as where the walls meet the floor and where two walls meet, can be left rounded. Cleaning can be carried out very effectively, and there would be no corners to collect dirt. Further, should a piece be dropped—even the best watchmaker drops a piece occasionally—there would be fewer hiding places for the elusive piece.

By the way, keep hanging under the bench, in a convenient position, a brush for sweeping the bench, a useful form being the one used by painters for dusting before painting. It is also useful for sweeping the floor should a piece fall.

The Stool

The type of stool used is of no particular moment; for appearance sake, however, they should all be of the same style. The type used extensively in Switzerland is of the metal stand variety, with round wooden top which is adjustable and can be raised or lowered by revolving the top, similar to some types of piano stools.

Light

When the occasion arises for artificial light to be used, electricity is, generally speaking, the best. It is clean, dustless, gives off very little heat as compared with gas, and is more convenient.

The most useful form of application is by the long two- or three-jointed arm bracket, which is secured to the right-hand side at the back of the bench.

It does not occupy any room on the bench, and can be easily folded back to the right-hand side when not in use; in this position it will not obstruct the light during the day-time. By means of the adjustable arms the light can be placed in any position to suit requirements.

The shade should be of the bell-shaped pattern, made of metal, and enameled white inside and green outside. Some advocate the green and white lined cardboard shades, but I find they fade and the white inside turns brown very quickly and consequently does not reflect the light to the best advantage.

The power of an electric lamp should be such as not to cause eye strain, but at the same time there are limits; a 60 watt lamp gives quite a good light and should meet most requirements.

General Notes

A bright, clean, cheerful workshop must have its effect upon the workmen, and subsequently upon the work. Environment such as this has a clear, cool effect on the mind, and one could not for a moment imagine inferior work being turned out from such a workshop.

My readers may say that such a workshop is impractical, and it would not pay. I maintain that conditions such as these do pay, as the upkeep is small, and the influence is great.

Further, it would be an advertisement to show customers the conditions under which their watches are repaired. In England we are accustomed to find the watch workshop a much neglected, dust-ridden back room, as it were. Let us learn a lesson from Switzerland, the factories and workshops there being almost perfect.

Those who have read Henry Ford's book *Today and Tomorrow* will remember that all his workshops and machines are white. This color is used so that any dust or dirt shows up against the light background, and can then be easily removed.

Similar methods to those in Switzerland and advocated by Henry Ford are now being adopted in England by the modern factories, and I understand from those responsible that the results are excellent.

Ventilation

Ventilation is a very important matter, and much consideration must be given to it. When the workshop is free of people all the windows and doors should be opened, this applying both before and after business hours, and every effort should be made to do the same during the luncheon hour. During working hours ventilation is sometimes difficult, especially in large workshops, as very often the men near the windows want them opened at the top and the men at the back benches complain of draught. In such cases the best method to adopt is to fix a board about 1 ft. down from the top of the window, the board to be about 18 in. deep and tilted slightly upwards to the ceiling. The window can then be opened 1 ft. and the air will be allowed to enter the shop quite freely and draughts avoided.

I once knew of a workshop which faced the sea, and when the window was opened only a very little, the wind was troublesome. This was overcome by making a false ceiling, about 1 ft. down from the original, a number of holes of about 3 in. diameter being made, and the ceiling terminated about 3 ft. from the back of the shop.

The result was good, the window could be opened on to the false ceiling, and even on a very windy day no disturbance was noticed and the shop was always fresh.

Storage of Material

In large workshops and factories great care and attention are given to the storing of material, all pieces being so arranged that they can be easily found. It will be appreciated that unless some order is organized in this direction the time wasted in finding the necessary piece will be considerable.

Interchangeable Material

Several manufacturers accommodate the small workshop in the following manner. The vast number of machine-made watches now on the market call for a stock of material. The majority are so accurately made that the interchangeable parts fit without alteration.

Some of these Swiss factories supply material in boxes, the movement being given a series number, or a name, and in some instances the size of the movement, such as "17 ligne dress."

The box is fitted up with a number of smaller boxes, with an illustrated chart showing the actual movement both under the dial and the other side, and also an illustration of each piece; these pieces are given a number and the number placed on the box containing that piece. In some cases the material is contained in small glass top boxes through which the pieces can be seen.

It is advisable to keep in stock as much material of the popular models as possible, as it makes for speed and good service. The finest advertisement the watchmaker can have is to repair watches entrusted to him quickly and efficiently.

The Le Coultre movement (the hand-made type), return springs, etc., can be purchased from the tool shops, partly finished, to suit this type of movement; a small alteration is all that is usually necessary to make the piece fit perfectly. Shafts also can be bought partly finished, and in such cases as these small stocks only are necessary. These pieces should be stored in boxes with description of the contents on the outside.

To use the material made by the makers for their watches makes for efficiency and, further, is a stamp of good workmanship. Nothing is more objectionable than to come across a watch, say, fitted with a mainspring, hands, or other parts which are not original; it has the appearance of a makeshift job.

Balance and Mainsprings

These springs are best stored in a cupboard or a cabinet kept especially for the purpose, mainsprings being kept in greaseproof paper and, balance springs in lime. The tool shops store balance springs in their original packets as supplied by the makers in Switzerland, but they are continually using them. The workshop where balance springs are wanted only occasionally would consequently keep the stock for a longer period, and the springs therefore stand a greater chance of rusting. Once such a spring shows even the slightest signs of rust it is useless and therefore wasted.

Unnamed Movements

We all know the difficulty of obtaining material for some watches—the Swiss in particular—the movements of which are not named and are generally unknown.

There are in Switzerland hundreds of watch factories where watches are finished. In comparison, there are few actual makers of the movement itself, the frame or ébauche, as it is known, being made in one factory and sold to the other factories, who use their own methods of finishing.

There are factories where the escapement only is made— the "assortment" factory—there are of course many grades. In this manner a factory buys the ébauche, which comprises the movement with the exception of the escapement, hands, and dial. You will see, therefore, that one particular type of movement can be finished in many ways and grades.

In some instances, the factory buying the ébauche request that the top plate or bars and cocks shall be of an original cut, in order that the movement shall have an appearance exclusive to that factory, and it is this factor which makes the maker so elusive. On the other hand there are a few factories where the movement complete is made, including the escapement, and it is quite a simple matter to find material for such movements.

An American System

Now the Americans take advantage of this fact, and cabinets of material are compiled in such a manner that one cabinet can contain all the material required to repair such movements entering America.

The method adopted is this: A chart is made

illustrating many designs of the small bar which holds the intermediate wheel or wheels in position, and sometimes this bar forms the check spring combined. Should, say, a click spring or any other piece be required, match the bar, or "yoke," as the Americans call it, on the chart, and this forms the key to the make. All the material is then at hand in a similar manner to the boxes supplied by some of the large factories, who make their own ébauche. The bar or yoke referred to is standard, i.e. say an 8-3/4 in. movement is supplied to several factories, who require some individual treatment, the bar or "yoke" is in each case the same shape.

Swiss Watchmaking Towns

Once, when in Switzerland, I made inquiries as to why most of the watch factories were in a particular part of the country, and was told that the original Swiss watchmakers were farmers. By reason of the inclemency of the weather during the winter months it was quite impossible to do any work out of doors, and their attention was therefore turned to some form of indoor labor.

Some men, more enterprising than others, started workshops, and employed people to finish some small parts in their own homes, returning them upon completion to the workshop for assembling, etc. I understand that even quite young children used to be employed in minor operations. One can well imagine, for instance, that on the approach of winter, the man would apply to one of the workshops or factories for, say, wheels and pinions to finish. At home he would set up a small workshop, and the family, maybe for the want of something better to do, would help. The result was that the cost of production was small—mass production in its infancy. Switzerland here begins where England left off as regards watchmaking.

Much the same principle is still carried on in Switzerland; the small "one man" workshop has grown into a good-sized factory, and occasionally its sole production is mainsprings or balance springs, escapements, etc. Young children are, of course, no longer employed on such work.

The above is the explanation my Swiss informant gave me, and although I cannot vouch for its absolute accuracy, it is quite feasible.

When one looks round such places as La Chaux-de-Fonds, in Switzerland, in the summer, and sees the vast number of factories there, and then pays a visit in the winter, one can well understand the necessity for some form of livelihood other than that of farming. Nowadays, of course, the watchmaking in these parts predominates, and farming is of secondary importance.

Switzerland Compared with England as a Watchmaking Country

This has taken us a long way from the storage of materials, but you will understand now how so many different finishes are given to the same movement. After all, the principle of manufacture is the same in Switzerland as it was in England years ago, always with the exception, of course, of the very large factories, although even in these mainsprings, balance springs, jewel holes, pallet stones, dials, hands, cases, buttons, and glasses, etc., are not made, such pieces being left to special factories. Even watch case factories do not make both gold and silver cases, there being the gold case maker and the silver case maker, etc.

In England, the rough movement, or frame, was made by one man, or concern. The watch manufacturer, so called, would procure such a rough movement; he would then send it to the finisher, who would pivot and face the pinions, etc.; then this partly-finished movement was sent to the jeweler, who would fit the jewel holes; then to the escapement maker, to have the escapement fitted. This last-named man would, in turn, employ the services of the pallet maker; the balance maker in turn employed the services of the balance screw maker. Then, back to the keyless maker. The manufacturer was usually the springer and adjuster, and the balance would be sent to the balance spring maker for a spring. When the movement was nearing completion, it would be sent to the case maker, who in turn employed the services of several other tradesmen, such as springer, boxer-in, joint pinner, pendant maker, polisher, etc.

All the various operations mentioned were separate trades, and the work was carried out on the workman's own premises. One could go on *ad infinitum*.

That is why material for English watches is always difficult to obtain; the pieces are handmade, and the movement supplied by the movement maker is not as complete as the movements now supplied by the Swiss movement makers.

There are one or two factories in England. Watches made in them are more or less interchangeable, and material can be obtained ready finished.

Maintain the High Standard

As the majority of watches that pass through our

workshops today for repair are machine-made, when it is necessary to fit new pieces these are in most cases interchangeable and more often than not very little alteration is required to make them a good fit.

Should, however, the occasion arise to make a new piece entirely, the standard is set by the machine-made piece, which, as we all know, is not always of the same standard as the hand-made piece.

I do not agree, for instance, in making a balance staff for a machine-made watch of the same high finish as a better quality hand-finished watch would demand. Make the staff to the same standard as the watch. Watches should be repaired in such a manner that they will not look as if they have been through the hands of the repairer at all. In short, they should look as new.

Occasions do arise, however, where a higher standard of work is required, and if the student has not had that particular training which is necessary to carry out this work, he is lost. A man may be quite a good turner, but when it comes to *finish*, is wholly ignorant.

The Swiss recognize the necessity for maintaining the high standard when training their boys, so do not let us shut our eyes to it. Therefore, I maintain that it is essential that the apprentice should be taught the better way; the other way comes all too easily.

In this book I propose to take the student through the various operations in the better way, so that should the occasion arise, he will be able with ease to adjust his work to all requirements.

I shall attempt to sit at the bench with him, as it were, to give him, so far as I am able, the advantage of the apprenticeship as it should be given.

CHAPTER 2

TRAINING METHODS

There can be little doubt that the best course to take, when giving instruction in the art of watchmaking, is to adopt the one and only method, and that is the *ideal*. By the word ideal, I mean the *proper* way, not makeshift or patchwork methods; the latter are all too readily picked up.

The general and only recognized principle of the workshop should be: *There is only* ONE *way to do work, and that is the correct way.*

A good standard should be set, and steps taken to see that the standard is maintained.

This supervision may seem to be unnecessary, but unfortunately the human element enters into the workshop; men will err. Such supervision must not be taken as a slight upon one's capabilities. No buyer, for instance, would purchase goods just because the label said that the contents were good value and of fine quality without examining them first; supervision, therefore, is a form of examination.

The principle of a standard should be drilled into all beginners; ours is the highest standard. "Good enough" is not good enough, it must be the best and nothing but the best.

In the case of the apprentice, a certain time should be allocated for work at the bench, which should be of such a nature as to benefit the beginner. Generally speaking, a boy leaving school (at the age of from 14 to 16 years) is not fit to "touch" a watch, and a year or two spent in the clock workshop is time well spent, both to his and his employer's advantage. It breaks him in, as it were; he understands the handling of tools, and learns unconsciously what "touch" means.

In many workshops, watches and clocks are repaired in the same shop, and in one-man businesses by the same man. If it is at all possible, the two sections should be kept separate, and at least watches should not be repaired on the same bench as the clocks.

Time should be set aside for practical instruction; for instance, the actions and functions, etc., of the escapements should be fully explained to him. Depths, etc., likewise dealt with, and as fresh items come along they should be explained. The student's interest must be stimulated; there is no tonic like enthusiasm, for when he is keen the best can be expected.

Nothing is more disheartening, both to the student and the instructor, than lack of enthusiasm. It is just as important for the instructor to be keen as it is for the student.

I propose first to deal with such matters as filing, turning, polishing, etc., and assuming that you are by my side, I shall endeavor to show you how these things are done.

Polishing Materials and Their Use

Before we start making new pieces I propose to talk about polishing materials and how they are used.

Oilstone Dust. To grind steel.

This can be purchased in the dry form from the tool shop. It is advisable, first of all, to wash the oilstone dust. Into a receptacle of convenient size pour some water and on it sprinkle the oilstone dust; let it settle for a few minutes, and then gently pour the water off.

Benzine, petrol, or alcohol can be used instead of water. They have the advantage of drying out the powder more quickly. The oilstone dust left is then spread on to a sheet of paper to dry, making sure to cover it to prevent dust from settling. I would mention here that it is almost as important to keep oilstone dust clean as it is diamantine.

Some prefer to wash oilstone twice, but this is as a rule unnecessary. You will notice that this dust is generally sold as "double washed" and the object of our washing again is to ensure that there is no objectionable gritty substance present; curiously enough the water floats this off.

To prepare for use, take as much oilstone dust (washed and thoroughly dried) as can be placed upon a sixpence; turn this on to a block made for the purpose (see Fig. 1). The same style of block is also used for diamantine. Mix with a drop or two of clean clock oil. The consistency should be fairly thin, similar to that of cream or a little thicker. The quantity mentioned here will last the average watchmaker some considerable time, and it will not be necessary to mix a fresh lot for each time used, so when not in use replace the cover provided for that purpose. The method of application to the polisher is to present the polisher itself to the mixture and in the case of the facing tool dab the business end on. Sufficient of the oilstone dust and oil will adhere. If we are using the plate for underhand polishing or the lap, apply a little with the tip of a knife and then smear over the surface with the knuckle of the thumb similar to the method shown in Fig. 1. It may be necessary to add a little oil occasionally to the oilstone dust to keep it moist.

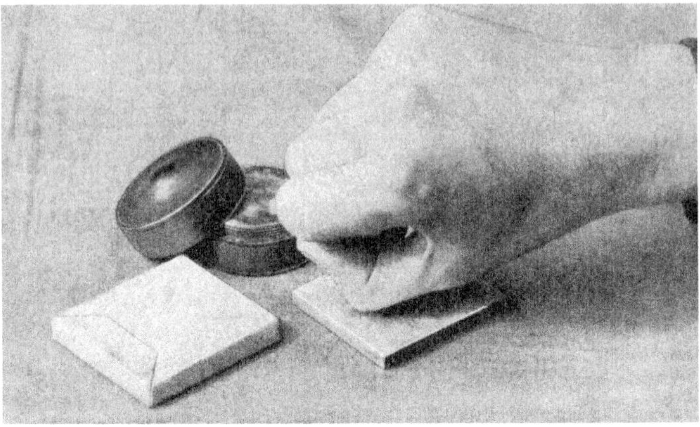

Fig. 1 – Method of Dressing Zinc Block with Diamantine

Diamantine. To polish steel.

This substance, also purchased from the tool shop, is sold in bottles and is a fine white powder. It is made from ammonia alum, a sulphate of aluminum and ammonia. The alum is calcined in a furnace at an exceedingly high temperature, and this powder, known as alumina, is the basic material used in the production of artificial stones and has the same chemical properties as the sapphire.

To prepare for use, place as much as will lie on a sixpence on to the block similar to the oilstone dust block. These blocks can be purchased in two tiers, one for oilstone dust and the other for diamantine. I prefer to use two separate single blocks, as this ensures that the oilstone will not get into the diamantine. On to this small quantity of diamantine place one drop of *watch* oil, using a clean dipper and also clean oil. Well clean, on the emery buff, the small flat pivot end burnisher. Wipe the burnisher on a clean linen rag and begin to mix the oil and diamantine; use considerable pressure, and press the oil into the diamantine. You will eventually have to add another drop of oil, but usually two drops will be sufficient for this amount of diamantine. It will need a lot of mixing, pressing, and beating, and it will eventually have the consistency of putty. One mixing will last the average man weeks. Some advocate that the mixing should be done with a glass rod as the steel burnisher leaves the diamantine very dark, but from experience this does not affect its efficiency.

The application to the polisher and facing tool is the same as for oilstone dust and oil. To apply to the polishing block or lap, knock the thumb knuckle on to the diamantine and then on to the polishing block or lap. The correct amount of diamantine will thus be transferred (see Fig. 1). If you have used the knuckle for oilstone dust, make sure that it is quite free of this before applying diamantine. Finally, be as particular with the diamantine as you are—or should be—with the watch oil; always keep it well covered when not actually in use. You cannot be too particular about diamantine to keep it clean; any dust or grit mixed with it will produce a scratchy surface.

Red Stuff. To polish gold and brass.

This is rouge and is mixed in a similar manner to oilstone dust and is applied as diamantine. Diamantine also can be used to polish brass and gold.

Polishers

Now the material on which the polishing medium is used.

Iron. Used with oilstone dust and diamantine to polish steel.

Iron polishers are made in various shapes and sizes

and will be described as used.

The metal is ordinary soft iron and is used to hold both oilstone dust and diamantine. As an instance, to show that no special metal is necessary, some of the old English "finishers"—the men who did that beautiful pinion turning, polishing, and facing—used an ordinary French nail for a facing tool (see Fig. 33A).

Bell Metal. Used with diamantine to polish steel.

Some prefer, in the place of the iron polisher, to use bell metal for diamantine. I have seen good work done with both metals; oilstone dust is not used with bell metal. Usually laps, as supplied with the screw head tool, are made of this metal.

Zinc. Used with diamantine to polish steel.

This metal is used with diamantine only. It is not used usually for small polishers, being rather soft, but is the ideal medium to hold diamantine when underhand polishing. Fig. 1 shows the zinc block and the sheath in which it is kept to keep it clean.

Tin. Used with red stuff to polish gold and brass.

Pure tin is used, in the form of a block similar to the zinc block, and the method of procedure is similar to that of diamantine on the zinc block. Tin is much softer than zinc and it is not possible to apply the same pressure. The article being polished is inclined to bite into the tin. Tin can also be used in the form of a bar, about 6 in. long, 1/2 in. wide, and about 1/8 in. thick. Similar to zinc in this respect, it is too soft to use as a small polisher.

Boxwood. Used with diamantine to polish steel.

This is a close grain hardwood and it usually used in the form of a slip and also as a lap as supplied with the screw head tool. Boxwood is used as a final finish, after the metal polisher.

Filing

Let us start with filing first. The acme of perfection in filing is to file perfectly flat and true. The correct way in which to hold the file, when using the large or pillar file, is shown in Fig. 2. When using this file, give a firm even pressure and the strokes are from the tip of the file to the heel. The forward stroke does the cutting—it is actual cutting, not rubbing—and a firm decided stroke is necessary; this must not be too quick. The backward stroke can, and should be, light, for it is just a means of getting the tip of the file back again; no cutting is expected from this stroke. In some instances, when filing a small surface, it is better to lift the file quite free of the work on the backward stroke, and then to bring it down smartly on to the work and start the forward stroke immediately. Try this out on a piece of brass first; screw it firmly in the vice, and holding the file in the right hand steady the tip with the left hand. Now give the file a steady, firm, forward movement, when you should "feel" it cutting; a file should not just rub.

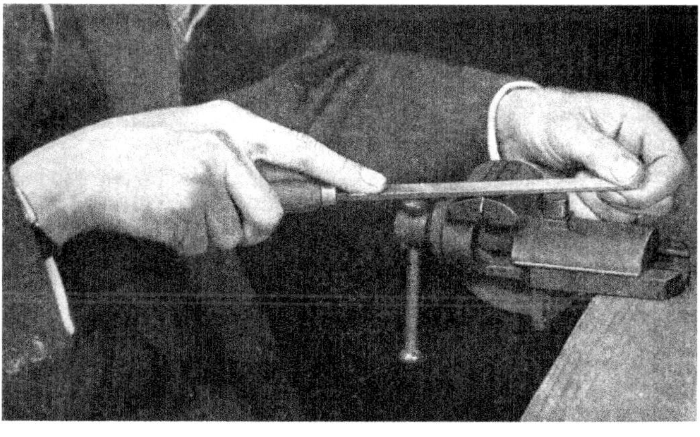

Fig. 2 – Using Large File

Take the pressure off and bring the file back again; it should hardly touch the metal. We have not the same control over the backward motion and there is every possibility of the work becoming rounded if metal is removed on the backward stroke. I have seen men rubbing metal backwards and forwards quickly, with a file, but they can never file flat and most certainly not true. By filing true, I mean filing, say, a step in a piece of metal so that the line or edge so made is perfectly straight.

When filing, half the battle is won when the metal to be filed is held in the correct manner, so as an example we shall file up a cock or bridge. Take a piece of brass, the size of which is immaterial, and file the top and bottom flat and have these surfaces parallel; this can be done with the brass held in the vice. While still in the vice, file a step as indicated by the dotted line (Fig. 3). To finish off this step remove from the vice and hold in the left hand as indicated (Fig. 4), allowing the part to be filed to rest on a piece of cork which is held in the vice. We are now only able to use one hand to hold the file; use pressure on the file in the forward strokes, holding the piece lightly on the cork while so doing. By this means the work will find its own level, and after practice you will be able to "feel" that the file is filing flat and making a full cut, and not cutting on one side only. When this step or shoulder has been filed flat and true proceed to file another step as shown in Fig. 5. To do this the piece is reversed in the vice and the procedure is as before. Pillar files have, as a rule, one edge which is also a cutting edge and the other edge is left smooth. It is this smooth or "safe" edge which is brought up against the shoulder, as we do not want to cut the side of the step.

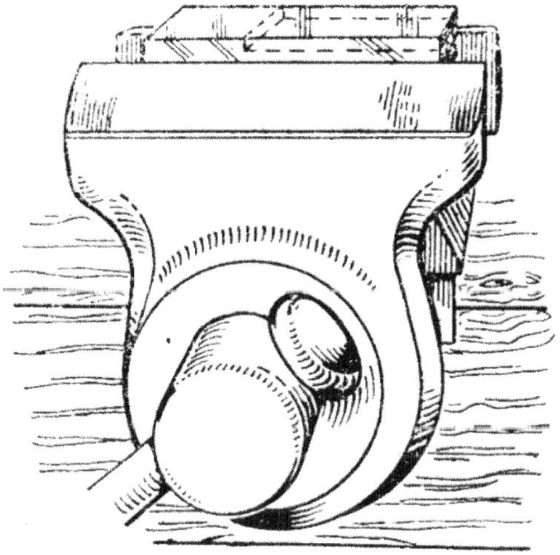

Fig. 3 – Dotted Lines Indicating Step to Be Filled

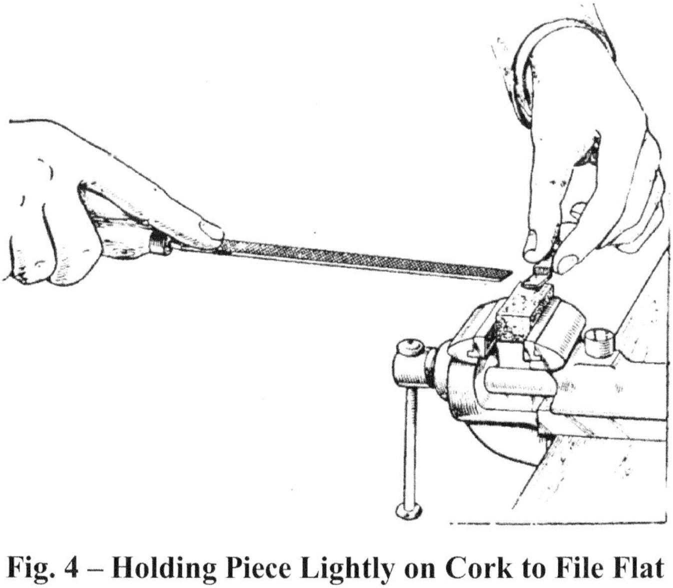

Fig. 4 – Holding Piece Lightly on Cork to File Flat and True

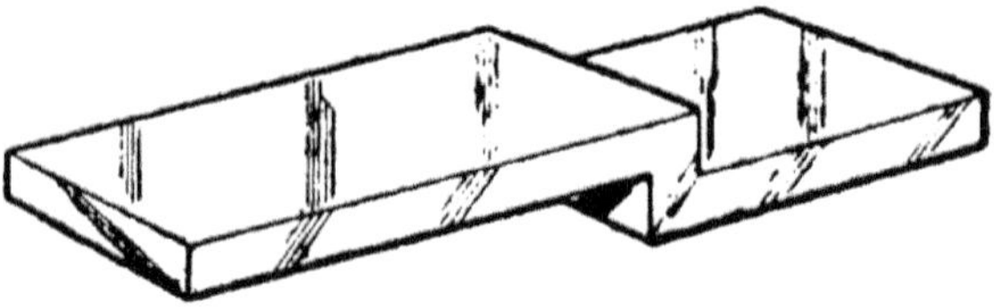

Fig. 5 – Showing Second Step Filed

The sides of the cock are filed by holding the piece in the left hand as shown (Fig. 6) and here we bring the file *away* from the surface on the backward stroke. Holding the work very firmly in the left hand, place the tip of the file in position and give one steady forward movement, using considerable pressure; the left hand will "give" under the pressure and by so doing the file will find its own level and a flat surface assured. You will feel the file actually cutting the metal. It may be necessary to file the cock to a certain shape as shown in Fig. 7. This being the case, hold in the vice to do the rough work first, using another piece of metal under the cock so that it will not be distorted (Fig. 8) and a piece of thick paper on the top of the cock so that the serrated face of the jaws of the vice do not mark the surface.

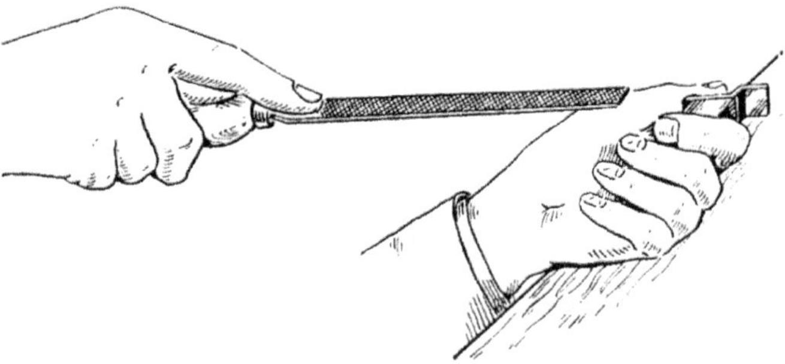

Fig. 6 – Method of Holding Piece to File Flat

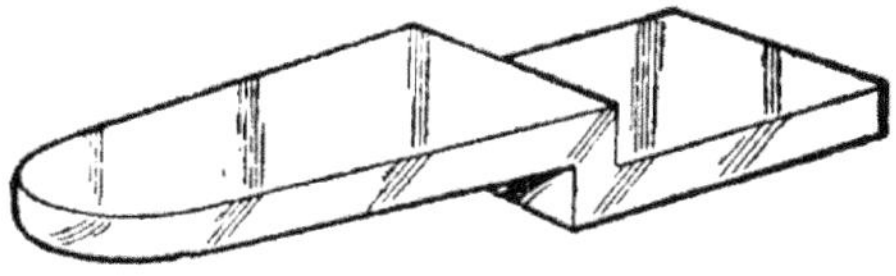

Fig. 7 – Showing the General Shape of Cock

To finish the cock to make the surfaces fine, either use a finer cut file or an emery stick, holding the piece as already explained.

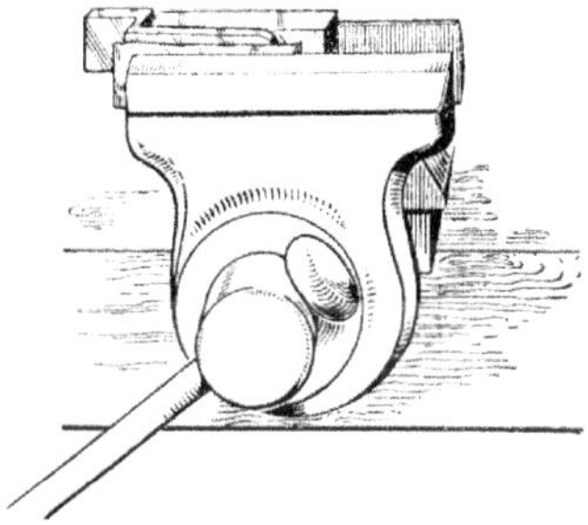

Fig. 8 – Showing Packing Used When Holding Cock in Vice

Filing Steel

When a good deal of filing is to be done on steel it must be soft. Hardened and tempered steel places too great a strain on the file; small surfaces can, however, be filed, but more accurate work can be done when the steel is soft.

So when fashioning new steel parts for a watch, silver steel is used, the new piece being hardened and tempered before final finishing.

As an example we shall make a return spring. Procure a piece of silver steel a little thicker than the finished spring is to be and wide enough for it to be cut out of. We shall assume such a piece of steel is 6 in. long, 1/4 in. wide, and 1 mm. thick. If you have the old broken spring, proceed as follows. Make smooth and bright with an emery buff the top of this steel bar at one end. Slightly warm this end and smear with beeswax so that a thin film of wax covers the surface. Place the old spring on the waxed end, the spring towards the end as illustrated (Fig. 9); if there are two or more pieces place them in their correct positions. Now hold this piece of steel over the flame of a spirit lamp until the bright end turns blue, then remove and allow to cool. Remove the spring from the piece of steel and we shall find that a white outline of the spring has been left. The wax has excluded the air and not allowed the part under the spring to change color.

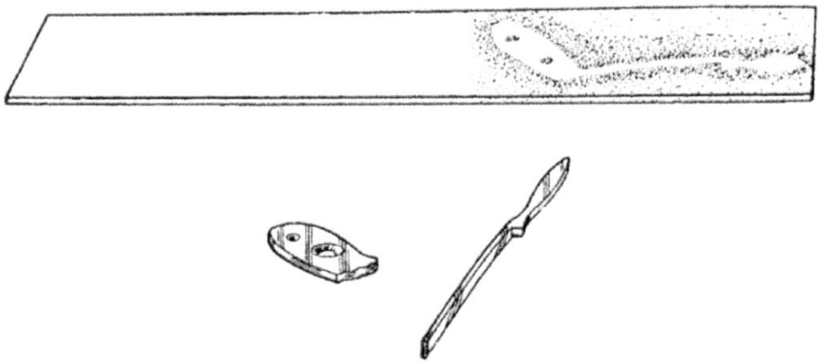

Fig. 9 – Broken Return Spring and the Outline Made on the Bar of Steel by Bluing

We now proceed to file to shape, using the pillar file first and finally using needle files, three square and half round. When near to size, draw file the sides, i.e. instead of cross filing just draw the file along the whole length as shown in Fig. 10, by this means any irregularity will be revealed. Do not cut the now partly finished spring from the bar until the spring is nearly finished as the bar forms a convenient handle. When practically finished cut the spring away from the main part as shown in Fig. 11 and finish the end off, holding the spring in the sliding tongs. Drill the hole for the screw and also the hole for the steady pin. File to the correct thickness; to do this, place on a soft wood block, holding the spring in position with a short brass pin in the screw hole. File lengthwise (Fig. 12), using the pillar file, and giving long, steady strokes. The steady pin is not placed in position until after hardening and tempering (see hardening and tempering).

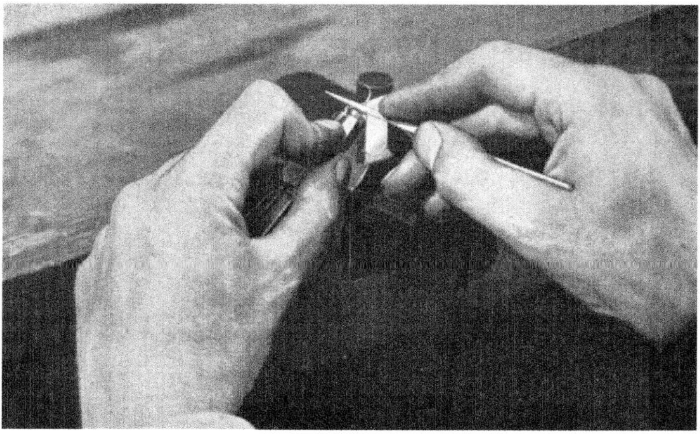

Fig. 10 – Using Needle File to Draw File

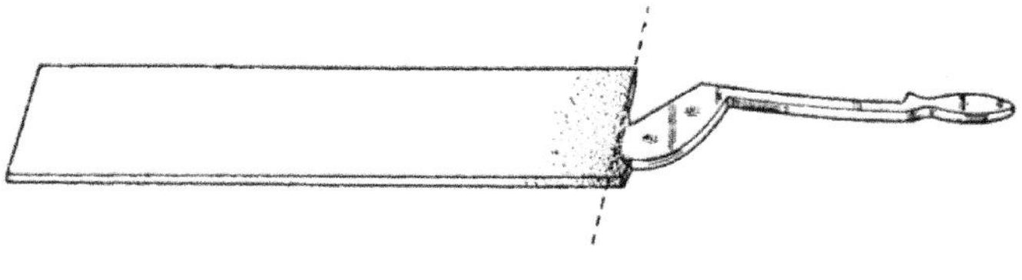

Fig. 11 – Dotted Line Indicating Where Partly Finished Spring Is Cut Away

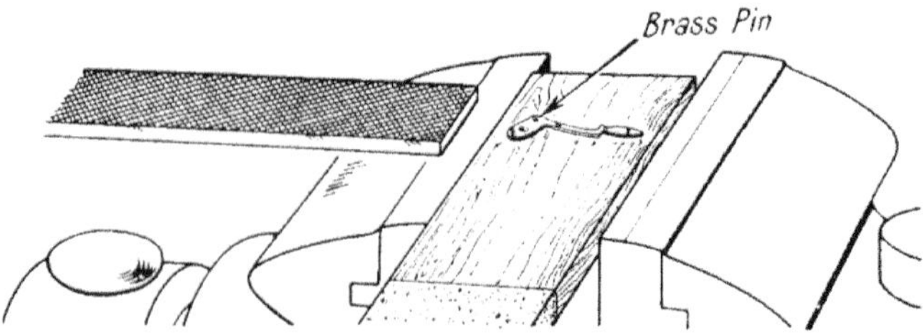

Fig. 12 – Indicating Position of Spring When Filing Lengthwise

When making the impression of the spring on the steel, the screw hole and steady pin hole—if the steady pin was first removed—may be indicated. If so, we can drill. If, however, the marking is not distinct enough, place the old spring on the new one and mark their positions with a pointer and drill. Sometimes the screw head is sunk to the level of the spring. To make this sink proceed as follows. Drill up a piece of round silver steel a hole the diameter of the thread of the screw. Turn the outer diameter of the rod to the size of the head of the screw. File the end to shape as indicated in Fig. 13.

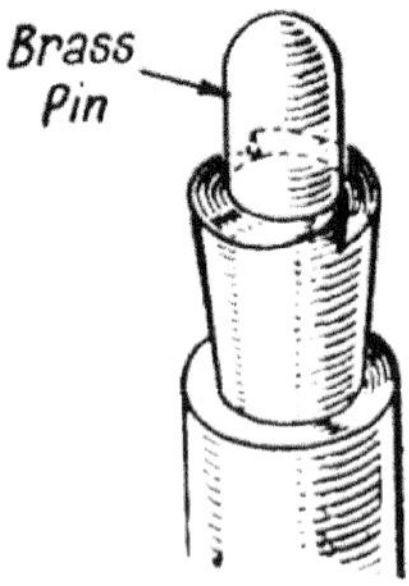

Fig. 13 – Tool for Cutting Recess for Screw

Now harden the end and temper to a straw color. Pit a short brass pin in the hole just drilled. This brass pin should just fit the hole in the spring we are making and if the rod is made to revolve as a drill, it will cut a sink the size of the screw head. We can now harden and temper the spring, and to finish, stone the underside, using an emery stone, place the spring on the cork held in the vice and give one or two long, firm strokes, similar to those made with the pillar file.

Make sure the strokes are lengthwise of the spring, as cross cutting may cause the spring to break easily. The edges are finished by stroking them with an Arkansas slip, a similar motion to that employed when draw filing. Sharp bends and corners, etc., can be treated with the iron polisher charged with oilstone dust and oil.

Now fit the steady pin, driving it in from the top side, cut off as near the top surface as possible with the cutting nippers, stone the superfluous pin with the Arkansas stone. Place the spring on the cork and give one or two steady strokes with the fine emery stone, lengthwise again. This will leave a bright straight-grain finish.

Sometimes in fine quality watches, the steel work is finished with the edges broken, i.e. the top edges of the sides cut at a slight angle. This is quite simply effected by drawing the Arkansas slip along these edges, afterwards burnishing the edges with a small oval burnisher (Fig. 14). Cut the other end of the steady pin to size and finish off with an finally making the end round by twirling over the end a rounding tool, which is similar to a chamfering tool, but reversed.

Emery stones can be purchased from tool shops; they are a composition stone, varying in size from about 1 in. sq. and about 6 in. long to slabs of 4 in. wide, 1 in. thick, and 6 in. long. No oil is used with these stones and the surfaces are made flat by rubbing two similar stones together, allowing water to drip on to them whilst so doing. They are cleaned by rubbing with a rag and benzine. They are made in various degrees of fineness and are a most useful adjunct to the watchmaker's equipment. A flat-faced piece of pumice-stone can also be used for the same purpose. The pumice-stone is made flat by rubbing it on a flagstone, or plate glass with fine sand, or pumice-powder and water.

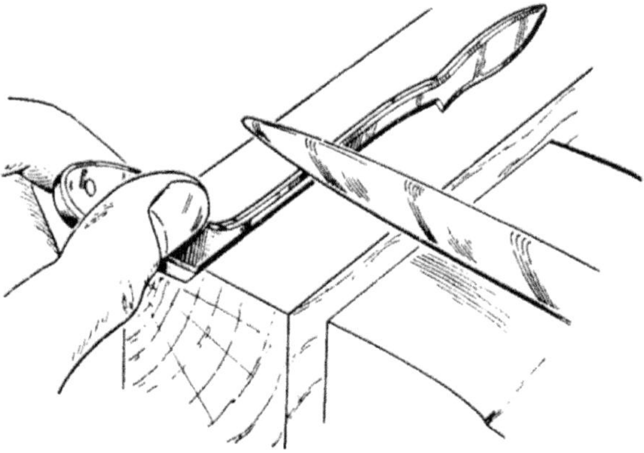

Fig. 14 – Showing Bevel or Chamfer Being Burnished

The Arkansas stone is a fine white natural stone, somewhat similar to marble in appearance. Slips of this stone are sold in various shapes: square, three square, lozenge, etc., about 3 in. long and 1/4 in. sq., etc. The larger stones of the same material used for whetting the gravers on, are about 6 in. long, 2 in. wide and 1 in. thick. Oil is used on these stones and they are cleaned by rubbing with a rag and benzine.

Whilst the instruction refers to the making of a return spring, the same procedure is followed when making any small steel piece requiring flat filing, etc.

As I have said, it is not so much the actual work but the method of holding the piece; all methods are employed so that the work finds its own level. For instance, when holding the work in the left hand and filing with the right, the left hand gives under the pressure of the right hand and thus a flat surface is assured; in a similar manner the cork gives to the pressure.

Other Methods of Finishing Steel Work

For instance, the top surface of a Swiss balance spring stud. Having made it, hardened and tempered, fit in the tool here illustrated (Fig. 15), which is known as a bolt tool. The end of the tool is detachable and is held in position by two screws, thus forming a jaw. Between these jaws grip the stud with the surface to be polished downwards; at first do not tighten the screws but leave them finger tight. See that the two adjusting screws are projecting through the underside of the tool an equal amount and about the same distance as the stud projects. Place the tool on a piece of plate glass and bring a little pressure to bear on the top of the tool so that the stud is pressed into position. The surface of the stud presented to the glass should be full, thus forming one foot, as it were, and the ends of the two adjusting screws the other two feet, then tighten the two jaw screws to hold the stud firmly. Transfer the tool to another piece of plate glass dressed with oilstone dust and oil. Give the tool one or two circular rubs on this dressed surface, using a fair amount of pressure. This will grind the surface of the stud dead flat; it may also grind the ends of the screws, if they contact the oilstone dust, but that does not matter. When you are satisfied that the surface is ready to be polished clean off well with pith to remove *all* traces of the oilstone dust.

Fig. 15 – Bolt Tool

Transfer the tool to a zinc block dressed with diamantine and give one or two similar rubs; examine before you proceed, to see that a *full* surface is presented to the zinc block. The block may not be as true as the plate glass, and here the two adjusting screws may come in useful.

It may, for instance, show that one side only of the surface touches the zinc block, in which case one of the adjusting screws must be either screwed in further or drawn out so that the side not showing signs of polish is brought down on to the zinc. When a full surface is presented proceed to polish.

Rub backwards and forwards, tracing a circle, then an oval, then a few straight strokes. Keep the movement up, covering a surface on the zinc of about the size of a half-crown, exerting at first some little pressure and gradually lessen the pressure. With a little practice you will be able to "feel" that the surface is "up." The reason for the diverse quick movement during polishing, is to break the grain; if you were to rub backwards and forwards only, fine lines would appear. The finish required is a black, flawless, polished surface, and this is easily and quickly obtained.

The same tool can also be used to polish an index or similar piece. In this case the index is shellacked in position. Warm the end of the tool in the flame of a spirit lamp, smear a little shellac on, then place the index in position and apply a little more heat; whilst the shellac is still soft turn the tool quickly on to the plate glass and apply a little pressure. By this means the full surface of the index will be presented to the plate. The same precautions as regards the depth the adjusting screws are screwed in applies as when adjusting the tool to suit the balance spring stud.

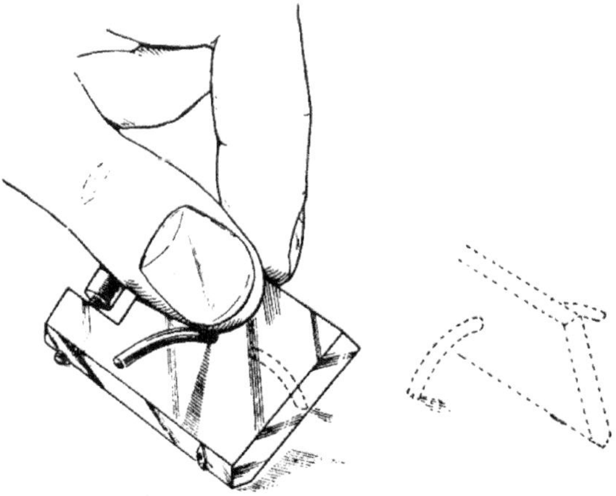

Fig. 16 – "Rocking" Tool for Polishing an Edge Rounded

The heads of screws can also be polished in this tool. The large flat headed screws, such as the transmission wheel screw, etc., are treated in this manner. In such cases the thread of the screw is gripped in the jaws, as we did the stud. The smaller screws can be lapped, using the screw head tool described elsewhere.

Another tool (the "Rocking" tool), useful when polishing, is shown in Fig. 16. It is used generally to polish the round end of the balance spring stud of English watches. It may not be used to any extent today, but I shall describe it as it may be useful for other purposes where a true rounded surface is required. The piece is shellacked in position as indicated. The piece of wire can be bent to suit the curve you wish to make. Hold the tool as shown and wipe it backwards and forwards on the glass plate dressed with oilstone dust, letting each end of the brass wire touch the plate. A perfectly true rounded surface will be the result. To polish, clean off with pith and repeat the operation on the zinc block.

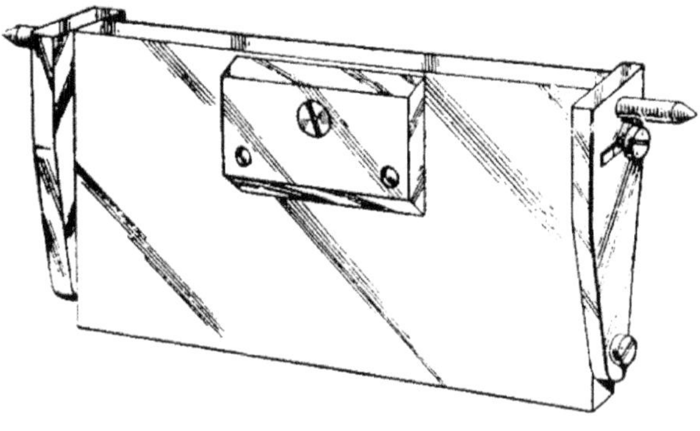

Fig. 17 – Swing Tool

The tool shown in Fig. 17 is useful to obtain a small flat surface, its original use being to polish the edges of the lever, but other uses are to be made of it, it is known as a "swing tool." Screw the piece in the jaws, presenting the surface to be polished uppermost. The tool is held in the turns or lathe between centers and allowed to swing quite loosely. An iron polisher charged with oilstone dust and oil is used. Hold the polisher in the right hand as you would a pencil or pen, work up and down the full length of the piece, at the same time moving the polisher backwards and forwards exerting a fair downwards pressure. The tool will give, and a flat surface will ensue. To polish, clean off with pith, refile the polisher and charge with diamantine and repeat the operation; a highly polished flat surface can thus be obtained.

Yet another tool, which can have other uses than the original one it was made for (Fig. 18). Its original use is to polish the crescent of a roller and the horns of the lever. Say you wanted to polish a segment, half-round, for instance. File to nearly the size required, then hold the piece in the jaws as indicated. The rod is made of soft steel or iron and the hole at the other end of the tool is adjusted so that the rod is parallel with the body of the tool. The end operating on the piece is charged with oilstone dust and oil. The rod is made to revolve and at the same time moved backwards and forwards; the end of the rod opposite the acting part is, while operating, lifted upwards and this makes the acting end bear down on the piece. A flat and true surface is thus obtained. If it is desired to polish the surface, the piece is cleaned with pith and the rod cleaned and filed and dressed with diamantine and the operation repeated. The curve of the horns thus formed may not be correct, but for our purpose it is quite satisfactory. I have mentioned these one or two, maybe obsolete, methods of polishing primarily to illustrate that it is the method of holding the work which is important, and further, that such methods can be adapted and used to good purpose today.

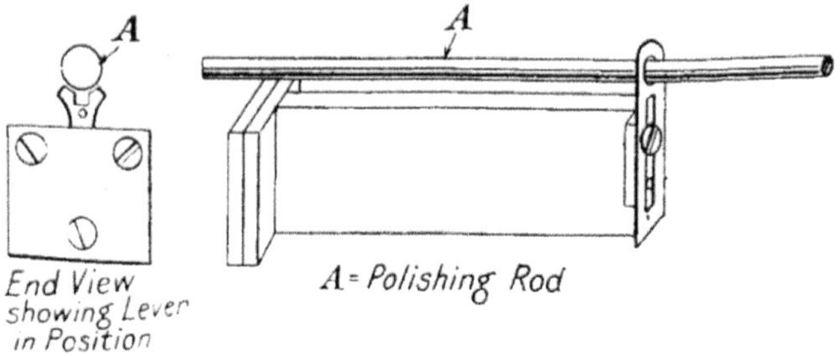

Fig. 18 – Lever Polishing Tool

To polish a small surface, such as the ball of a minute hand or an index center, a pointer can be used. To polish the ball of a minute hand, for instance. Place the hand on the glass plate dressed with oilstone dust and oil, hold the pointer, which may be the rounded end of a piece of peg-wood or a tool made especially for the purpose. Use reasonable pressure on the pointer and give motion similar to that employed when polishing the stud; a flat surface will result. To polish, clean off with pith and repeat the operation on the zinc block dressed with diamantine.

If it is not possible to manipulate the index center with a pointer, shellac it on to a piece of brass, about the size of a sixpence, chamfer a sink in the center of the upper surface and use the pointer in this sink (Fig. 19) and proceed as for the minute hand center.

To Finish Brass

We shall consider first the bridge we made previously. A medium fine emery buff is used and the procedure is precisely the same as when filing. Using the emery buff is inclined to make the surface rounded, so it must not be used for too long a period on the same surface. The object is to give to the brass a fine straight grain, so when you come to the end of the stroke lift the buff off the work quickly, otherwise a cross scratchy surface will be the result. The emery stone can be used instead of the emery buff.

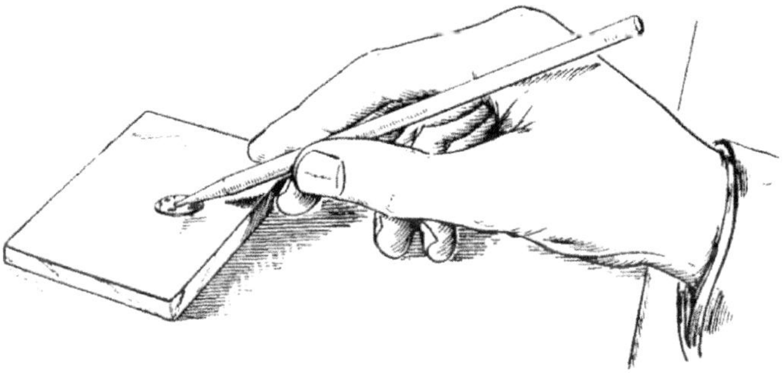

Fig. 19 – Underhand Polishing, Using a Small Plate to Which the Piece Being Polished Is Shellacked

Water-of-Ayr Stone

Water-of-Ayr stone is a similar substance to slate pencil and is sold in the tool shops in various sizes—1/4 in. square up to 1 in. square and about 6 in. long. This stone imparts a fine, almost grainless, surface and is an ideal ground for gilding.

The method of using is to dip the stone into water and rub the surface to be stoned, give a circular motion to keep the surface flat, and apply a little water as the surface becomes dry. The work is cleaned off by washing with water.

When a small surface is to be treated, an ordinary slate pencil can be used. The acting part of the pencil is filed with a file, so that it can so shaped as required. Quite a good finish can be given to brass by stoning with Water-of-Ayr stone first, then dusting on to the surface dry oilstone dust. Now sharpen a piece of peg wood chisel shape; making the peg to revolve on the surface, lift the peg up and apply again; repeat this operation continuously all over the surface to lie treated, and a pleasing frosted finish will thus be imparted, known as "spotting."

To Polish Brass and Gold

Small surfaces, such as the top edge of a jewel hole setting, the ball of a gold or composition minute hand, etc., can be polished dead flat quite easily. One method is to polish on a tin block dressed with rouge and oil, using it on the tin block in a similar manner to that employed when polishing steel on the zinc block dressed with diamantine. Another method is to burnish the surface; we shall take a jewel hole setting as an example. Place the piece to be polished on a piece of soft wood, such as the handle end of an emery buff, and hold the wood in the vice. Make sharp a flat burnisher on a medium emery buff, very slightly smear the burnisher with oil. Hold the burnisher on the top of the jewel setting and apply a little pressure. This will cause the piece to sink into the soft wood slightly. Now rub the burnisher backwards and forwards, using a little pressure; three or four full strokes of the burnisher is generally sufficient. When removing the burnisher take care not to lose the setting; it may be stuck to the burnisher. By this means a perfectly flat, highly polished surface can be obtained. Another method is to use a flat piece of agate, or jasper, faced by grinding with fine diamond powder. This surface acts as a burnisher, and the piece to be polished is held underhand, as already explained.

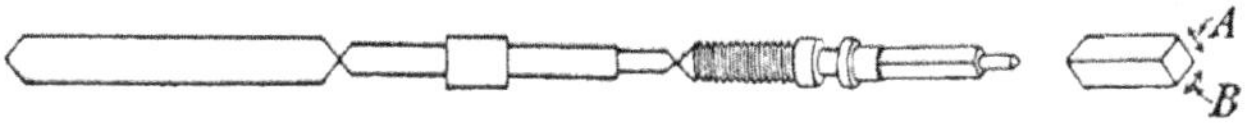

Fig. 20 – Stages of Making Shaft

Turning

Turning takes more practice, perhaps, than filing and it is certainly equally important, especially in watch work. As the first example I do not think I can do better than to turn a winding shaft (Fig. 20), for here we have turning, filing, and thread cutting. We shall first of all turn in that old-fashioned tool, the turns (Fig. 21). The Swiss still use the turns for the finest turning and always for training purposes. (Turning in the lathe will be dealt with elsewhere in this book.) First procure a piece of silver steel rod, a little longer than the finished shaft is to be and also a little larger in diameter than the largest part of the finished shaft.

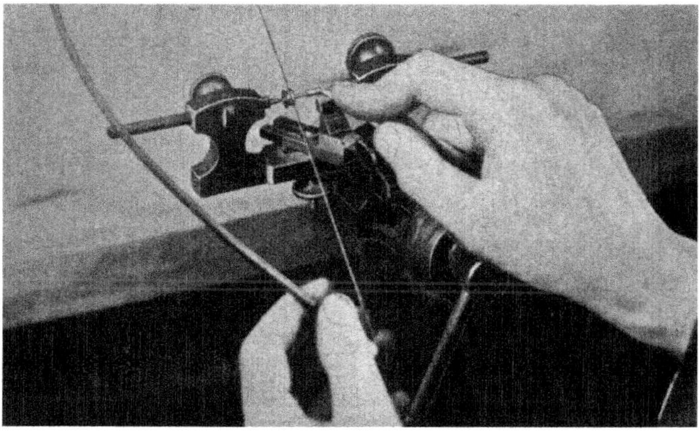

Fig. 21 – The Turns

The Graver

Fig. 22 shows the shape to which the graver should be whetted. A graver so shaped enables the work to be seen, and we are able to turn exactly where wanted.

Fig. 22 – Shape of Whetted Graver

Sometimes we find a graver so sharpened that the work is almost hidden. Such methods are clumsy, and good work cannot result. When whetting the graver (i.e. sharpening), hold firmly and, with a long circular movement, trace on the stone an oval. This ensures flatness of the whetted surface.

The feather edge produced is removed by holding the graver flat on the stone and giving one or two rubs. The graver should not be tilted during this operation. A test to find whether the graver is sharp is to dig the point gently into the thumbnail; it should dig in as a needle does. Finally, before turning, dig the graver into soft wood, such as the leg of the bench, to remove the fine feather edges. I have seen the bench of a finisher with the leg practically eaten through with this digging.

To turn with a graver having a feather edge would have the tendency to burnish, and if tempered steel is the subject under treatment) such as a balance staff, this burnished surface is troublesome to remove.

However, if the surface continually becomes burnished, satisfy yourself that the graver is quite hard, or that the steel is not too hard. Sometimes, when sharpening on a carborundum wheel or stone, the friction is such as to soften the cutting edge. The remedy is to harden the graver, re-temper, or to discard it altogether and use another. The best kind of stone to use for whetting the graver is the Turkey stone, finishing off on an Arkansas stone. The Arkansas stone is fine, and the cut is therefore smoother, which has the advantage of leaving less work for the polisher.

To proceed with the shaft. If you have a lathe the conical pivots can be turned in this, but failing the lathe the pivots can be filed up in the turns, using the runner made especially for that purpose (Fig. 23). Place the ferrule in position as indicated, having first filed by hand that end to a conical pivot. Rest the other end on the runner and hold it down with a fairly smooth file. Draw the bow and at the same time file the pivot, holding the file at an angle as shown; 45° is considered the best wearing angle for the conical pivot. As the round body of the rod rests on the V-shaped runner the pivot so formed will be reasonably true, provided sufficient steady pressure is brought to bear on the file. It is an advantage first of all to file the end of the rod square. The file is then not so inclined to jump.

Having made this pivot, place the ferrule on that end and proceed to make a true pivot of the other one. To ensure this, see that the original body part of the rod rides in the V runner as before. When both pivots are made, place in the turns between female runners the ferrule on your left side as before. There should be *no* play of the rod or arbor between the centers, but at the same time the arbor must be free to revolve. Apply a spot of oil to each pivot. Bring the T-rest up fairly close to the work and at a height so that when the graver is resting on it the cutting edge of the graver is just a little *above* the line of centers (Figs. 24, 25, 26). If this point is observed in all turning there is little risk of the work breaking because of the cutter getting under the work. Furthermore, at this point, the greatest pressure can be exerted on the cutter to the best advantage.

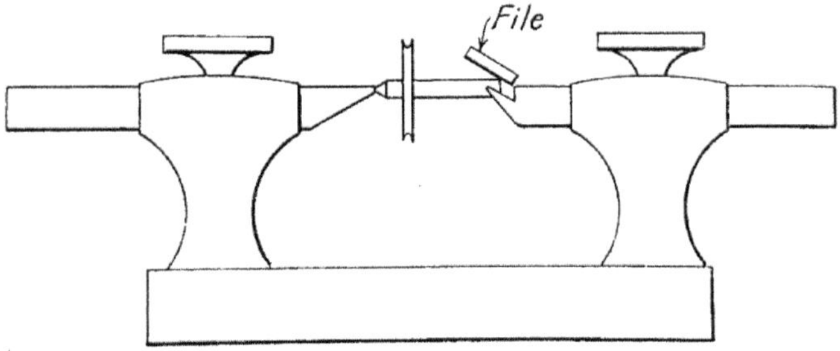

Fig. 23 – Filing Conical Pivot

What really happens when we cut with the graver is to wedge or peel the metal off, and the diagrams illustrate the necessity of a particular cutting point. We now turn the arbor true the full length, and to do this it is vital that the graver should be held firmly on the rest and also to use the point of the graver only. When using the turns, as with the lathe, the cutting only takes place when the work is revolving towards the cutter, so, unlike the lathe, when the bow is drawn upwards, the work will reverse its motion and the graver is held away. A very little practice will make this movement quite natural, and you will unconsciously hold the graver free of the work whilst it is revolving backwards. Now bring the bow downwards and at the same time hold the point of the graver to the work; it may not make a full cut. If we imagine for a moment that the arbor is oval, we shall, if we hold the graver firm enough, be able to cut at two points only, eventually making a full continuous cut when the work is true, that is, perfectly round. When the whole length of the arbor is running true, we bring the side of the graver into play and present to the work as much of the cutting edge as we wish. Practice alone will teach when to apply the full cutting edge. We can now turn down the part which is to fit into the movement that is from the shoulder that works between the bottom plate and the barrel bridge.

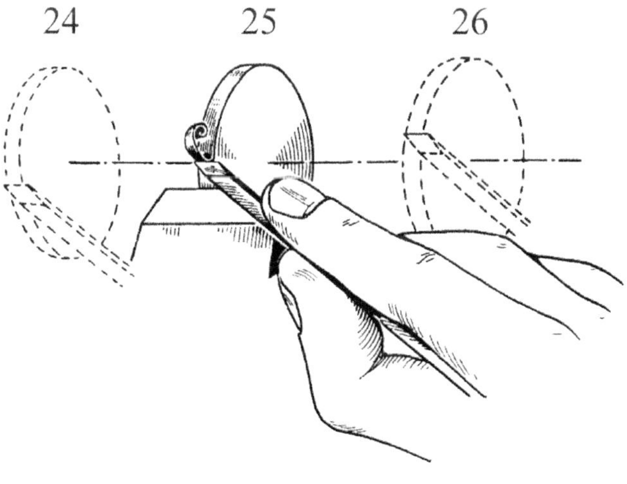

Fig. 24 – Position of Graver Too Low
Fig. 25 – The Correct Position to Hold the Graver
Fig. 26 – Graver Held Too High

The fit must be very tight in order to allow a further reduction when polishing and still then be a good fit. Now turn the pivot at the end of the shaft and so allow the first shoulder to move further into the movement by an amount equal to the length of the pivot. Just a word here about turning the shoulders. Using the same shaped graver (Fig. 22), hold it as indicated (Fig. 27), the shoulder being at right angles to the cylindrical part of the shaft; see that no pip is left; it should have the appearance of a separate collet driven on to the shaft. This will require a little practice and is an important accomplishment to good turning; all shoulders must be square. We can now turn the shaft to let the crown wheel on, or, to be correct, nearly on; polishing will give the requisite freedom.

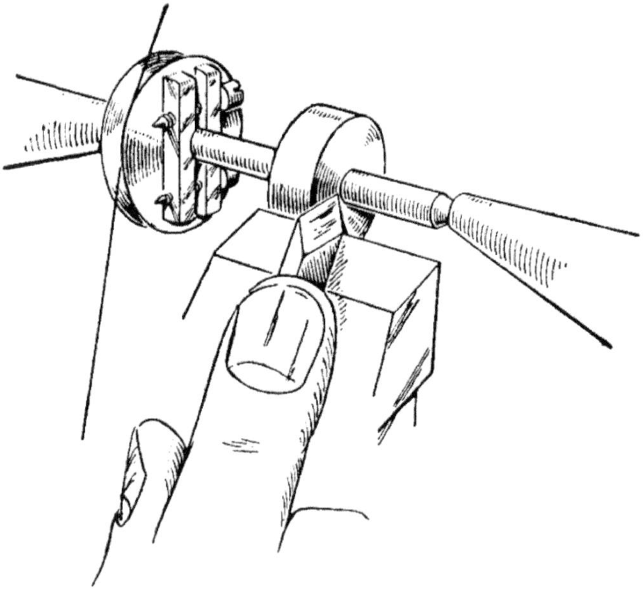

Fig. 27 – Showing Correct Position of Graver to Cut a Square Shoulder

Mark the arbor the length this last bearing is to be and turn a nick; we can turn the remaining part to the pivot down a little, that is the part where the square is to be for the castle wheel to work on. Having done this, remove from the turns and remove the ferrule. Place the shaft in the pin tongs as shown in Fig. 28 and file a flat, not too much at first.

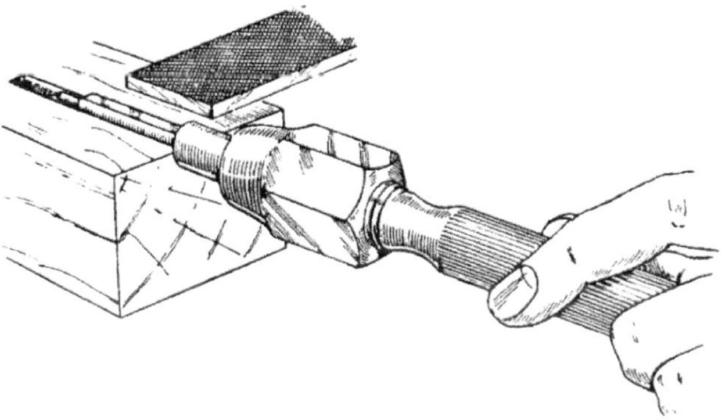

Fig. 28 – Showing Winding Shaft Square Being Filed

If the shaft rests in the groove of a filing block held in the vice it will be found convenient. Now reverse the shaft and hold it on the filing block so that the flat just filed rests flat on to the flat part of the block and proceed to file another flat of the same amount as the first. We now have two flat surfaces which should be parallel. Remove the block from the vice and hold the shaft in the jaws with a rounded surface uppermost, now file another flat of the same amount, reverse in the vice and file the fourth flat. If due care has been exercised a good square should be the result. The castle wheel should not yet begin to go on and the square may not be full; the edges may still show the original cylinder. Remove the shaft from the pin vice and replace the ferrule on the end where the thread is to be cut. Fit up in the turns, but without the bow. Hold the ferrule with the left hand and with, a fine 3-square needle file proceed to file each of the flats, using a motion similar to that employed when polishing, just a little to each flat at a time. Remove from the turns occasionally and see if the castle wheel fits and continue this process until the wheel goes on the square about half way. It is as well to measure all four flats to ensure a perfect square, as *A, B* (Fig. 20). It will be noted that the nick we turned to determine the length of the square has become useful. We are thus able to keep clear of that shoulder and at the same time make a clean job. By holding the shaft between centers, filing, and at the same time holding the ferrule, we are able to ensure a flat surface; the flat presented to the file finds its own level, and steadying it with the hand enables the file to be used. We now remove the shaft from the turns and placing the ferrule on the square part, turn down the end to be threaded so that it will enter the hole in the screw plate two holes larger than the hole we intend to use, to cut the thread. Make the end taper so that it enters the correct tap hole. We are then able to start the thread.

Fig. 29 – Iron Polisher

Having done this, remove the ferrule and grip the shaft in the runner of the screw head tool, using a brass chuck and holding it as near the part where the thread is to be cut as possible. Proceed to cut the thread. (See Screw Making, pg. 57)

The shaft is now ready to harden and temper, tempering it to a blue. It is always a good policy to finish new pieces made for a watch in the same style as the rest of the movement; if for instance the steel work generally is of a grey finish, we then finish the shaft grey. In this instance we shall assume that the shaft we have made is for a high-grade watch and that the steel work is polished. Place the ferrule on the extreme end of the tapped part of the shaft; this end which is tapped and has not a full thread cut on it will be cut off, otherwise the button will not screw on correctly. Fit up in the turns with the bow and first of all polish the bearing which works in the frame with an iron polisher charged with oilstone dust and oil. The iron polisher we use for this purpose and also for most polishing in the turns or lathe is made from a piece of iron or mild steel, about 9 in. long, 4 mm. wide and 2 mm. thick. One side is filed as shown (Fig. 29) so that when you hold the polisher in the right hand the left hand side is filed both to a taper and a knife edge. This enables the polisher to be held at an angle from the work, and the knife edge is the part that polishes the shoulders, as we shall see.

When using this polisher, close the left eye and with the right eye follow the knife edge of the polisher and see that this edge operates square to the work, to ensure that the shoulder is square; as the bow is brought down the polisher is worked forward, and backwards on the upwards stroke of the bow; the work is then always revolving against the direction of the motion of the polisher. A little practice will make this diverse motion quite simple.

In this manner polish the first bearing until it fits tightly in the plates. Then proceed to polish the bearing for the crown wheel, again leaving the fit tight; at the same time watch the shoulders, leave them flat and square. We can now polish the pivot in a similar manner. The square is polished with the same polisher; remove the bow, and work the polisher up and down each flat of the square, a little to each flat at a time, using the same motion employed when filing it. It will not be necessary to hold the ferrule, as the polisher will not "bite" as the file does. Again leave the fit tight.

Remove the shaft from the turns and also remove the ferrule. Hold the shaft in the screw head tool as we did when tapping, but gripping the square. Split a piece of soft wood (the end of an emery buff does well), open the split, and apply a little oilstone dust and oil in the split.

Place the thread of the shaft in this charged split, screw in the vice so that the soft wood closes in on the thread. In this position screw the shaft up fully and unscrew, several times, so that the thread is cleaned. When this is completed, clean the shaft well in benzine and brush to remove all traces of oilstone dust and oil. We can now proceed to polish with diamantine.

Replace the ferrule as before and fit up in the turns with the bow. Wipe the polisher with a clean rag, then refile the acting surface, giving the surface a cross grain to retain the polishing medium; this equally applies when refiling to charge with oilstone dust and oil. The polisher is now charged with diamantine and exactly the same procedure is followed. Sufficient of the polishing medium finds its way to the knife edge to ensure the shoulder receiving its share. This final polishing will give the requisite freedom of the shaft and at the same time give the black polish so desirable.

Polishing a pivot or bearing flat and parallel, with a good square shoulder, and the shoulder with a good flat surface and well-polished, is an accomplishment that needs some practice.

Turning in a Pinion

As an example we shall turn in a new fourth pinion; it has a seconds pivot and calls for some special care on this account. In order to embrace the full curriculum I propose to explain the procedure when turning a new wheel and pinion. Usually the wheel is supplied with the pinion already riveted to the wheel.

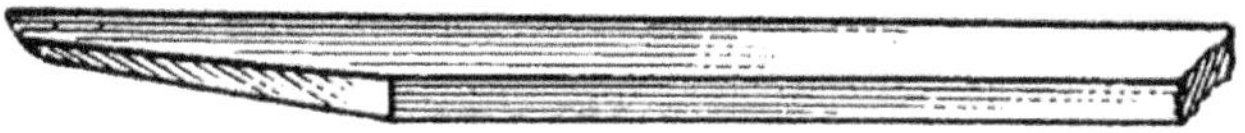

Fig. 30 – Ogee Cutter

We first of all start by giving both faces of the wheel a surface with the Water-of-Ayr stone; to do this, fit up in the turns with the ferrule and bow, make the wheel revolve fairly quickly, and hold the stone, dipped in water, against the face. Do not move the stone and we shall give a circular grain finish. Remove from the turns, and, with a brush, remove all traces of the Water-of-Ayr stone. We then cut the ogees, that is, the turned parts on both sides of the wheel itself. Fit up in the turns again, and use the cutter here illustrated (Fig. 30) to turn the ogee on the pivot side. After whetting the cutter, polish it on the zinc block with diamantine. The surface cut will then be polished and no further treatment is necessary. Keep this, and the other cutter to be mentioned later, especially for ogees; they will not require sharpening frequently if this is done.

To cut the first ogee *D*, bring the T rest up close to the work with the broad side facing the wheel (Fig. 31). Hold the bow on the up stroke and then place the cutter in position and make the first cut; three or four cuts should be sufficient. This work is carried out slowly and decisively, just a firm steady cut, no chattering; the result will be a polished surface. Hold the cutter at an angle so that the corner nearest you cuts first and by the time the full cutting edge comes into operation the ogee will be finished.

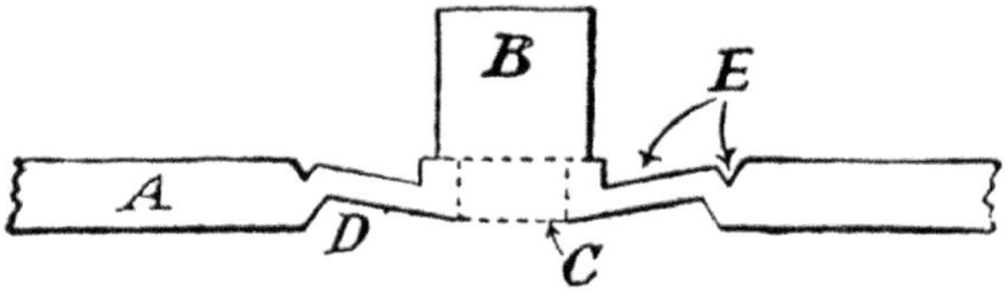

A = wheel *B* = pinion head *C* = rivet

Fig. 31 – Wheel, Showing Shape of Ogees

Reverse in the turns and cut the pinion side with the cutter, which is the shape of an ordinary graver but polished. Here we make two cuts as shown in Fig. 31 at *E*, taking the same precautions as when cutting the other side.

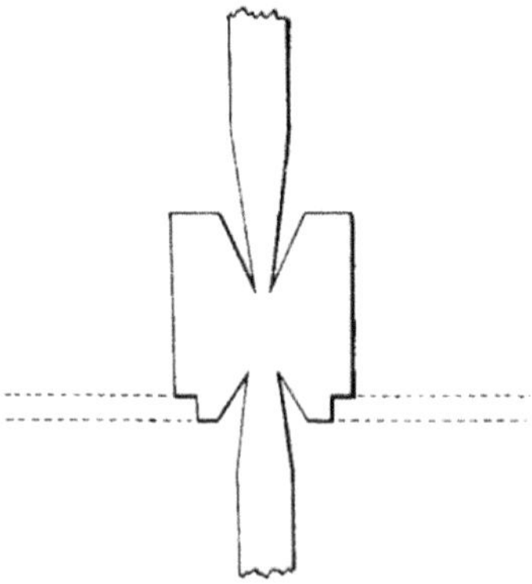

Fig. 32 – Pinion Showing Undercut

We are now ready to start on the pinion. (If necessary, turn down the pinion head to correct height.) First we cut the undercut into the pinion head, starting on the pinion end first (Fig. 32). Whet the graver to make the first cut and as we cut deeper whet the graver to a longer point to enable a deeper cut to be made and at the same time not widening the cut. Our aim is to make a reasonably deep cut but not too wide at the mouth, so that when finished a ring of metal is left at the roots of the pinion leaves. Reverse the pinion in the turns and cut the undercut on the bottom side, the riveted part. The prime object of the undercut at the top is to free the facing tool, and the bottom one is to trap the oil at the pivot. Undercutting has, however, developed into a test of craftsmanship, and, while deep undercuts are a pleasure to inspect, there are limits—stability must be considered. This done we can proceed to face the pinion. Drill up a piece of iron or mild steel a hole large enough for the arbor of the pinion to fit quite freely, the diameter of the facing tool, as it is called (Fig. 33), to be larger than the diameter of the pinion head. File the end flat and charge with oilstone dust and oil. An ordinary lock key (Fig. 34) makes a very good facing tool, the portion as indicated by the dotted line being cut away. The large hole gives ample freedom to the arbor. A good facing tool can be made from an ordinary French nail (Fig. 33A), in fact, some of the finest facing I have seen has been done with the aid of such a tool. Fit up in the turns as shown (Fig. 35) and make the wheel revolve fairly quickly. Apply a fair pressure to the facing tool and at the same time make that revolve about a half turn, backwards and forwards.

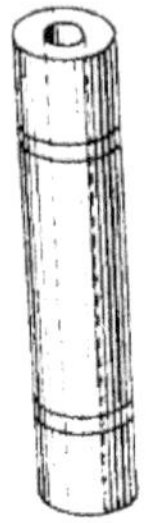

Fig. 33

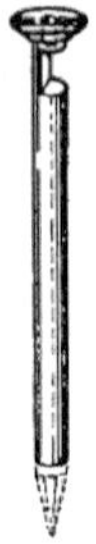

Fig. 33A

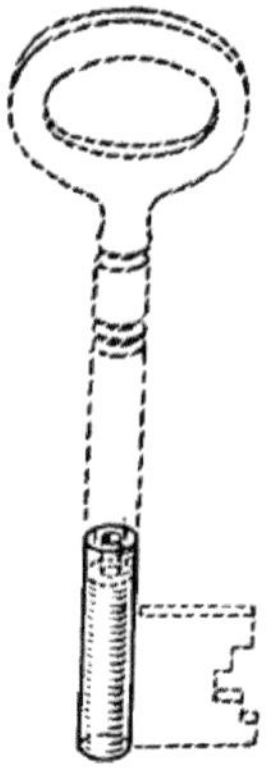

Fig. 34

Fig. 33 – Facing Tool
Fig. 33A – Facing Tool Made From a French Nail
Fig. 34 – Showing Facing Tool Made From a Key

In this manner the face of the pinion will be ground quite flat. Let the facing tool follow the work as it were, and it will find its own level. Grind both faces in this way, and then clean well to remove all traces of oilstone dust. Clean the facing tool well, refile the end and charge with diamantine and repeat the operation as for grinding. The face is "up" or fully polished when the tool squeaks; it takes some little practice to face a pinion well. Turn the arbor as shown (Fig. 36) and polish with oilstone dust and oil, finishing off with diamantine; see that the shoulder is square. When fully polished, turn down the pivot; by cutting into the highly polished arbor we shall give it a very square appearance.

Proceed to polish the pivot as we did the arbor; do not shorten the pivot until it is fully polished. Particular care must be taken to see that no pip is left in the corner of the pivot shoulder, otherwise it may bind in its hole.

Finally, with a finely whetted graver, cut the extreme sharp edge, as indicated; do not polish this last cut as it gives the pivot shoulder an appearance of extra flatness.

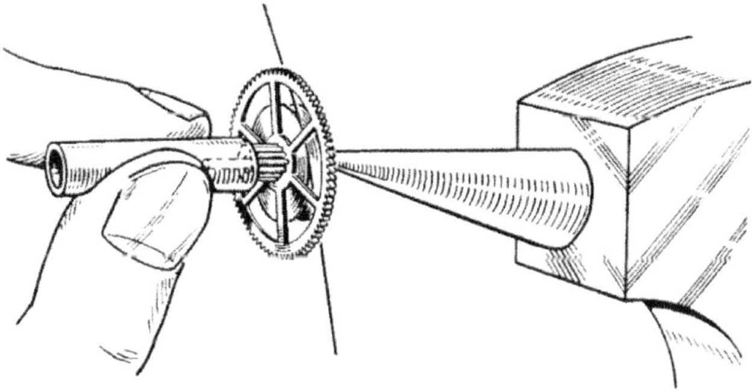

Fig. 35 – Method of Holding Facing Tool When Facing Pinion

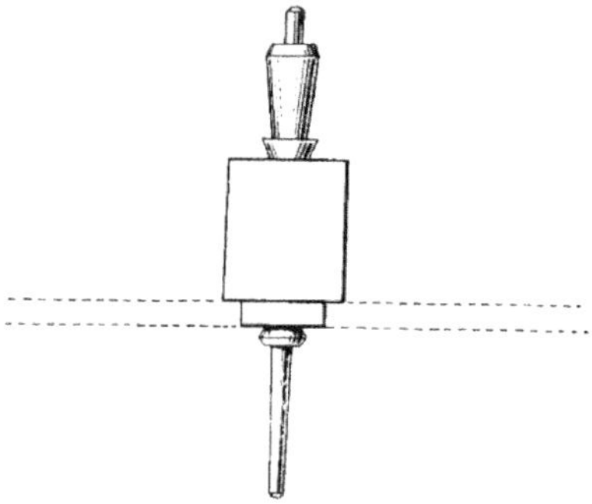

Fig. 36 – Finished Pinion

Turn the other pivot in a similar manner and we can now cut the pivots to length and round the ends. The pivots are finally finished by burnishing. The burnisher hardens the surface, and forms a hard skin. To round the ends, place in the runner here illustrated (Fig. 37), rough down with an Arkansas slip and finish off with a flat burnisher.

To give an extra finish to the arbors finally polish with boxwood slip charged with diamantine, or a piece of ordinary watch peg wood cut flat answers well. Use very little diamantine and polish until dry; a black velvet finish will be imparted. The finished pinion is as shown in Fig. 36.

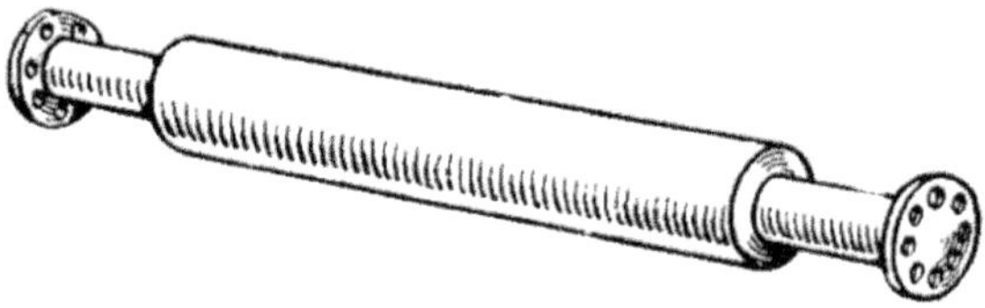

Fig. 37 – Runner to Round off Ends of Pivots

To Turn a Balance Staff

Balance staffs can be purchased in the rough from the tool shop. They are, as a rule, ready hardened and tempered down to a blue and are known as "blue staffs," which means that they have been roughed out. On the other hand, the staff can be made from the rod, turned as illustrated (Fig. 38) and hardened and tempered, but generally speaking it is not economical so to do.

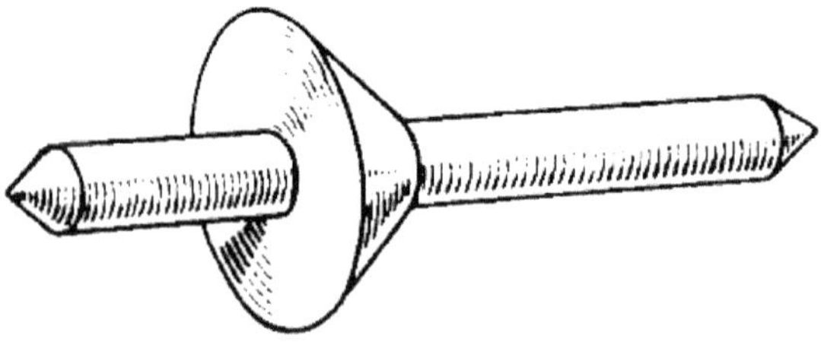

Fig. 38 – "Blue Staff"

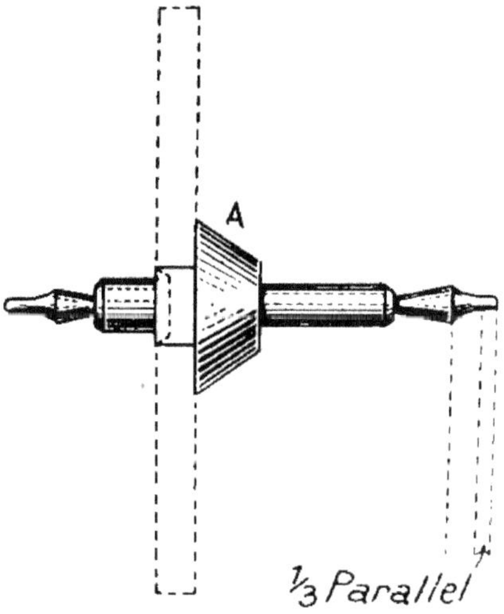

Fig. 39 – Finished Balance Staff

However, to start with a blue staff. First turn the back slope true (Fig. 39 at A) and polish with oilstone dust and oil and finish off with diamantine. Now cut into this polished back slope, turn down so that the roller just begins to go on, reverse the staff in the turns and again cut into the back slope to let the balance on. By making these two cuts into the polished surface of the back slope, the remaining part will have a square appearance. Polish the arbor to let the roller on into its correct position, watching the shoulder, to keep it square and flat, first with oilstone dust and oil, then with diamantine. Into the polished arbor cut for the back cut of the pivot as shown, break the sharp corner as we did when making the pivot of the pinion; do not turn the pivot yet. Reverse in the turns and turn down and polish the shoulder to take the balance spring collet. Undercut the rivet for the balance and rivet the balance in position. Turn the top pivot to shape, using the graver shaped as illustrated (Fig. 40). In order to expose as much of the pivot as possible to facilitate turning use the runner (Fig. 41). Small dot holes are punched on the extreme edge with a pointed punch before hardening and tempering.

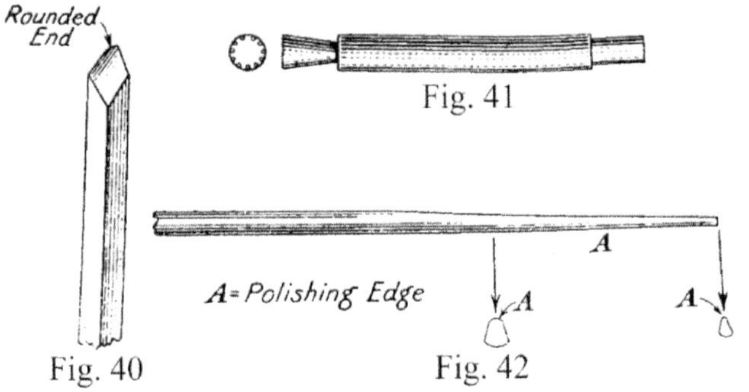

Fig. 40 – Graver for Balance Pivot
Fig. 41 - Runner for Pivot-Making
Fig. 42 – Polisher for Balance Pivots

After hardening and tempering, the end is stoned flat and the edges are also stoned away as required. By this means it is possible to turn quite a small pivot. The shape of the pivot is important. There should be one-third of the pivot, measuring from where the cone starts, parallel, and two-thirds to form the cone. This shape is considered the most suitable to give strength and freedom. To polish the pivot, use an iron or mild steel polisher made of a piece of round rod about 9 in. long and 3 mm. wide. File one end as shown in Fig. 42.

By making the polisher taper it will be found convenient to manipulate, and further it will serve for various size pivots. The runner for polishing the pivot (Fig. 43) is similar to the Jacot tool runner. First use oilstone dust and oil and when polishing not only give the polisher a backwards and forwards movement but also an inclination to twist the polisher so that it has the tendency to cut the grain as much as possible. The final finish is given with the same polisher, cleaned, refiled, and charged with diamantine. A burnisher, similar in shape to the polisher, is now used to form the hard skin, as already explained.

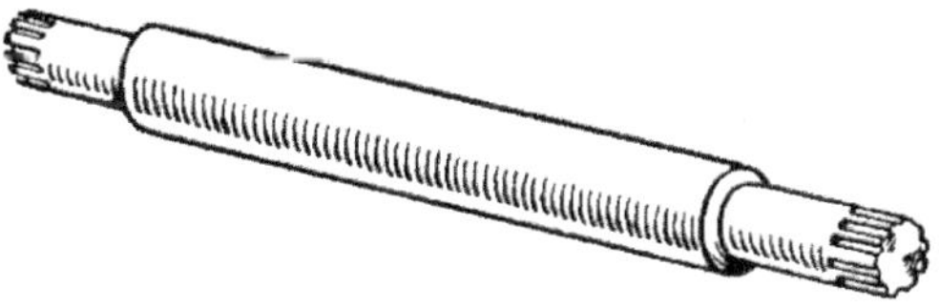

Fig. 43 – Runner for Polishing Pivots

Some watchmakers make a small steel plate with an aperture cut to the shape of the polisher; this tool is hardened and the face is finished with a fine stone. The tool is held in the vice (Fig. 44) and the polisher drawn with the polishing edge presented to the shaped part, thus remaking the polisher by cutting it on the sharp edge, always to the same shape. If we are making always the same size pivot such a procedure is quite good, but for general work, filing in the ordinary way suffices. We now proceed to make the lower pivot. The ends of the pivots are finished off in the same manner as the pivots to the pinion we have previously discussed. A word as regards measurements; if the old staff is available the procedure is quite simple, providing the old staff was correct. The principal measurement is from the end of the bottom pivot to the seat of the balance; the balance must be free of the pallet cock and at the same time as much freedom as possible allowed for the balance spring. The other measurement is the distance the roller is to be let on to the staff, otherwise the rest is fitting.

Fig. 44 – Tool to Remake Pivot Polisher

Bread as Cleaner

In connection with the cleaning of steelwork during polishing I would like to mention here a method which was, and probably still is, used by escapement makers and other workmen who are continually polishing steelwork.

In order to ensure that all traces of oilstone dust are removed from the subject under treatment—and this is very important—the center part of a piece of bread is kneaded with oil to the consistency of putty, and with this substance the steel piece under treatment is dabbed.

This is very searching and removes without doubt all traces of oilstone dust, but as the average watchmaker today does so little of this form of polishing, it is hardly worth while going to this trouble to make a special preparation. But, nonetheless, it is still equally important that all traces of the oilstone dust should be removed before attempting to polish with diamantine.

Screw Making

Whilst it is rarely necessary today to make a screw, the ability to be able to make one is useful, not only to make the screw itself but to be able to apply the skill in other directions. We then proceed as follows.

Procure a piece of steel the diameter a little larger than the head of the new screw, turn down for the thread about twice the length the thread is to be and leave the end slightly tapered. The diameter of the arbor to be tapped should be such that it just fits the tap hole two sizes larger; if this is observed a fill thread will be ensured. The actual thread is not cut, but burred up. In mass production of screws, more especially with the larger screws, the thread is cut and metal is removed, but with the watchmaker making just one screw such is not the case; the individual thread thrown up is really drawn up, similar to drawn pinion wire. So when "cutting" the thread use great care. The screw to be tapped can be held in the lathe, or if turned in the turns, in a pin vice. In either case make sure the screw plate is square to the arbor being tapped, apply plenty of oil, and work the arbor backwards and forwards, "cutting" the fresh thread slowly. Continue thus until the arbor has been tapped to its full length. Then reduce the head of the screw to the required diameter and height. Shorten the tapped part as required. Cut the slot in the head with the slotting or screw head file and we are ready to harden and temper. (See Hardening and Tempering, pg. 63)

Most screws in watches are left with a blue finish, so after hardening proceed as follows. Clean the thread between wood as already explained when making a shaft. The head is finished in the screw head tool (Fig. 45). Make the side of the head smooth with an Arkansas slip and treat the end of the head in a similar manner. Then use a fine emery buff on both these surfaces, well clean the head with pith and peg the slot to ensure that all traces of emery are removed. To polish, use a bell metal polisher, a fairly large one, about 9 in. long and 1/2 in. wide and 1/8 in. thick. Charge with diamantine which is moister than that ordinarily used to polish steel work; if the diamantine is dry a good blue is not obtained. Finish off with the boxwood slip, charged with moist diamantine, do not continue the polishing until the diamantine is dry. The handle of a watch brush answers well in place of the boxwood. To clean the handle of the watch brush, before charging with diamantine, scrape with a sharp knife, this equally applies to the boxwood slip.

Fig. 45 – Screw Head Tool

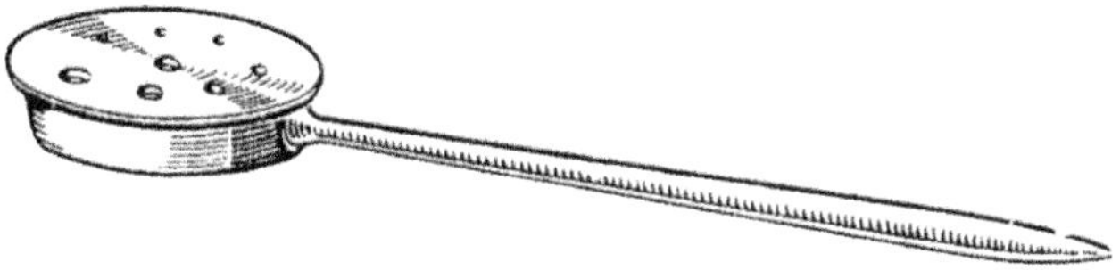

Fig. 46 – Bluing Pan

Remove the screw from the tool and place in benzine and brush well, there must be no trace of grease to obtain an even blue and on no account touch with the fingers. To blue, use a bluing pan (Fig. 46) and hold over the flame of a spirit lamp and while heating tap the handle near the pan. This will cause the screw to jump about very slightly in its hole and help the even distribution of heat and so an even blue. When the desired blue is obtained, remove the screw immediately from the pan with the tweezers, otherwise the bluing or tempering will continue even if the pan is removed from the flame. The stages of coloring are pale straw, deep straw, red, and then blue: after that the metal turns green; watchmakers are not interested in this latter color. Some makers finish the screws of their watches red, others white.

If the screw we have just made is to be white, then temper to a blue after buffing, finishing with the diamantine as already explained. To finish the end of the head as flat as possible by hand is known as a "tallow" head. If the head is to be dead flat, use the laps supplied with the screw head tool, using the iron lap charged with oilstone dust and oil first, then the bell metal lap charged with moist diamantine, and finally the boxwood lap. The "bolt tool" can also be used for this purpose, as already explained. In high-grade watches the edges of the slots are "broken" with an Arkansas slip (Fig. 47), no further finish being necessary to this part. If the slot is too narrow to admit the use of the Arkansas slip, an old, worn pivot file answers well. First, out with the file, and then a stroke or two with the burnisher side of the file. The edges of screws are "broken" to preserve them; you will not find such screws with burrs thrown up. The ends of the screws are rounded and polished, and the lantern chucks supplied with the screw head tool are used for this purpose.

Screws that have been burnished do not blue well; they have a mottled appearance, and screws that have been polished with diamantine too dry have a milky appearance; the only way to rectify both these is to harden again and polish as directed.

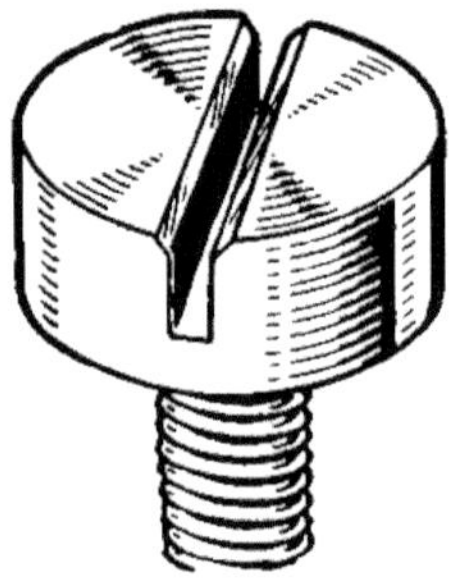

Fig. 47 – A Well-Finished Screw Head

The Swiss Method

It is interesting to note that the Swiss method is precisely the same as ours, only, of course, in the large factories special arrangements are made to carry out the work expeditiously.

I saw, when making a tour of one of the largest factories there, a very interesting tool used for polishing the heads of screws—a plate of about 2 ft. in diameter, drilled with hundreds of holes, of a size to allow the thread part of the screws to drop in.

This plate is placed on the bench and the screws are dropped in each hole, and another plate of about the same size, but without holes, is then placed over the heads of the screws. The two plates are then reversed, the underside of the plate, with the holes, uppermost.

The holes on this side are countersunk; the plate is then heated, and a wax similar to brown sealing-wax is poured over the plate to fill these sinks. When cool the plate is lifted off, and the screws are all held securely in position and, of course, quite flat.

This plate, which has a tapped hole in the center, is then screwed onto a machine and the latter is so arranged that immediately under the plate with the screws another plate is fixed, which is made of iron or bell metal. The procedure is as follows: The lower plate is charged with a sharp cutting medium, such as oilstone dust, and is then made to revolve. At the same time the other plate containing the screws is made to revolve, but in the opposite direction. The upper plate is then lowered on to the grinding surface, with the effect, of course, that the heads of all the screws are ground perfectly flat. The operation, as you can realize, is very speedy and several hundred screws are so ground in a few minutes.

The method of applying the polishing medium is very interesting. The material is made up into sticks resembling large sticks of sealing-wax, and this method not only applies to the sharp cutting medium but also to the diamantine. It is, of course, very clean, and an economical method of using these materials.

Now when the heads of the screws are in such a condition as to be polished with diamantine, the plate containing the screws is thoroughly cleaned off, and the iron or bell metal plate is then substituted by a zinc one which is charged with diamantine. The operation is then proceeded with as before until the surfaces of the screws are polished.

When completed, the plate is unscrewed and dropped on to a bench, when all the screws come out and are collected and transferred to another room, where they are boiled in a solution of caustic soda. After this they are transferred to metal barrels containing boxwood dust, which are tilted to an angle and kept revolving over a lighted gas jet. When perfectly dry, the entire contents of the barrel are turned into a sieve, and the screws, all with white threads, are thus separated from the sawdust.

The object of the tilting of the barrel is to ensure the boxwood dust moving and so not burning. At the same time, the screws are subjected to the heat without fear of tempering and are at the same time thoroughly dried.

The reason for the white threads is due to the special hardening and tempering, which I will explain later.

I have described screws, taking one instance, but the method of procedure is precisely the same when dealing with springs, etc. You will see that the same principles are used in the modern factories in Switzerland as were used in England years ago by the hand-workers.

While in Switzerland, I endeavored to obtain from the tool-shops some of the solid form of diamantine and sharp cutting medium, but found that it was unknown. I presume, therefore, that this method is the property of that particular factory.

Cleanliness

Just one final word about polishing. Cleanliness is absolutely essential. Keep your diamantine always covered, as you would your watch oil. Also keep all polishers and polishing blocks, etc., in cases or sheaths, the same, of course, equally applying to oilstone dust. It is always advisable to keep the oilstone dust away from the diamantine.

I would like to emphasize the importance of using watch oil when mixing diamantine. Do not get the diamantine mixed with your stock of oil, otherwise this will spell disaster to the pivots of watches, etc. To keep a bottle of watch oil especially for diamantine is a much safer plan.

We have not discussed all the parts that are turned in a watch but, I think, sufficient to show the method of procedure; the ground we have covered, together with the notes on the lathe, embody all branches of turning the watchmaker is likely to encounter and should enable him to carry out any work of a similar nature.

Hardening and Tempering

There are many ways of hardening and tempering, books having been written on this subject alone, and engineers lay down laws governing it. For watchmakers, however, we need confine ourselves only to one or two methods.

When hardening screws, shafts, etc., the object should be heated to a cherry red and plunged into water. The piece can with advantage be covered with ordinary soap first. Some workers are of the opinion that it is inclined to toughen the steel if the water is hot, while others maintain that if a film of oil is floated on the water first, this has the tendency to prevent distortion, etc. These, of course, may be fads of the individual, and I recommend everybody to do just what suits him best. The main object, of course, is not to burn the steel, and how this is achieved is, so far as we are concerned, of secondary importance.

With such pieces as springs, keyless wheels, etc., where there is a certain amount of strain, a toughness is required, and a better result is obtained by plunging into oil. There are other methods of cooling in mercury, cyanide of potassium, etc., when an extra degree of hardness is required, but we very rarely require this high standard of hardness, so we can confine ourselves to water or oil.

To harden some pieces, such as a long click spring, special care is necessary to prevent distortion; in such cases the piece should be plunged into the cooling medium lengthways. It is advisable, as an extra precaution, should the piece be very long and thin, to bind it well with iron binding wire; it is important that the wire should be of iron, because this will not harden.

Use plenty of the binding wire to form ample protection, and leave a piece that can be used as a handle. Now cover the whole piece with ordinary soap, heat to a cherry red, and plunge into the quenching medium as advised. If the piece being hardened has a thick part, and then tapers off, as a solid click spring would do, it is advisable to apply the heat first to the thick part. Then the fine portion will not burn. You can well imagine that with such a spring, if held in the flame at, say, the center, the fine spring end would become white-hot by the time the thick end was red.

It is advisable to hold the piece in the quenching medium for a moment or two before withdrawing.

In some instances, where the piece is of a very

delicate nature, more elaborate precautions must be taken. For example, when hardening a chronometer detent it is advisable to make a small tube of steel into which the detent can be placed to its entire length. Fill the tube either with graphite or charcoal (preferably from burnt leather), seal each end with soap and proceed to harden the whole piece as explained.

You will find, in hardening in this manner, there will be no tendency to distort; furthermore, the piece will not have changed color and, consequently, will not have scaled.

Some chronometer makers use a piece of steel rod of about 6 in. or 7 in. in length, with a hole drilled in one end of sufficient depth to receive the detent, and pack the one end as explained, using the other end as a handle. In these circumstances, the best method of tempering is to immerse the whole rod—do not remove the piece from inside—in a pan of oil, holding the pan over a flame until a black smoke issues; then remove the rod from the oil and allow it to cool naturally. Carefully unpack the end, and the piece will be found to be hardened and tempered. By using a steel container we are able to test with a file to ensure hardness before tempering, without removing the object, since if the tube is hard the contents also will be hard.

It is advisable, after hardening all steel pieces, to test to see that the piece is actually hard. Just try it carefully with a file and if no impression is made you may take it that it is satisfactory, that is, pieces other than the detent, as already explained.

A Swiss Method

Advantage is taken by the factories in Switzerland of the fact that if air is excluded during the hardening and tempering no oxidization takes place, and the pieces retain their color as finished by the machines. The method utilized in the factories is to place the pieces in a spoon-shaped tool. The bowl is used as the receptacle, and another bowl is then clamped over this and material is used for the edges to ensure it being airtight.

To the end of the handle a wire is attached, and the whole piece is heated by electricity. When the desired temperature is reached—this is shown on a gauge dial—the whole spoon is plunged into the cooling medium. The current is, of course, turned off before the plunge.

Upon removal from the liquid the current is again turned on until the temperature has been reached for the purpose of tempering. It is then switched off again and allowed to cool naturally. Upon opening the spoon the pieces are perfectly white as when placed in there.

Hardening in Air

Small drills and other fine pieces, for which it is necessary to harden only the extreme point, can be hardened effectively by holding in the flame until cherry red and then suddenly blowing the flame out. The sudden chilling is sufficient to harden.

In such circumstances the tempering must be done very carefully. Make the hardened end bright with a fine emery buff, and hold the thicker part of the piece in the flame. You will find that the heat will travel along the piece until the hardened end is tempered. In the case of a drill a light straw color will be sufficient.

Hardening and Tempering Small Pieces

Small pieces, such as clicks, return pieces, pull-out

pieces, etc., are best hardened as follows: Bind a piece of iron binding wire round the article, leaving sufficient of the wire to act as a handle. Harden in the usual manner in oil, and try it with a file to ensure that it is quite hard. To temper, just dip the piece again in the oil, and with the oil still clinging, pass quickly backwards and forwards over a flame; do not hold the piece still in the flame, otherwise too much heat will be applied and it will soften. The tempering is complete when a black smoke issues from the oil clinging to the piece. We have, in effect, boiled the piece in oil.

A convenient method to hold screws is to file the end of a piece of brass wire, about the thickness of a steel knitting needle, filed to a taper, for about an inch, to the thickness of an ordinary sewing needle; bend this tapered end to a "V" shape about a quarter of an inch from the end. We now have a convenient holder that will take all sizes of screws likely to pass through our hands for hardening.

To Harden Brass

Brass is hardened by hammering or rolling, and in the case of wire, by continual drawing through a draw plate. During hardening of brass, care must be exercised to ensure that the piece is not cracked or fractured. To temper brass apply heat.

Drilling

The principal points to be observed when drilling are the shape of the drill blade and its temper, the speed at which the drill should be made to revolve, and lubrication. The shape of the blade of the drill for brass and steel is as shown in Figs. 48 and 49. If the bow is used, the blade may be shaped to form a double cutting edge; that is, it will cut both during the backward and forward motion.

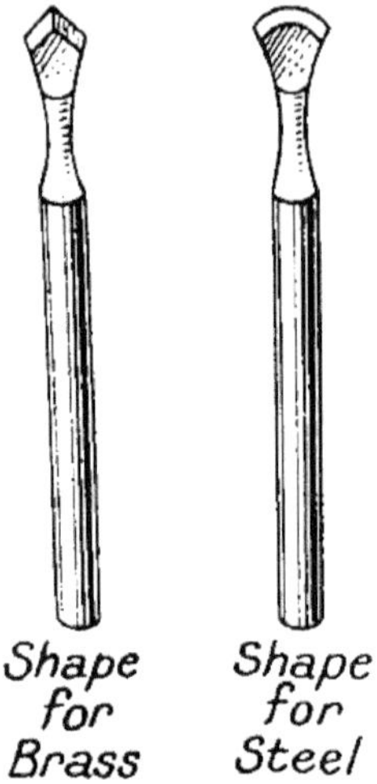

Figs. 48 & 49 – Drills

If the drill is used in the lathe, the blade need be sharpened to cut only in the one direction.

The drill, whether for steel or brass, should be so shaped as to allow the metal cut away to be emitted from the hole; also the stock of the drill must be smaller than the blade, otherwise the drill will bind when the hole is of any depth.

It is obvious, of course, that the drill must be harder than the metal you are to drill; so you will see, therefore, that it is useless to try and drill a piece of hardened and tempered steel with a hardened and tempered drill. The drill must be left hard.

It is preferable to use a tempered drill, this being stronger, not so brittle, and less liable to break. To break a drill in metal is sometimes a difficult matter to rectify.

Where possible, therefore, it is advisable to soften the piece before drilling. There are certain pieces, however, which cannot be softened, and in these circumstances the drill of suitable temper or hardness and shape must be used.

To Remove Broken Drill

Should you happen to break a drill in the work, it can sometimes be removed with beeswax. Roll a piece of the wax to a point, and insert the point into the hole and withdraw sharply. The broken piece must be loose to enable you to do this. Should the piece be wedged tightly, there is no alternative but to make quite soft and re-drill. Such a procedure applies when steel is being drilled.

If you wish to remove a broken drill or any piece of steel from brass, such as a broken screw, etc., it can be removed in a solution of alum. The procedure is this: Make a saturated solution of alum, i.e. take as much water as is required to submerge completely the entire article, and dissolve as much alum as the water will take. Into this place the article and allow to stand for about 12 hours, after which you will find the steel piece has rotted. The method can be accelerated by heating, or very slowly allowing to boil. If the article is gilded, it will be necessary to re-gild, as the alum badly discolors the gilding. Should it be necessary to remove a screw from a watch plate in this manner, it is obviously advisable to remove all other steel work before immersing in the alum solution.

To Drill for New Pivot

What I particularly wish to point out is that when drilling the drill must be suitable for the individual requirements.

I do not advocate the drilling of pinions and staffs to fit new pivots, but I know, of course, such things are done when it is a question of economy. The only alternative, from a good workmanship point of view, when a pivot is broken, is to fit an entirely new piece. However, in view of the fact that this form of pivoting is practiced, I propose, for the help of those who require it, to describe the method of drilling. We will take a pinion, for example.

Having removed all traces of the old pivot, select or make a drill a shade larger than the finished pivot. Select the runner of the pivoting tool that just allows the drill to pass through freely. Fix the revolving drum with the runners by the peg provided for that purpose. Apply plenty of oil to the chamfer sink of the runner. Place the pinion in position and bring the back runner up sufficiently tightly to ensure there being no shake, but, at the same time, it must be free. Place a spot of oil to the pivot running in the back runner (see Fig. 50).

The illustration shows the simple hollow runner type. The procedure is the same, but there is no drum to lock.

The bow should be in position before the wheel is placed between the runners. Adjust the pin in the ferrule to engage with the wheel. Now make the wheel revolve slowly and evenly and place the drill in position and apply a fair amount of pressure, at the same time making the drill revolve slowly. You should be able to feel the drill cutting.

Remove the wheel occasionally to see that all is progressing satisfactorily, and it is advisable to clean out the hole with a sharpened peg before replacing in the tool. Apply plenty of oil again to the countersink guide into which the arbor being drilled is fitted.

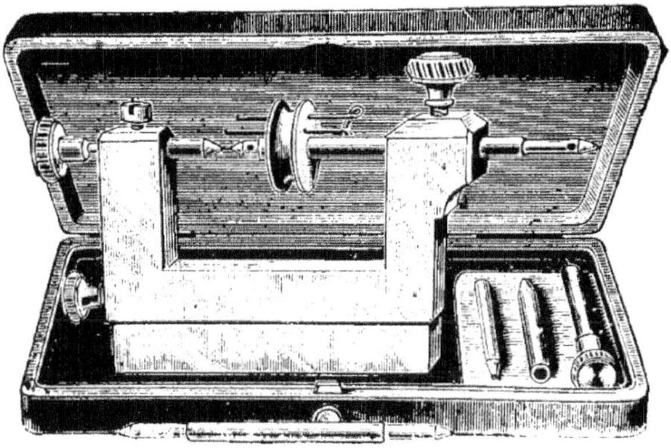

Fig. 50 – Pivoting Tool

Should you find the drill is not cutting, ascertain why. Do not carry on unless a decided cutting is shown, otherwise the surface to be drilled will be burnished, and this surface is sometimes very difficult and troublesome to remove. We must remember that the pinion should not be softened, and it may be that the drill is not hard enough or the blade is not sharpened enough to an obtuse angle.

Sometimes hard surfaces require the cutting edge of the drill to be flatter or blunter, to enable the drill to stand up to the hardness. To obtain a good result, you must experiment. Having drilled the hole to a depth at least equal to the length of the finished pivot, proceed to file a piece of hardened and tempered steel wire to a very slight taper.

File the wire so that the end just commences to enter the hole drilled, then draw-file with a fine file until two-thirds enter the hole.

Make the end flat and square with an Arkansas slip, to ensure that all the pivot in the hole is gripping the sides, and that a sharp point is not preventing the pivot going quite home, thus serving no good purpose.

It now remains for the end so filed to be dipped into dry oilstone dust, and forced into the hole so far as possible. Now cut the new pivot nearly to length, and place the pinion on a stake and lightly tap the pivot quite home with a punch and hammer.

The new pivot is finished in the jacot tool, using the file first and finally burnishing. Round up the ends with an Arkansas slip and burnish, and the job is complete.

Let me repeat that this form of watch repairing is not good workmanship and is not tolerated in good workshops.

As a general rule it may be accepted that brass and similar metals can be drilled with considerable speed, but with steel a slower speed must be used and the harder the steel the less the speed.

Drilling Tools

The acme of perfection of drilling is to be able to drill straight a hole of some depth. There are in existence automatic means to enable this to be done—tools, such as the upright drilling machine (the pivoting tool just described), and various contrivances, worked in conjunction with the lathe. Should none of these devices be available, and you wish to drill a hole to some depth, this can be carried out to a marked degree of accuracy by placing on the drill stock a loose collet. The hole in the collet should be sufficiently large to allow ample freedom whilst the drill is revolving.

By this means we shall be able to see that the drill

is held straight in one direction—the horizontal position—as the drill must be lowered or lifted to keep the collet in the center of the drill stock.

If, for instance, the hand holding the article being drilled were lowered, the collet would run down towards the drill blade.

You will see that we now have only one direction to observe by eye to ensure straightness of the hole drilled, and that is to see that the drill is running parallel to the work.

Engineers pay great importance to drilling, and rules are laid down governing the speed of the drill with respect to different metals, etc., also the constituents of the oil used and the exact shape of the drill, using various forms of twist drills, etc.

I do not think the watchmaker need concern himself with these matters. The main points that he must observe are the shape of the blade, to ensure ample clearance, the hardness of the drill, and lubrication. The rest must be left to his experience and skill.

Twelve Watch Points

The following hints will be of assistance to the student, and should help him to turn out work of the highest class—

1. Honesty in all things; a watch botched because it cannot be seen by its owner is dishonesty.
2. Remember that when the watch leaves your hands your reputation is with that watch, so make the best possible job of all jobs.
3. It is as important to keep a promise as it is to do the work well. If you make a date, keep

it.

4. Good value is always a good policy; charge fairly for good work.
5. More watches are ruined by probably well-meaning but incompetent workmen than are actually worn out.
6. There are no short cuts to good watchmaking, no "royal road." Concentrated application is the motto.
7. Rigidly maintain the high standard.
8. Too much oil is as harmful as none at all.
9. With the index in the center, and the watch running to time, is how all watches should leave the workshop.
10. The movement should have that new appearance, and not look as if it had been repaired.
11. Use the original material where possible; otherwise copy faithfully.
12. Always remember that more watches stop because of lack of attention to detail than through actual constructional faults.

CHAPTER 3

EXAMINING THE MOVEMENT

Examining the watch movement embodies a vast field, and, in order to arrive at something definite, I propose to give here, in detail, the examination of a Swiss keyless movement and whilst so doing we shall talk about other subjects which are kindred.

Now, by examination, I refer to the complete and full overhaul, and, in this instance, we will assume that the movement under review is in a bad state of repair.

The remarks referring to this movement and the method of adjustment equally apply to all movements, since the active principle is the same—except for the escapements, with which I will deal under separate headings.

The Case

It is advisable to adopt a definite system to ensure that nothing is overlooked. In the first place, when you receive the watch, examine the case closely with the aid of an eyeglass to see if there are any bruises, that the joints fit well, and that there are no openings likely to allow the free entry of dust. These points are important.

If you notice the case is bruised, special attention should be given to see if parts of the movement are damaged as a result of a blow or fall. If, on the other hand, the movement is full of dust, it would be useless to clean it and extend a guarantee knowing full well that the case does not give sufficient protection to the movement. Such a procedure would be injurious to one's reputation.

In such matters a note should be made, and the owner of the watch advised.

Dust in Cases

It is sometimes very difficult indeed to understand why an apparently well-fitting case should allow dust to penetrate through to the mechanism. The experiment noted here clearly explains what happens.

A watch is submitted to many changes of temperature, and, assuming we start with a temperature of 60 degrees, the air inside the watch is, of course, of the same temperature. During wear the temperature will rise approximately to 90 degrees. Consequently, the air inside the case will reach this temperature also, and, in expanding, a certain amount will be emitted from the case, since even the best made cases are not airtight. This does not refer to waterproof cases.

Now the trouble commences when the watch is transferred to a lower temperature. The watch immediately commences to suck in more air and, consequently, dust. It has been put to the test that a watch, the movement of which was in a perfectly clean condition, was brought to a certain temperature and then placed in a vessel containing flour of a lower temperature, and it was found that, after a time, upon examining the movement, a certain amount of the flour had found its way inside. This is a point well worth remembering. If you are troubled with a watch that lets the dust in and the case appears to be well fitting, smear a little wax on to the snapping edges of the case, so that when the case is closed it is sealed. For this purpose, melt a piece of beeswax with about three times its weight of vaseline, and stir well while hot. When cold, and ready for use, this wax is a sticky, non-setting substance, and will not chip off and fall into the movement. Dust cannot penetrate this film of wax.

The Hands

Having obtained all the clues possible by an external examination, which will subsequently help us respecting the movement, proceed to examine the hand work.

Before you open the bezel, satisfy yourself that the glass is high enough to free the hands; if you are in doubt, open the bezel and examine the underside of the glass. Usually, if the hands have been touching the glass, either a light mark will be shown round the edge where the point of the hand has rubbed, or a more decided round mark in the center of the glass where the minute boss has touched.

If you have suspicions that the hands do touch, and yet there are no marks upon the glass, it is as well to make quite sure by smearing the doubtful parts with a thin mixture of rouge and oil. Snap the bezel in position, and turn the hands round two or three times; open and again examine the underside of the glass. If it is quite free of rouge, you can rest assured that the hands do not touch. Another test is to breathe on the inside of the glass and the steamed surface thus produced will show up plainly the rubbed parts of the glass.

The next step is to see that the hands themselves are quite free, that the hour wheel has up-and-down shake, as well as the freedom of the pipe on the cannon pinion, and the back lash of the teeth of the hour wheel in the nut of the minute wheel is perceptible.

If the hour wheel has a collet fitted to it to correct an excess of up-and-down shake, it should, even then, be perfectly free, both as regards the back lash already referred to and the pipe on the cannon pinion.

Now turn the hands, and, whilst so doing, observe that they are free of each other at all hours of the dial. The hour hand should rotate parallel to the dial, and the minute hand should do the same. There should be no up-and-down movement. If you observe an up-and-down movement of the hour hand only, and the minute hand itself travels quite flat or parallel to the dial, this is due to the cannon pinion arbor being bent. But should the minute hand also show an up-and-down movement, say, free of the dial on one side, and touches on the other, this denotes that the center pinion is out of upright. Now to correct the former trouble is a comparatively simple matter. The cause of the trouble is due to the center arbor being bent from the bottom pivot. The minute hand will in these circumstances rotate at an even level from the dial. The hour wheel, however, will rock up and down, and with it the hour hand; it will be up on one side and down on the other. It only remains for the arbor to be made straight. Care must be exercised whilst doing this, as the arbor is usually hardened and tempered. Spin the wheel in the calipers and note carefully where the bend is. Place on a brass stake and peen the arbor as indicated (Fig. 51). This will cause the arbor to curl, as it were, and at the same time the risk of breaking is eliminated.

To Upright Center Wheel

But to upright the center wheel is a somewhat longer operation, and calls for very accurate work. The method of procedure is this: we must assume for the moment that the movement is in pieces; to make the wheel upright it will be necessary to fit a new hole, and it is usually better to fit the top hole rather than the lower.

The amount necessary to displace this hole is slight, and this movement will not, as a rule, affect the barrel or third wheel depths. But if, owing to circumstances, the top hole is jeweled, and it is necessary to alter the lower hole, care must be taken to ensure that, after the new hole has been fitted, the minute wheel depth with the cannon pinion and the hour wheel with the minute wheel nut are correct.

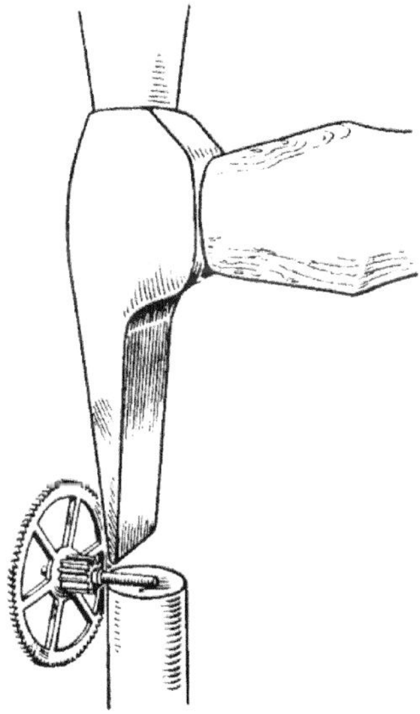

Fig. 51 – Peening the Center Arbor

I mention this in particular, because these depths are sometimes overlooked. Should, however, both holes be jeweled, it would be advisable to have a new jewel hole fitted to the top.

Now to make upright, place the lower plate in the mandrel, using the pump center in the center hole; clamp the dogs in position, removing the pump center or centering rod, as it is known, and bring the “T” rest into position near the plate. Adjust the rest to within about 1 in. of the plate, and at a height about equal to the center hole.

Select a straight piece of watch peg wood, and sharpen one end to a long taper. Place this tapered end in the hole and give the mandrel one or two turns, holding the peg wood while turning. This is to ensure that the peg will run smoothly in the hole.

Now, on the other end of this peg wood place a pair of pliers or something similar, straddle wise, to hold the peg steady. Revolve the mandrel slowly and observe the extreme end of the peg wood closely; there should be no up or down movement (see Fig. 52). It is not likely, however, that there will be, since we have used the centering rod to center up this plate, but this forms a check.

Should there be an inaccuracy in the tool, however, and the peg has an up-and-down movement, the plate must be slightly tapped to adjust correctly.

If, for instance, it is found that, when revolving the plate, the peg has a slight tendency to move, and if when doing this movement the plate is stopped when the peg is at its lowest point, it will be necessary to tap the plate slightly at the point that is uppermost. It will require only a very slight tap, which will have the effect of bringing the peg up. It will not be necessary to loosen the dogs during this adjustment.

We will assume the plate is now absolutely true; place the top bar or bridge in position on the plate, without removing the plate from the mandrel, and screw firmly in position.

Now try the peg wood test again in the top center hole. You will notice that there is a decided up-and-down movement when the plate is made to revolve. To correct this, the hole itself must be caught true; bring the "T" rest quite close to the bridge, and with a long cutter (as illustrated in Fig. 53) catch the side of the hole until a full cut is obtained. The cutter must be held very firmly on the rest to ensure absolute truth.

Fig. 52 – Mandrel Showing Method to Upright

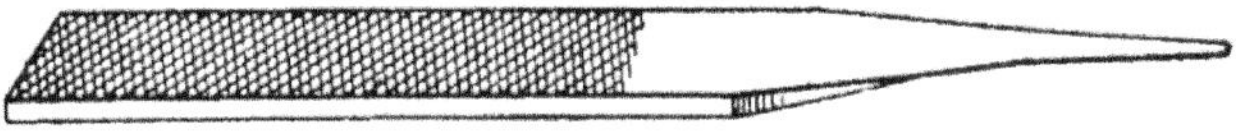

Fig. 53 – Hand Cutting Tool, Made From Old File

To Rebush Hole

Apply the peg wood test again to see that all is in order. We can now remove the whole plate from the mandrel. Take the bridge or bar off, and proceed to re-bouch the enlarged hole to fit the center wheel pivot. Very slightly broach the hole, only just sufficient for it to be able to take the same taper as the broach itself. The broaching is done from the inside.

Select a piece of bushon wire with the hole

somewhat smaller in size than the finished hole. Cut off a piece about three or four times the length ultimately required; place on an arbor, and turn between centers, true, and to a taper equal to the taper of the broach.

Proceed until it fits the hole—from the inside—mark, and cut off from the top end, so that when the bush is placed in position tightly it does not project but leaves sufficient for the final living home by the hammer. Gauge the length required for the other side, and cut off. Turn this end quite flat, but turn the other end with a slight chamfer for riveting.

Remove from the arbor and place the bar or bridge on a flat polished stake, with a hole sufficiently large enough to allow the rivet to project. Place the bush in position, and drive home with a polished flat-headed punch and hammer.

It now only remains for us to reverse the bar on a smaller flat stake held in the vice, and with a polished round-end punch rivet the chamfered end. It is advisable, before placing the bush in position, to chamfer the top side of the hole to receive the rivet. If the bush has been cut carefully to length, and the other points observed as I have mentioned, it will not be necessary to do any further finishing to either side of the hole.

Now open the hole with a sharp cutting broach until the pivot fits tightly, finishing off with a round or burnishing broach until the pivot is quite free. This burnishing not only leaves a polished and free hole, but has the effect of hardening it.

During broaching, check continually to see that the broach is in an upright position. Remove with a chamfering tool (Fig. 54) any burrs the broaching may have caused.

Fig. 54 – Chamfering Tool, Made From Old Round Needle File

We are now ready to try the wheel in the frame. Place the wheel in position and screw the bar or bridge on, giving the wheel a spin to make sure that it is quite free. Place the cannon pinion on, dial and minute hand in position, and, upon testing, you will find that the hand will rotate at the same distance from the dial in all positions. The wheel is now upright.

If the holes were jeweled, remove the hole to be replaced, proceed as for a brass bush, and, after the hole has been caught true, fit a new jewel hole, which will, of course, be of a slightly larger diameter.

We must now go back again to the examination. Having satisfied yourself that the hands are perfectly free and sufficiently tight to carry, proceed to remove the movement from the case.

Tighten Hands

Just another word or two respecting the adjustment of the hands, etc. I would like to mention here that the fitting of the dial and hands, etc., is considered such a simple matter that the correct adjustment is often overlooked, and I think I am quite right in saying that, at least, 10% of the watches that stop do so because of faulty hand adjustment. The greatest care can be given to the actual movement, which may be in a perfect condition, but this is all lost if the hands bind or foul, thus causing the watch to stop, or to behave in an erratic manner.

We must always remember that a watch is judged upon the service it gives, and it is for the watchmaker to see that all steps possible are taken to ensure a satisfactory result.

The hands should be tight enough to carry without any doubt at all. If you are at all doubtful do not hesitate to tighten them, as it is a waste of time to attempt to regulate a watch with the hand work loose. It must, however, be borne in mind that the hands must not be as tight as to endanger the teeth of the minute wheel during setting. There is no hard and fast rule to determine the tightness the hand work should be; experience alone can teach.

Should the hands be loose, it is quite a simple matter to tighten them. If the cannon pinion is fitted to an arbor and this arbor fits into a hollow center pinion, the arbor itself must be in some manner slightly enlarged. This is usually best effected by making one or two slight burrs with the cutting edge of a flat burnisher. It must always be remembered that the cannon pinion itself must fit the arbor tighter than the arbor fits in the hollow of the center pinion. Otherwise the cannon pinion will revolve on the arbor and ultimately become quite loose, and at the same time the minute hand will remain stationary when setting the hands, because the hand is fitted on to the center arbor.

A tool is made for carrying out this work, and is in the form of a stake with a half-round base (Fig. 55). The illustration shows the tool with the punches for the snap cannon pinion; these can be replaced by the half-round bed and the pointed punch. The arbor is placed on this base or stake, and directly over the arbor a pointed punch is held in the tool. A slight blow with a hammer on the punch will effect a spreading of the arbor.

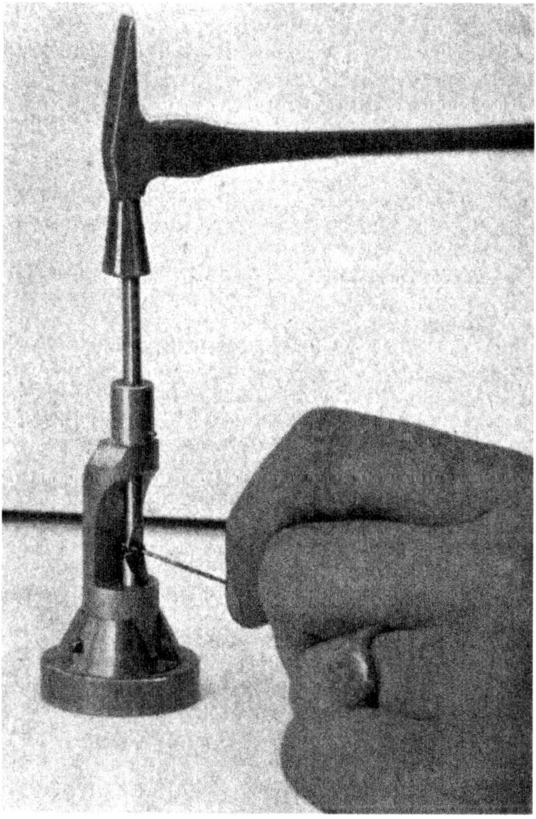

Fig. 55 – Cannon Pinion Punch

It is most important that whichever method is adopted the arbor must not be bent. If the cannon pinion is of the snap-on variety, the pinion itself must be closed in, and on no account should the arbor itself be touched.

Fitting Snap Cannon Pinion

In order that this form of fitting shall be thoroughly understood, I think it will be better if I now explain how a new snap-on pinion is fitted. You will then be able to see what alterations are necessary both to tighten the pinion and to correct in the case of the cannon pinion rising during hand setting.

We will assume that the arbor has been turned to a taper, and this taper should be such that if the cannon pinion is opened with a broach and it is then presented to the arbor the wrong way up, it will go into the end of the cannon pinion by the same amount it will project if the cannon pinion were placed on the arbor the right way up. In other words, the arbor must fit the hole in the cannon pinion for its full length. There must be no doubt about this; if it is found that the arbor is too tapered there will be a tendency for the cannon pinion to rock on the arbor.

Finally, the arbor is stoned down with oilstone dust and oil until the cannon fits comfortably; if too tight, the cannon will ride up, and if too loose it will rock. It should just fit and be free.

You should be able to press the cannon pinion home without any undue pressure. This done, place the cannon pinion on an arbor and turn a groove to a depth of about half the thickness of the pinion pipe; place in the vice a punch with a chisel-shaped end. Now place the pinion on a piece of brass wire upon which two flats have been filed, holding the pinion on this chisel punch in such a position that the flats will present themselves to the chisel punch below and also to the chisel punch we are going to use above.

With a hammer, give a reasonably sharp blow to the top punch. This will have the effect of making two slight indentations, and if the pinion is removed from the wire we shall find that this has made two slight projections on the inside.

The tool already referred to for spreading the center arbor of the hollow pinion can be utilized for the same purpose, replacing the half-round base by a chisel punch and the pointed punch by another similar chisel punch, as illustrated in Fig. 55.

Having left the center arbor grey from the oilstone dust, place the pinion on the center arbor with a firm straight downward movement; you will find that it is a little stiff, but avoid, as far as possible, any twisting movement to get the pinion on. Make sure it is quite home on to the shoulder of the pivot of the center wheel.

Holding the wheel in the left hand, give the cannon pinion several complete turns with the brass-nosed pliers held in the right hand. Now carefully remove the cannon pinion with a straight upward movement, no twisting, and we shall find that the center arbor has been marked with a ring made by the burrs thrown up.

We now proceed to turn a little above this mark first of all a groove the shape as illustrated in Fig. 56. Try the cannon pinion on again and proceed to turn this shoulder back—that is, the highest point turned—until the pinion snaps on, and this snap should not be effected until the pinion is quite home.

You will now see the object to be achieved if you meet with a rising cannon pinion. Also, should it be necessary to tighten the cannon pinion, the burrs already referred to must be re-punched in the same position as originally.

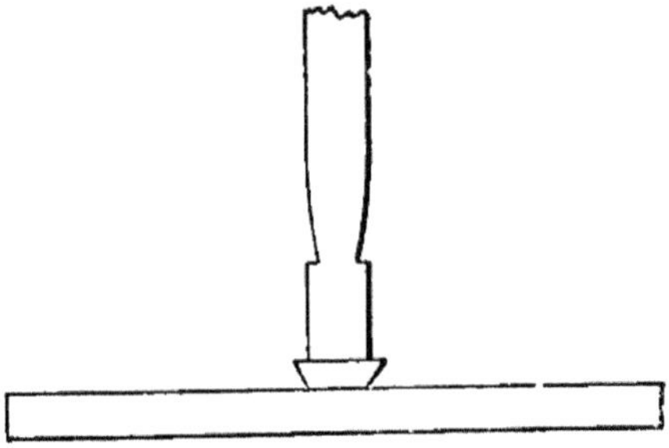

Fig. 56 – Center Arbor Showing Snap Cannon Pinion Groove

To refer to the rising cannon pinion fault again, this is somewhat difficult to correct in certain instances; it may mean that the burr on the inside of the cannon pinion will have to be placed a little higher than the original one, and the arbor turned back to suit it, or the cannon may fit the arbor too tightly before the pips were made.

To Polish Cannon Pinion

While on the subject of cannon pinions, I will explain how the polished hollow end which is met with in some of the finer quality watches is obtained.

The acme of perfection, as regards the finish of this portion of the handwork, is for the end of the center arbor to be polished as nearly flat as it is possible by hand—for this to be lapped dead flat would spoil the effect—the end of the cannon pinion to be hollowed and polished so that the center arbor forms the bottom of the hollow. The result is that the arbor is very slightly rounded, and this is met by the curve of the hollow and the piece is completed with a nicely polished boss of the minute hand and forms a good piece of work.

To polish this hollow is quite simple Place the

cannon pinion on an arbor with a ferrule attached, the size of the arbor to be such that it will not permit the pinion to fit on fully; the pinion should just stick on the end (see Fig. 57).

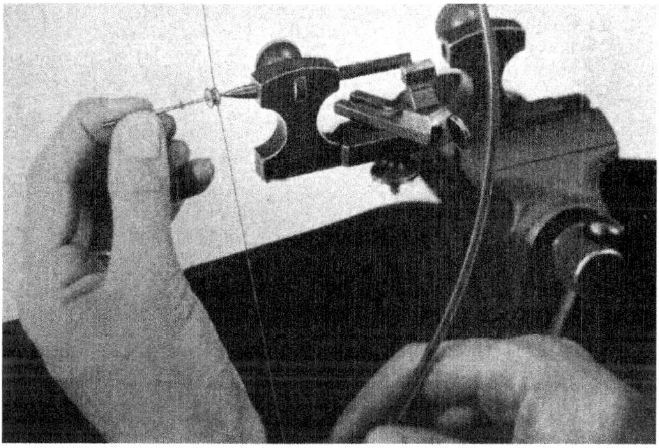

Fig. 57 – Method of Holding Cannon Pinion When Polishing End

Now prepare a piece of iron wire with a rounded end; the size of the wire depends on the size of the pinion and the extent of the roundness of the end upon the size required for the hollow.

With a bow on the ferrule hold the cannon pinion in position and with our polisher—the end of which has been charged with oilstone dust and oil—in position, make the pinion revolve quickly, and, at the same time, move the polisher slightly backwards and forwards and up and down. Continue this until the hollow required is obtained. Thoroughly clean off all traces of oilstone, clean the end of the polisher by refiling, charge with diamantine and proceed as before until the black polish is obtained.

The movement of the polisher helps to keep the hollow true, and any slight irregularity of the rounded end polisher is not reflected in the work; at the same time, this movement breaks up the grain and materially helps the polishing.

The cannon pinion is, of course, hardened and tempered before the polishing and finishing are attempted.

To Remove the Hands

We will now resume the examination of the movement again. We must go back for a moment to remove the hands; the best way to do this is to use the hand levers (see Fig. 58). These are quite simply made from a piece of brass of about 8 in. long, 5 mm. wide, and 3 mm. thick. Cut this piece of metal into two, which leaves us with two levers 4 in. long. File the ends as shown in the illustration. Place a piece of tissue paper on the dial under the hour hand boss, fit the levers under the hand, and slight pressure on the ends of the levers and the hands will lift without fear of damage, either to the hands themselves or to the dial. The tightest hands can be removed in this manner, and should the dial be made of enamel there is small risk of cracking it.

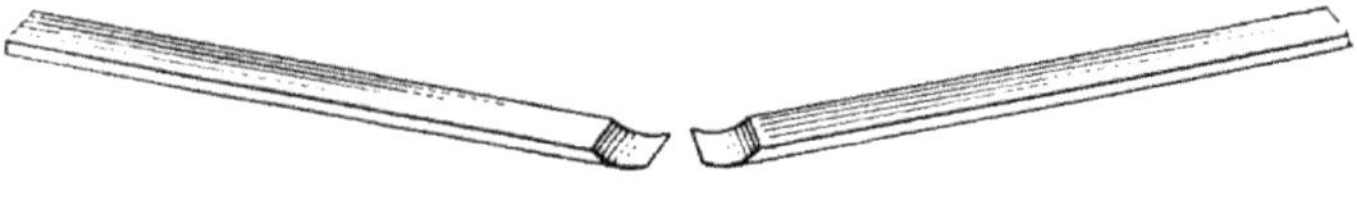

Fig. 58 – Hand-Removing Levers

Another method of using the same tools is to place a piece of tissue paper over the hands, then place the levers in position as before. The paper so arranged forms a hood, and should the hands fly off there will be no fear of loss. The disadvantage of this method, however, is that the work cannot be seen, and sometimes when the hands are fitted close to the dial it is more difficult than if the former method is adopted. To remove a seconds hand: if there is sufficient room the levers can be used, but should the seconds hand fit closely to the dial, loosen the dial and lever up with a knife near the seconds hand and the hand will come away quite safely.

The Motion Work

Remove the dial and carefully examine the motion work. Examine the depth of the hour wheel in the minute wheel nut; the minute wheel in the cannon pinion; and also the minute wheel with the intermediate wheel.

These depths are as important as the train depths, and any binding here, while it may not cause the watch actually to stop, will certainly have a detrimental effect on the timekeeping properties of the watch.

Observe that the minute wheel stud is quite firm; this can be a source of trouble, and, if not habitually checked when examining, can be an elusive fault.

It will be found that these studs have a tendency to become loose, and steps must be taken to remedy this. Examine the underside of the dial and see that the motion work has not been running afoul of it. You will sometimes find the minute wheel nut has marked the dial, and steps should be taken to rectify this. Such binding retards the freedom of the train and faults of this description are difficult to detect when the watch is assembled.

They are, however, apparent by the erratic time-keeping of the watch itself. In some instances the dial can be reduced, and should it be enamel, stone the mark away with a carborundum pencil. If the dial is made of silver it can be scraped either with the edge of a flat burnisher or a knife, care being exercised to ensure that too much is not removed, otherwise the front of the dial will be marked and such defacing cannot be removed effectively.

It must, however, be ascertained that the wheel is quite free, and the best method to do this, if you are at all doubtful, is to smear the top of the nut with a little rouge and oil, then place the dial in position and set the hands—in order to make the minute wheel revolve—two or three times, removing the dial to examine if there is any trace of rouge on it.

Another method to correct this fault is to reduce the height of the minute wheel nut itself. Place the wheel on a turning arbor and cut sufficient of the nut away with a graver. Finish by polishing under hand with oilstone dust, and finally with diamantine.

The Train

When examining the actual movement itself, it is usual to commence with the escapement but, as the latter is such an important matter, I propose to deal with it separately, and we will therefore deal with the remaining portion of the movement.

We must assume that the escapement has been removed, and we are left with the train from the fourth wheel. First examine all the end-shakes, and then see that the pivots fit their holes correctly. Sometimes a faulty depth can be caused by an ill-fitting pivot. To be correct there should be no perceptible side-shake, but, at the same time, it should be free beyond doubt. When dealing with watches or clocks used in the air that are subjected to extreme temperature such as -20° C, then the end shakes and the side shakes should be generous, especially if the holes are of brass.

The rule adopted by the old finishers was that when a wheel was in position in the frame or between cocks, it should be sufficiently free to fall from one side to the other by reason of its own weight. For instance, place the fourth wheel, say, in position, and note that the lower pivot is resting fully on the lower hole. Now carefully turn the movement completely over, and by this time the shoulder of the top pivot should be resting squarely on the top hole and the end-shake of the wheel should be visible by the space between the lower pivot and its hole.

Another test is that if the wheel is lifted it will drop into its former position.

Depths

The next step is to ascertain that the depths are correct. If you are in doubt as to any particular depth, place the doubtful wheel and pinion in the frame by themselves and make quite sure that all is in order. (I shall deal with the question of depths separately.)

It is always a good plan to make a note of all the defects of the movement during examination, either mentally, or, should you not be possessed of a good memory, in a book. It is much to be preferred to carry out the necessary repairs before the movement has been cleaned, rather than to realize that after cleaning and reassembling some further repair is necessary.

To Upright Fourth Wheel

It is essential that the fourth wheel should be upright, especially if it carries a seconds hand. It is equally necessary for all the train wheels, including the barrel, to be upright but not to the same extent, perhaps. The fourth wheel out of upright, carrying the seconds hand, is much more accentuated.

I mention the fourth wheel in particular, because not only is it incorrect for the wheel to be out of upright, but you will experience the same difficulty to free the hands as is experienced if the center wheel is out of upright.

A very slight error in this direction is magnified when the tip of the seconds hand is examined when it is rotating. The method adopted to correct this want of uprightness is the same as when fitting the center hole.

If the hole is of brass, it will not be possible to catch the sides owing to its size. In these circumstances open the hole considerably more than you would if you were just rebushing the hole in the ordinary way. Instead of a bush with hole in it, we will fit a plain piece of brass, and then drill the hole in the correct position. The position of the hole can be determined in one or two ways, one being with the aid of an uprighting tool (Fig. 59). In this tool, clamp the bottom plate of the movement on to the plate of the tool lightly, bring the centering rod up into the lower fourth hole, and then clamp the plate firmly in position, moving the plate, if necessary, to accomplish this.

Now place in position the top plate or bar, as the case may be, without removing the plate from the tool and bring the upper rod down on to the top hole, and this will indicate the exact position for the hole. If it is desired to rebush the lower hole, the rod can be brought into position on to the top hole and the plate clamped firmly; now remove the top plate or bar, when the rod will show the correct position of the lower hole. With the tool illustrated drilling can be proceeded with immediately.

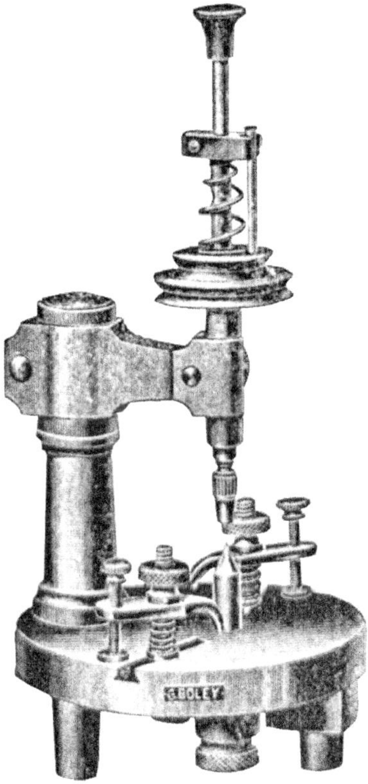

Fig. 59 – Uprighting Tool

Some uprighting tools are not provided with these clamps or "dogs." The escapement maker's tool shown in Fig. 60 is fitted with two centering rods, one top and bottom. In this case, the drilling for the lower hole, say, is effected by just placing the frame on the tool with the top plate screwed in position. Bring the upper centering rod down so that the point enters the top fourth hole. Hold the movement firmly with the hand, now manipulate the lower centering rod upwards so that its point will mark the position for the new hole.

Fig. 60 – Escapement Maker's Uprighting Tool

To drill a new top hole, secure the top plate or bar in position, place the frame so assembled on the tool and bring the lower centering rod up to the lower fourth hole. Hold the movement firmly with the hand and then bring the top centering rod down, marking the position for the new hole.

The drill used must be smaller than the pivot. Open the hole the required size with a cutting broach, and finish off with a round broach to harden, as already explained.

It will be necessary to chamfer the sink for the retention of oil; sometimes, when working on a plate which is gilded, the gilding may become damaged.

Should the holes be jeweled, the hole to be replaced is removed, the setting caught true, as when fitting the center hole, and a new hole fitted. In these circumstances the frame is fitted up in the mandrel, as we did when fitting the center hole.

Finishing

If after fitting the new hole it is found necessary to finish the surface, say in the case of the fourth hole, it may not be desirable to turn in the mandrel. It is considered good workmanship to leave the surface grey after stoning with Water-of-Ayr stone; do not stone a bigger surface than is necessary. The piece can be further finished by "spotting," as explained elsewhere.

You will sometimes meet with the top plate of English watches so treated, the reason for this being that the actual maker has not manufactured the watch to a definite order. The movement has been gilded with this exception, and it is not until the name of the vendor has been engraved that the plate is gilded to match the rest of the movement.

To Continue

The object of the examination of the movement should be to assure yourself that when it is cleaned, repaired, and reassembled, it will function satisfactorily. We shall now consider the barrel and mainspring.

CHAPTER 4

THE MAINSPRING AND BARREL

It is essential that the barrel and the mainspring in the barrel shall be as free as any part of the watch. Because of the force at the barrel this is sometimes neglected. Any binding or other cause that prevents freedom is due to friction, and since friction is a variable quality it should be eliminated as far as possible.

Whilst the watch may go with the barrel or mainspring binding a little, the best results cannot be obtained because of the variation of the force transmitted to the train. This fault is sometimes difficult to elucidate because, when the mainspring is wound up, it has the tendency to distort the barrel, with the result that the fault is there only when the mainspring is wound; when unwound the barrel is quite free.

Examine the Barrel

In such an instance, a thorough examination of the barrel is necessary, particular attention being given to the arbor to see that it fits well; this is most important. Should the holes be wide they should be rebushed without hesitation. It is important that the arbor itself should have sufficient end-shake in the barrel to be just free.

Place the arbor in the barrel and fit the cover in position, holding the arbor by the square in the sliding tongue, and so arrange that the barrel is just free of the jaws of the tongs.

Now give the barrel a spin, and make certain that it runs quite true; the jaws of the tongs will serve as a guide. It may be that either the cover or the barrel itself has become damaged, causing it to run out of truth, and if such is the case the damaged parts must be straightened by tapping with the hammer, finishing off with water-of-Ayr stone to remove any bruises there may be. It is not considered bad workmanship if such pieces are left from the stone as already explained. Regilding sometimes is not convenient, and, further, it has a tendency to soften the metal. I prefer the barrel and the wheels of the train left from the stone and not gilded at all; leave such pieces with a circular grain.

Having made what adjustments are necessary to ensure the barrel running flat and true, place in the frame and give it another spin to see that all is true and free here.

You may find that although the barrel tilts a little, it will run quite true—that is, it will not rock up and down—but always on one side: this shows that the barrel arbor is out of upright in the frame, and the only way to correct this is to proceed as when uprighting the center wheel.

Should you, however, find that the barrel runs out of flat, that is, up on one side and down on the other, this indicates that the barrel arbor in the barrel is out of upright. In this case upright and rebush the hole farther from the barrel teeth.

The fitting of the arbor between the plates should be close, and there should be no perceptible end-shake; the freedom of the arbor here is only to facilitate the easy winding of the watch, and does not come into operation when the watch is going.

Stop-Work

If the watch has been made for stop-work, always see that the stop-work is replaced. It is the height of bad workmanship not to replace it.

There are one or two instances, however, where the omission of the star wheel is excusable. Sometimes in small movements you will find, where stop-work has been fitted, that by reason of the proportionately large winding button the stop-work gets forced quite frequently, with the result that the finger piece is jammed past the stop of the star wheel, which ultimately stops the watch.

In such an instance it is quite permissible to remove the stop-work. We must always bear in mind that the first and essential function of a watch is to go and keep time, and if some part is so arranged by the manufacturers that it is a hindrance rather than an asset, it is quite justifiable to remove it.

It should be removed in such a manner that the next man who repairs the watch will recognize that it is intentional and not accidental or the result of negligence. The best manner is to remove the star wheel entirely and to replace the star wheel screw. The finger piece can be turned down to a round boss or collet; it is essential to replace this piece, otherwise the square on to which it fits will cut a sink into the bottom plate, unless it is of the swing barrel type; even so, it makes a better job to finish as advised.

By the way, I can never understand why stop-work is fitted to watches of a size less than ten lignes; in such cases it is a menace. The primary object of the stop-work is to ensure that the best turns of the mainspring are used, and so transmit, as equally as possible, the force to the train. The object of the equality of force is to minimize the difficulty of timing in the long and short arcs. When dealing with timing of this nature, we are concerned with seconds and not minutes. This brings me to my point: if a wrist watch keeps time to, say, within 2 minutes per week, it may be considered to be going quite well; I know of many instances where a closer rate is obtained, but, as a general rule, 2 minutes per week is good; so why a device should be introduced whose object is to correct for seconds is a matter which calls for the attention of the manufacturers.

If the stop-work were sound I would say retain it by all means; any adjunct to help perfect time-keeping is admirable, but when that device is a source of trouble, and this coupled with what I have already stated, I say do away with it, but do it well.

Test the Stop-Work

It is essential that the stop-work should be tested to ensure that it is quite free. First of all, see that the star wheel revolves quite freely on its stud. Now, without the mainspring in position, place the finger piece on and hold in the sliding tongs by the barrel arbor square. Carefully make the barrel revolve, and observe that the finger piece enters the star wheel accurately and that there is no sign of binding during any portion of its functions.

As a final test, just give the barrel a light spin, and it should quite easily revolve the four or five turns, as the case might be, allowed by the stop-work.

When the mainspring is in position it should be set up so that the center turns only are used during the functioning of the watch. It is usual to find that the barrel arbor will make from five to six-and-a-half turns when a four-turn stop-work is used.

If, for instance, the arbor makes exactly six turns, it is best to wind one turn before placing the finger piece in position. This gives us one turn set up and one turn on the hook.

In some cases you will find that the finger piece is marked to be refitted on a certain square, and these conditions must be strictly observed, especially if the finger piece forms the pivot of the barrel. Otherwise, if this is not observed, there is fear of the barrel running out of truth.

Types of Hooking

If the barrel is fitted with stop-work, a hook in the side of the barrel and a hole in the mainspring is all that is necessary, since at no time does the mainspring pull direct at the hook. This form of hooking is quite simple and effective. A tool can be procured to punch the holes in the mainspring, but I am not in favor of this method, however; I prefer to drill and broach the hole, and to do this satisfactorily, proceed as follows.

The Hook and Eye

First of all soften the end to be drilled, taking great care not to allow the flame to touch the part of the spring not to be drilled; if the end is let down to a green color it will be sufficiently soft to drill easily. See that color change is gradual; if the softening is sudden there is a risk of breaking.

To drill the hole, first of all make a center with a chamfering tool (made by whetting the end of an old round needle filed pyramid-shape). Hold the spring against a piece of hard wood, such as the handle of a watch brush, and drill the hole.

Now broach the hole open to a sufficient size, finally cutting the hole to an angle as shown in Fig. 61; this ensures a sharp edge to fasten safely on the hook. Finish the end of the spring by filing round, and clean off with a fine emery buff the discoloration made by softening.

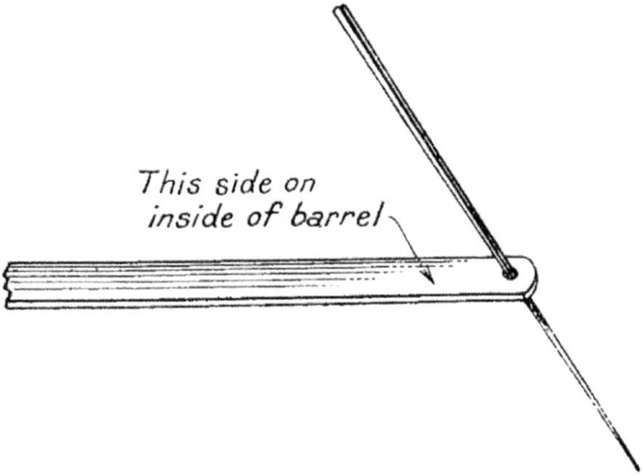

Fig. 61 – Broaching, Showing Angle of Hole in Mainspring

The end of the spring should now be bent to conform to the curve of the inside of the barrel. To do this without fear of cracking, place on a lead block and with the peen of the hammer give one or two blows; this hammering will cause the end of the spring to curl up (Fig. 62).

With regard to the hook in the barrel itself, should it be necessary to replace, this is best effected by screwing in a new one. Here, again, a special tool is obtainable which can be manipulated so as to press a piece of the side of the barrel inwards to form a hook:

but I am not in favor of this, as there is a serious risk of distorting the barrel, and even if the hook as made originally was of this description, I am of the opinion that a better job can be made by fitting one as follows.

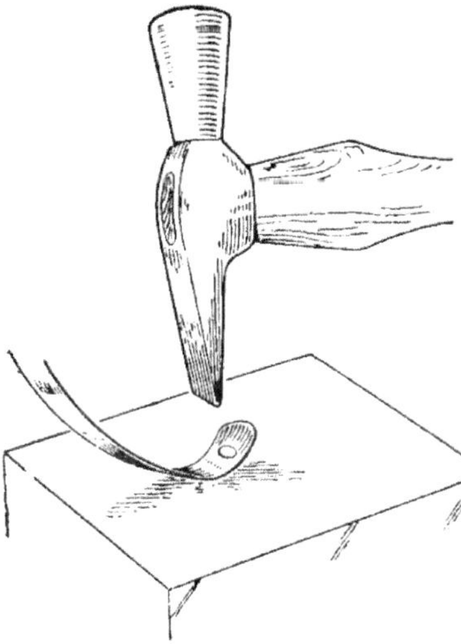

Fig. 62 – Mainspring, Peening End

First drill a hole in the side of the barrel at a distance so that it will be equal to half the depth of the inside of the barrel occupied by the mainspring. Broach this hole slightly at an angle in such a direction that the spring will hook on to the end of the broach projecting through to the inside of the barrel (see Fig. 63).

Not only does this add to the strength of the hook when the mainspring is pulling on it, but it will be possible to tap more threads for the hook, which again makes for security.

Now file a piece of silver steel wire to a taper. On this tap a thread, in the screw plate, and when a full tap has been cut, cut off and file the hook to shape while the piece still remains in the plate (see Fig. 64).

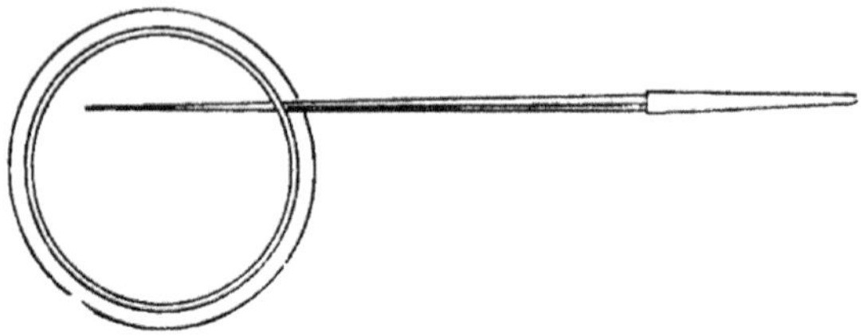

Fig. 63 – Barrel, Showing Angle of Hole

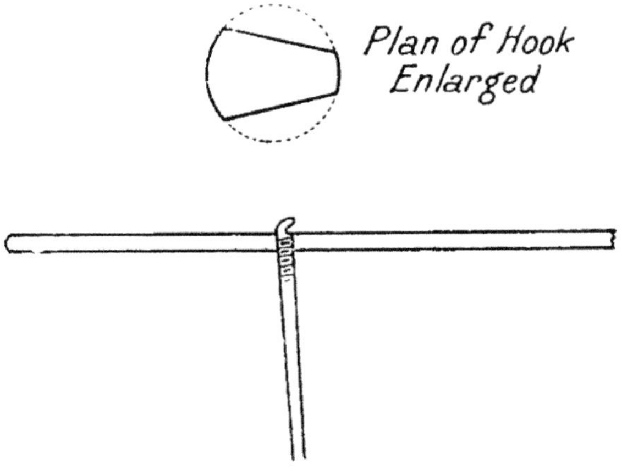

Fig. 64 – Barrel Hook

Now tap the hole in the barrel to the same size, and remove the hook from the screw-plate and screw into the barrel from the inside, holding the portion of the thread which is not fully cut and consequently will pass through the hole easily.

Screw the hook right home, drawing and turning anticlockwise. It now only remains finally to cut off the superfluous part of the hook and file, stoning flush with the barrel.

Pivoted Hook

In cases where the hooking is of the pivoted type, the same form of hooking should always be retained. You will sometimes find that, for some reason, a watchmaker has fitted a hook to the barrel where the maker intended that it should be pivoted. Remove this hook and fit a pivoted brace to the mainspring, as originally.

It is very rare to find that the holes in the barrel and cover of this form of hooking are at fault; if they are, however, it is quite a simple matter to drill two more.

This "T" end piece is used in some Swiss and American watches, and care must be taken when fitting these pieces to ensure that they are free to revolve when in the barrel, otherwise their object would be defeated.

Observe that the projecting pivots do not project beyond the barrel itself or the cover, otherwise there is a fear of them touching other parts of the watch. Usually this type of hook is supplied ready fitted to the mainspring, but should it be necessary to fit a new T-piece only, proceed as follows.

Select a T-piece and place inside the barrel; note that the height, if anything, is slightly lower than the height of the mainspring; this is to ensure perfect freedom. Reduce the length of the pivots if necessary, and just round and burnish the ends. This work is carried out before the piece is riveted to the spring. Now soften the end of the spring, and drill a small hole, smaller than the one ultimately required. File the end of the spring square, and reduce until the hole is the same distance from the end as the stud on the T-piece is from the end of the T-piece itself. In other words, reduce until the spring will fit the T-piece.

Now open the hole with a broach until the stud fits

tightly. Clean off all burrs with a fine file, finishing with a fine emery buff; slightly chamfer the hole on the outside of the spring. Lay the T-piece on the *inside* of the spring, place on a flat polished stake, and slightly rivet the stud; no further finishing should be necessary.

Square Hook

There is another form of hooking you may be called upon to do, and that is the "square hook."

This form of hooking is met with in some of the very old fusee movements and in most chronometers. It is very strong and has the advantage of holding the spring firmly against the side of the barrel, thus keeping the coils of the spring to a great extent separate, and consequently minimizing the friction of the mainspring.

As this is a somewhat unusual form of hooking, and an occasion may arise when it is necessary to fit a new one, I propose to describe the fitting. The procedure is quite simple when dealt with in the proper manner.

You will note that the hole in the barrel is filed at an angle (see Fig. 65); the reason for this is to draw when in tension. Procure from the tool shop some "hooking-in steel." This steel is still obtainable, but I doubt very much if it is sold today for the purpose for which it was originally intended. There are many uses to which steel of this shape can be put. It is useful for making polishers, new keyless pieces, etc., but the old name still survives.

File the end of a piece of this steel until it fits the hole well, always remembering to fit at an angle dictated by the hole. Finish all four sides with the polisher charged with oilstone dust and oil. Hold the steel firmly in the hole as far as it will go, and with a fine point trace on the steel both inside and outside the curve of the barrel; this will give us the thickness of the barrel, and consequently the height of the hook.

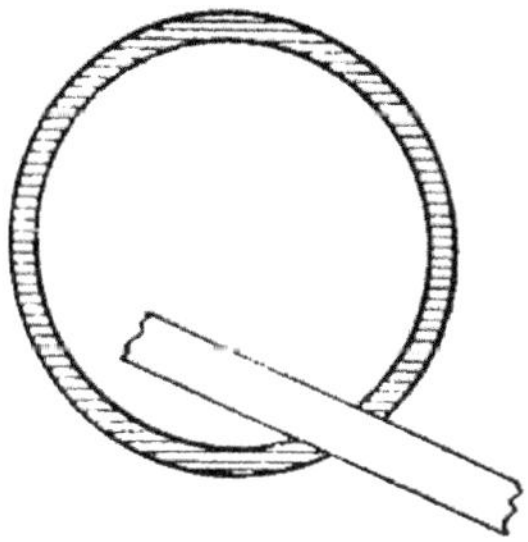

Fig. 65

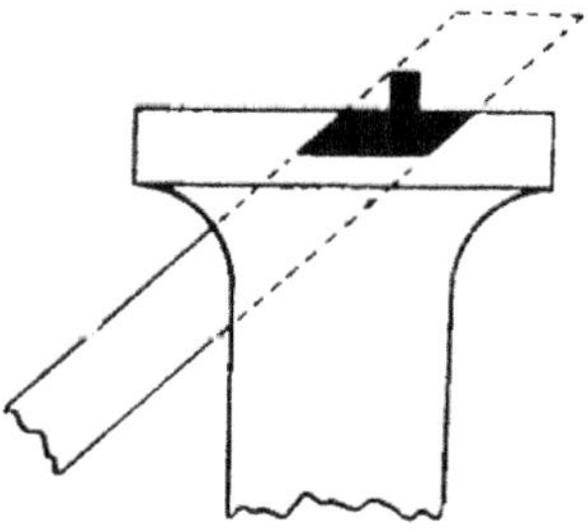

Fig. 66

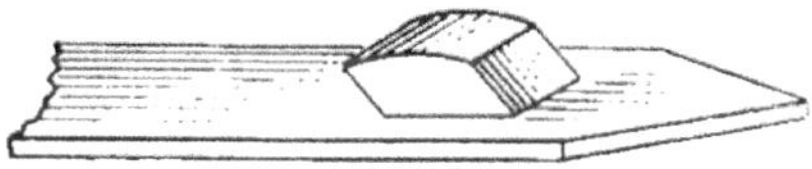

Fig. 67

Figs. 65, 66, 67 – Square Hook for Mainspring

The portion that projected into the barrel is to be pivoted, and will ultimately be riveted to the mainspring, so that portion which is projecting outside the barrel and is the major length of the steel will ultimately be cut off. When filing the pivot, see that it is at the front end of the square, because if it were placed at the back, that portion of the square in front would not act as a support, and the danger of being torn out would be greater than as advised.

Fig. 66 shows the procedure. When the pivot is made, drill a hole in the mainspring, leaving a small length of spring beyond the hook; open the hole until it fits the pivot tightly. Chamfer the hole on the inside, where the rivet will be; now hold the length of steel firmly in the vice, place the mainspring in position, and rivet, leaving a little rounded head as a further support. Fig. 67 shows the finished hook.

The end of the mainspring should, of course, have been cleaned with a fine emery buff before the spring was riveted in position. Now cut the square as near the line as possible, finishing the top with a fine file. Wind the mainspring into the barrel with the mainspring winder. You will notice that these spring winders are still sold with the device made especially for the purpose of winding the square hooked mainsprings in position, but it is necessary to file the end to shape.

The procedure is to wind the spring tightly on the tool, using the piece referred to for the square hook to catch; now place the barrel in position and put the hook so far as possible into the hole in the barrel (see Fig. 68).

Now reverse the click on the tool and allow the mainspring to unwind slowly, and when fully unwound pull the barrel away carefully from the tool and the hook will fly home; finally, tap the sides of the barrel near the hook with the back of a watch brush to ensure the hook reaching as far as possible.

Carefully file any superfluous metal there may be projecting, taking great care not to touch the barrel itself. It is advisable to stone finally with the Arkansas slip to remove burrs.

It now only remains for us to remove the spring from the barrel for the final finishing, and to do this place on a piece of soft wood with the square hook uppermost and polish the top with oilstone dust and oil, and, finally, with diamantine on an iron polisher. The mainspring can now be replaced finally as before.

Fig. 68 – Square Hook Mainspring in Mainspring Winder

Resilient Hooking

There are many ways of hooking in mainsprings, and some of the most popular met with in Swiss watches today are those in which a small piece of mainspring is either riveted to the spring itself or inserted to catch the bent-up end of the spring or on to a steel piece projecting from it.

In the case of the small piece of spring being attached to the spring itself, this is quite simply effected by drilling a hole through the two pieces and riveting together with soft steel wire. I do not advise this form of hooking for some of the very low springs, because drilling the hole is rather inclined to weaken the spring at this point. It is preferable to bend the end into the form of a hook, and to do this effectively proceed as follows.

The Bent-Over End

Hold the spring over a flame, first of all bending it back. You will find that it will not be necessary to bring it to red heat, as the spring will start to move directly when a slight heat is applied. Now, with a pair of thin, flat-nosed pliers, proceed to make this fold more definite; heat the pliers first, and, holding the bent portion of the spring in the flame, apply slight pressure; several applications will be necessary to ensure that the spring is not fractured.

When the spring has been bent almost double, place a small piece of the spring between the fold as near the bend as possible. Then heat again, with the piece of spring still in position, and give a final nip with the heated flat pliers.

The object of this is to ensure that the fold is as flat as possible, and yet not so close as not to allow the insertion of the loose piece of spring.

With the three-cornered file just nick the spring, leaving but a very short piece of the fold, and break the superfluous piece off; file up as illustrated in Fig. 69, and clean off all discoloration with a fine emery buff.

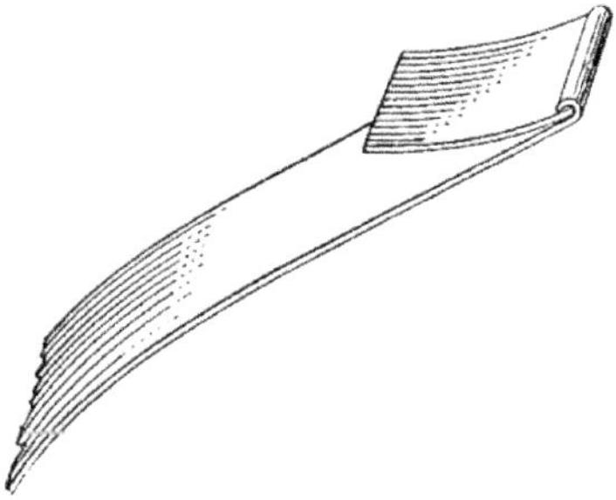

Fig. 69 – Mainspring—Bent-Over End With Loose Piece

Before carrying out this work you will have broken the spring down to size and there will be sufficient for both the loose we are now to fit and the piece used during bending. We now want a piece of the spring for the loose piece about 5 mm. in length; stone both ends square and one end stone at an angle, so that when the loose piece is in position the sharpened end will contact the barrel hook. We are then ready to wind the spring into the barrel. Take care that the bent end does not catch in the barrel hook, as we want to insert the loose piece for this purpose.

When in position you will see the advisability of (1) making the folds very flat; little space is then taken up by this hook; (2) the short bent-over piece; when the spring is wound, it will allow the loose piece to swing round; if a long piece had been left, the loose piece would press on this and a risk of breaking the bent-over portion would ensue.

The careful hooking of a mainspring is always worthwhile, and by observing the points referred to, the maximum force is ensured with the minimum risk of breakage. When buffing the end of a mainspring (or, for that matter, any spring) to clean it, always leave it with a straight grain, i.e. in the same condition as the spring was when originally made. This eliminates the possibility of breakage at this particular part of the spring. If a cross grain were left, it would constitute an invitation for the spring to break there.

Length of Mainspring

The correct size of the mainspring itself is very important. As already stated, in the average watch, the barrel arbor should make from five to six-and-a-half turns. To ensure this it is obviously necessary that, in the first place, the spring should be of the correct thickness and also of the correct length.

Watches with stop-work are generally calculated to run for thirty hours, and if no stop-work is used, they will generally run for thirty-six. The conditions to be complied with as regards the length of the spring are that the spring occupies one-third of the area of the inside of the barrel. For all practical purposes, we can say that the barrel arbor should occupy one-third of the space, empty barrel space one-third, and the portion occupied by the mainspring should be less than one-third of the space, as, by lineal measurement, the area is less.

Breaking Springs

It is sometimes found that mainsprings continually break, and this may be due to one or two reasons. The barrel arbor may be too small; the hook of the arbor itself projecting beyond the thickness of the mainspring, in which case the next coil of the spring will be made to kink at this point, and such a sudden bend will exceed its moment of elasticity, with the result that it breaks.

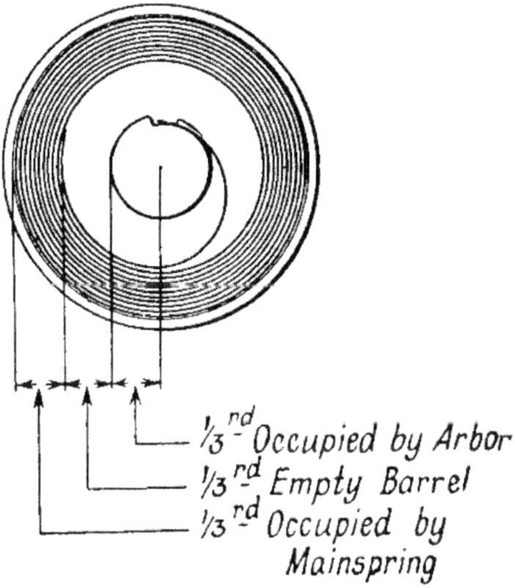

Fig. 70 – Correct Proportion of Mainspring in Barrel

The hooking at the barrel may project too far, which will cause a spring to break for the same reason as a long barrel arbor hook. You will find that most watches have the barrel arbor so made that the hook is part of the arbor; there is therefore no projection at all, and in some watches the hooking to the barrel is effected by a recess into the wall of the barrel itself. Here again there is no projection. This latter form of hooking, however, can be used only when the form of attachment is of the loose piece or riveted-on variety.

The "Gate" System

The gate form of hooking found in some Swiss and English watches has the advantage that the spring, when tightly wound, pulls on a post which is pivoted into the barrel and cover. In some cases an ordinary hook in the barrel and hole in the spring is used, and a little further along the pivoted piece is inserted. On the other hand, some of these gate pieces are fairly long; the portion fitted into the barrel, being flat, cannot turn, and the metal on either side acts as a bearing, thus, when the spring is wound up tightly, the pull does not come on the pivoted piece direct. This acts as the fulcrum and the portion of the gate piece nearest to the longer part of the mainspring acts as a spring. The advantage of this system is similar to that of the old English square hook. It is inclined to minimize the mainspring friction in the barrel.

The Stud Hooking

A system used largely by the manufacturers of the better-quality movements in which no stop-work is used is to rivet a stud to the end of the mainspring, and then insert a short piece of mainspring to operate between the stud and the barrel hook. When the spring is wound tightly, the short piece of spring is free to move, hinge-like, the hook at one end and the stud at the other, thus obviating the excessive pull on the hook, and not on the hook with the attendant tendency to tear the eye out of the mainspring, in a similar manner to the fold-over system already explained.

Fusee Mainspring

As fusee watches still pass through the watchmaker's hands for repair there are one or two points in connection with the mainspring worth mentioning.

Now, as regards the setting-up of the spring, this is determined with the aid of an adjusting rod. With the chain in position, set the mainspring up about half a turn, first of all.

Place the adjusting rod on the fusee square and wind fully—the escapement must not be in position, and if possible only the center wheel—some movements are so arranged that the third and fourth wheels can be placed in position afterwards. Very carefully let the rod unwind, and in so doing adjust the weight on the rod so that the pull of the mainspring will just lift it. Having adjusted the weight correctly for the top turn, allow the rod to come round for the next; the spring should now lift the weight without further adjustment, and so on to the last turn (see Fig. 71).

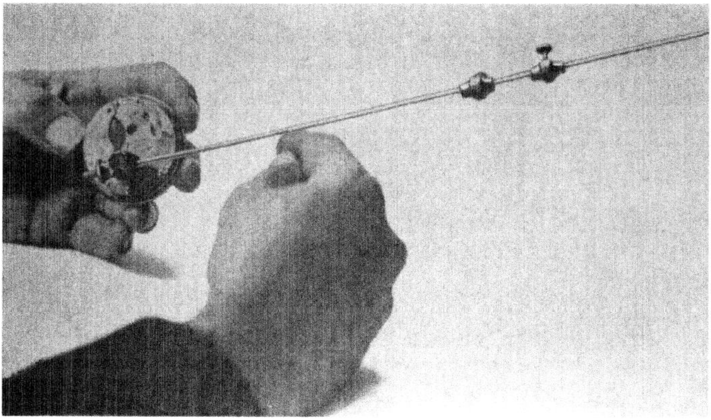

Fig. 71 – Adjusting Rod

If you find that there is not sufficient force on the last turn, set the mainspring up a little further and repeat the test. Should you find, however, that the top turn has the least pull, this generally indicates that the spring is set up too much. The adjustment should be such that the force is the same for each turn, but you will seldom find that this is the case, owing to the formation of the fusee cone. We must therefore compromise and make the pull as equal as possible, as it is inadvisable to consider re-cutting the fusee to the correct curve. When the adjustment is completed the ratchet click screw is then secured tightly.

Provision when Stop-Work is Removed

When no stop-work is fitted, or for some reason it has been removed, some provision must be made to prevent excessive pulling on the hook, as not only is there a danger of tearing the hole out of the mainspring, if the hole and hook system is used, but the extra force when fully wound will cause knocking; i.e. the escapement is quite safe if the balance vibrates one-and-a-half to one-and-three-quarter turns, but if much in excess of this, the ruby pin will knock on the other side of the lever, which is known as knocking the banking. An error of this kind will cause the watch to gain considerably. To prevent this excessive force when the spring is fully wound, a resilient form of hooking is introduced. Watches made for stop-work have not, as a rule, any form of re-coiling click. By means of this hooking the mainspring cannot be wound quite fully, and the result is that the spring does not, at any time, strain at the hook. Most modern watches not fitted with stop-work are fitted with a resilient form of mainspring hooking, i.e. the loose or riveted piece, and a recoiling click.

Progress in Mainsprings

Experiments are in progress in connection with the shape of the mainspring. It has been proved that if the spring is slightly curved, instead of being flat, more power is obtained (Fig. 71A).

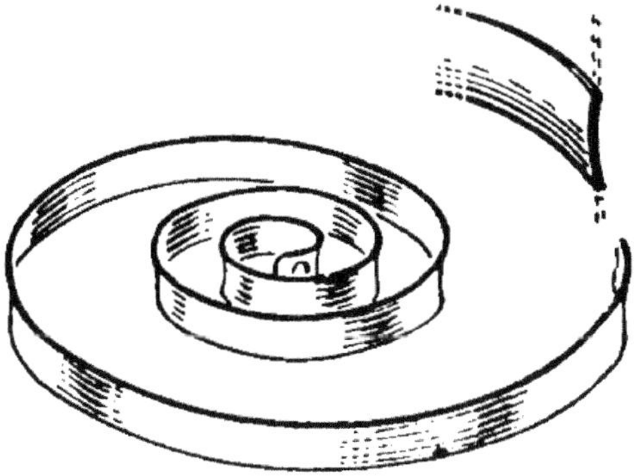

Fig. 71A – The New Cross Curve Mainspring
The curve is exaggerated to illustrate its form

This is readily understood, because we are then using, to a certain extent, the strength of the width of the spring. The strength of a spring varies directly proportionate to its height and to the cube of its thickness or strength. If, as an example, we consider a mainspring of say 1 mm. high and 1 mm. thick and were to use it edgewise (i.e. to lay it flat out and coil it thus, which, of course, is not practicable), our spring would be the strength of a spring 1 mm. thick and 1 mm. high, which would exert a force considerably in excess of 1 mm. thick and 1 mm. high, wound in the conventional manner. So in the new form of mainspring, a weaker spring can be used, which will give more turns and will give the twofold advantage of less liability to break and better facilities to rate.

A New Mainspring Slipping Device

The author has patented the device illustrated in Fig. 72 (Pat. No. 534,241). It has the following advantages when compared with the system of the mainspring slipping in the barrel—

It does not take up any space in the barrel, thus allowing the full length of mainspring to be used, with its attendant advantages of better timing at the end of the run, etc.

The tension of the mainspring is constant. There is no fear of the additional tension of the spring—as used when the slipping mainspring is used—coming into play, which is liable to cause knocking when fully wound.

There is no sudden jerking, which is associated with the slipping mainspring.

The same ratchet wheel is used. It is therefore not necessary to alter the design of the movement.

A disc indicates when the mainspring is fully wound. It revolves during the winding of the spring and remains stationary when fully wound.

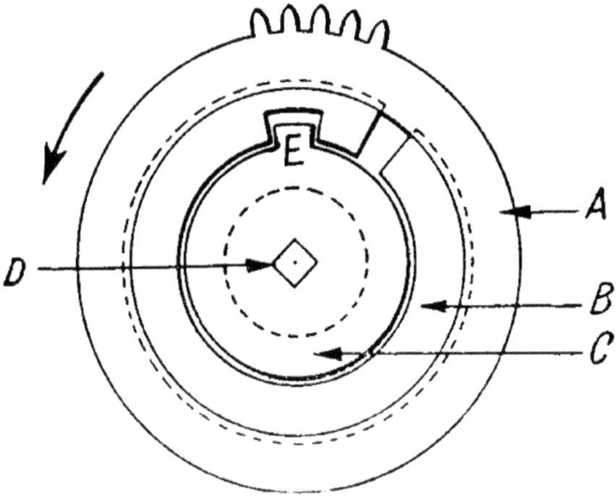

A = Ratchet wheel *C* = Boss squared to barrel arbor
B = Spring ring *D* = Barrel arbor square

Fig. 72 – De Carle's Mainspring Slipping Device English Patent No. 534241, Swiss Patent No. 218689, American Patent pending

Its action: The boss (*C*) is squared to the barrel arbor. The tongue (*E*) engages in the slot of the spring (*B*), the barrel arbor has an extended pivot, onto which fits the disc to indicate when the mainspring is being wound; the disc remains stationary when the spring is fully wound. As the ratchet wheel (*A*) revolves, and by virtue of the spring (*B*), it causes the barrel arbor to revolve. When a resistance, such as the mainspring being fully wound, is met with by the spring (*B*) the ratchet wheel (*A*) can still be made to revolve indefinitely with perfect safety.

CHAPTER 5

THE TRAIN

It would be futile for me to say that the train was the most important part of the watch. We are sometimes inclined to refer to parts as being the all and most important, but I do feel that the train does not receive adequate attention. It is essential that it should be free, and to ensure this a combination of adjustments must be correct.

Even in new watches we sometimes find a sad lack of care to the train: such matters as the uprightness of the pinions, shape of the teeth, and sufficient freedom. A combination of the smallest faults in each department can result in loss of power to the escapement, or an unevenness of the power transmitted.

In the less expensive type of watch these defects are overcome by fitting a strong mainspring. Therefore, if the watch is strange to you, i.e. the first time it has passed through your hands, give special attention to the train, and do not be satisfied that it just runs down, but ensure that all the depths, etc., are correct. Lack of power or intermittent transmission of power can give a deal of trouble during regulation.

This, to a greater extent, applies to the small wrist watches we are called upon to repair today. With such pieces it is desirable to obtain all the power possible and at a constant force to maintain the good action of the balance.

To Calculate the Train

As there are many books published which deal with the matter of calculating trains to a very minute and detailed extent, I will give only a rudimentary outline of the general procedure.

It will be readily understood that if a wheel of, say, sixty teeth drives a pinion of ten leaves, the wheel will make one revolution during six revolutions of the pinion. It is usual to calculate watch trains from the center wheel, as this wheel generally rotates one turn in one hour.

The center pinion itself does not enter into these calculations. Therefore, if the movement is fitted with a seconds hand to the fourth wheel, the number of teeth in the center wheel × third wheel teeth ÷ the number of leaves in the third pinion × the number of leaves in the fourth pinion will equal sixty.

It follows that if three numbers are known, the fourth can be determined by proportion, and if only two are known, the ratio of the other two can be ascertained thus—

The center wheel has 80 teeth, third and fourth pinions have 10 leaves each; find the number of teeth in the third wheel.

$$\frac{80 \times x}{10 \times 10} = 60. \quad \therefore \quad 80 \times x = 60 \times 10 \times 10$$

$$x = \frac{60 \times 10 \times 10}{80} = 75 \textit{ teeth in the third wheel.}$$

If, for instance, you wish to find the ratio of the teeth of the fourth wheel to the number of leaves in its pinion, which has been lost, then

$$\frac{x \times 75}{10 \times c} = 60 \qquad \frac{x}{c} = \frac{60 \times 10}{75} = \frac{8}{1}$$

That is, the wheel must have eight times the number of teeth of the pinion. In such circumstances, you would select a wheel which would gear well and that would be a wheel of 80 teeth and pinion of 10, if it were for the train as given before. Should you wish to calculate the whole train to determine the vibrations of the balance—the balance spring may be missing and you wish to fit a new one—then, assuming the train is as follows: center wheel 80, third wheel 60, third pinion 10, fourth wheel 60, fourth pinion 8, escape wheel 15, and the escape pinion 6—

$$\frac{80 \times 60 \times 60 \times 15 \times 2}{10 \times 8 \times 6} = 18{,}000$$

That is, 18,000 vibrations of the balance per hour. You will notice that the escape wheel was multiplied by two, because each tooth makes two beats, one on each pallet.

The table here will be found useful, and gives most of the modern trains—

18,000 Vibrations per Hour

Centre wheel	80	80	80	75	72
Third pinion	10	10	10	10	9
Third wheel	75	75	70	70	60
Fourth pinion	10	10	8	8	8
Fourth wheel	80	70	60	64	70
Escape pinion	8	7	7	7	7
Escape wheel	15	15	15	15	15

19,800 Vibrations per Hour

Centre wheel	80	66	55
Third pinion	10	8	6
Third wheel	72	64	54
Fourth pinion	8	8	6
Fourth wheel	55	60	48
Escape pinion	6	6	6
Escape wheel	15	15	15

21,600 Vibrations per Hour

Centre wheel	64	60
Third pinion	8	6
Third wheel	60	54
Fourth pinion	6	6
Fourth wheel	54	48
Escape pinion	6	6
Escape wheel	15	15

Table of the Motion Work Train

Cannon	7	8	8	8	9	9	10	10	12	12
Hour wheel	28	24	28	32	27	32	30	32	40	48
Minute nut	7	6	7	8	6	8	6	8	10	10
Minute wheel	21	24	24	24	24	27	24	30	36	30

Correct Depths

The ideal train would be the one without teeth to the wheels or leaves to the pinions. If two discs were mounted on arbors, and so planted that their edges just touched, movement given to one would cause the other one to move also. Should there be any resistance to one wheel, it would slip, and to correct this it would be necessary for the discs to be planted closer together. Such a procedure is not practicable, excessive friction at the pivots alone being sufficient to condemn it.

To correct this, the edges of the wheels are roughened, hence the teeth of wheels and the leaves of pinions. A wheel (in watch and clock work) is generally called a wheel if it has more than twenty teeth. If it has less than twenty teeth, it is termed a pinion, and the teeth are then known as leaves.

It does not always follow that the pinion is the driven, and that it is a pinion because it is driven. The rule above determines this. A correct depth should be as near the ideal as possible; with the ideal depth, as we have seen, there is little loss of power, no engaging or disengaging friction, only rolling friction, which is the least objectionable of all forms of friction. Fig. 73 gives definitions of terms in gearing.

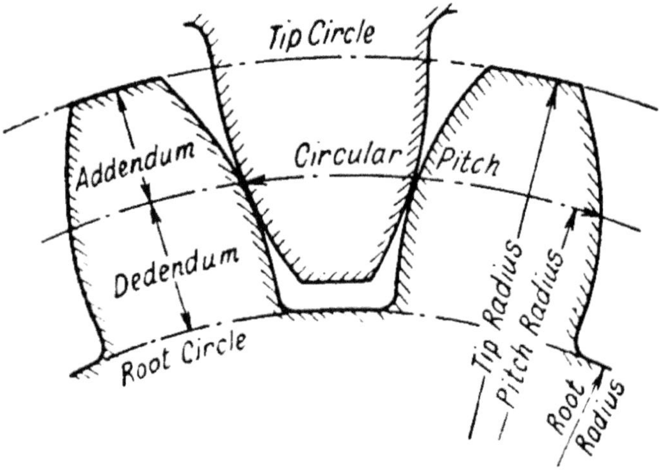

Fig. 73 – Definitions of Terms in Gearing

Correct Shape of Teeth and Leaves

If to the two discs already referred to teeth were added, and the discs themselves were cut into to give freedom to the projections, and certain mathematical conditions observed, such as the flanks of the teeth of the driven wheel being shaped to conform with the hypocycloidal curve, and this curve made by a circle of the same diameter as when used in shaping the teeth of the driver, the teeth of which were in turn made to conform with the epicycloidal curve, we should have as near a perfect depth as is practicably possible. The greater part of the friction, other than that of the pivots, would be rolling friction, and in a gear of this description there would be little disengaging friction and certainly no engaging friction.

If the size of one wheel, is considerably reduced, such as to the proportion of a wheel and pinion, disengaging friction is present, and in the instance of a low numbered pinion, such as one of six leaves, engaging friction takes place.

To realize easily the difference between the three forms of friction mentioned, you can well understand that the resistance of a plain wheel made to roll over a surface is negligible; the resistance of a rod drawn over the same surface would be light, but not negligible. If the rod were still held at the same angle, however, and pushed forward, the friction then would be considerable; here we have rolling, disengaging, and engaging friction respectively.

John Arnold

It has been stated that John Arnold was a past master at gearing, and that his gearing has never been surpassed. Arnold's chronometer escapement embodies the advantages of rolling friction; the teeth of the escape wheel are shaped to conform to the epicycloidal curve. It is said that Arnold's wife was a clever mathematician and helped him considerably in his calculations, etc. If it is ever your good fortune to have a John Arnold watch pass through your hands, examine the pinions of the train carefully; you will find that, unless it has been tampered with since it left the maker's hands, they will show little or no wear.

Gearing in Watches

It will be seen that low-numbered pinions are not desirable. A great deal of friction results, and, consequently, wear. On the other hand, there are limits to the high-numbered train. Stability must be taken into consideration, and, further, slight obstruction such as a minute particle of dust can cause the piece to stop altogether. We must therefore strike the happy medium.

The shapes of the flanks or acting portion of the leaves of the pinions are constructed from the hypocycloid curve. The line traced for the flanks of the pinions is straight, and as the flanks of the pinions used in watch work are radial the circle used to trace the curve for the wheel teeth and also for the flanks of the pinion to be driven by it will be equal to half the pitch diameter of the pinion. In large gearing the flanks of the driven and the driver take the form of a curve as well as the addendum, i.e. portion outside the pitch circle.

Not only do the mathematically-shaped teeth and leaves ensure the minimum of friction, but they also ensure the power being transmitted smoothly during the whole time of the operation of the tooth engaged on the flank of the pinion leaf.

For further information on this subject, I would refer the student to *Principles of Mechanism*, by Willis. Also an article on gears in *Modern Shop Practice*, Vol. VI, published by Chicago American Technical Society.

In a fairly high-numbered pinion the ends of the leaves can be shaped half round, but with the lower-numbered pinions the half-round end would form an obstruction, and a more pointed termination is adopted.

The circle traced by the discs, as mentioned in

Correct Depths, pg. 125, is known as the pitch circle, and when examining a depth these imaginary pitch circles should just touch. They are imaginary in the cut wheels and pinions, of course, since it would not be practicable to trace them, especially on the smaller pinions.

It is not sufficient just to feel that the intersecting piece has shake; if the train is to run smoothly, and all the power possible is to be transmitted to the escapement, and transmitted at a constant speed, *the depth must be correct.*

Involute Gearing

Involute curve, used in gearing, is the curve traced if we unwind a cord which has been wound round a central post or pin. Say, for instance, we wind a thread round a pencil and to the end of the thread fix another pencil, hold the first pencil still and trace with the second pencil the curve formed when unwinding the thread, that curve so formed is the involute curve, and is used in a modified form by some watch manufacturers. One such curve, known as the Mikron form, devised for the makers of gear-cutting machines of the same name, is much in favor in Switzerland. A similar curve is used for both the wheel and pinion. Usually this form has also the curve of a circle to form the dedendum of the tooth and leaf, and is much stronger than the parallel dedendum usually associated with the cycloidal curve gears. Fig. 74 shows the involute form of rack tooth, from which the curved forms of wheel and pinion teeth are generated or developed.

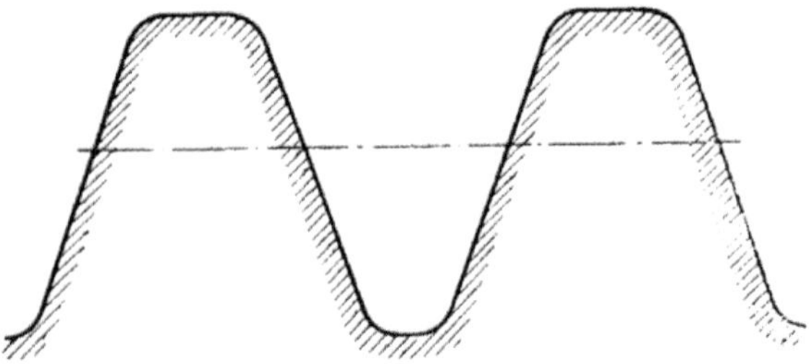

Fig. 74 – Involute Form

The Circular Arc Form

Yet another form, devised in England in recent years, and its primary object is to standardize gear cutting in this country so that there shall be some uniformity as regards the cutters and hobbing tools themselves.

In order to make this standard in England, the British Standards Institute has issued a specification. Few watches are made in England today, so this form of gearing may not be found in watches for some time, but clocks (and this also refers to the smaller type of clocks such as the calotte) will shortly be found with this gearing. The principle of the pitch circle equally applies, so when testing the depth you will know what to look for.

The foreword to the B.S.I.'s specification says: "In spring-driven escapement mechanisms for watches and clocks a high mechanized efficiency is necessary, and in this respect the involute tooth form is not necessarily the best, particularly if the pinion has fewer than thirteen teeth and is the driven member of a pair."

"For such a purpose the cycloidal tooth form or an approximation to it has been preferred, but from tests made at the National Physical Laboratory an alternative form, based on a rack tooth profile composed of two circular arcs, showed no appreciable difference in efficiency from the cycloidal form…"

The specification says—

"The tooth form shall be based on double circular arc rack tooth form, hereinafter called the circular arc form."

Fig. 75 shows the circular arc form tooth. The same cutter or hob is used for wheel teeth and pinion leaves. This form is not familiar to watchmakers, and we generally associate such gearing with large machinery, but there seems every indication that this will be the form of gearing for watches and clocks in this country.

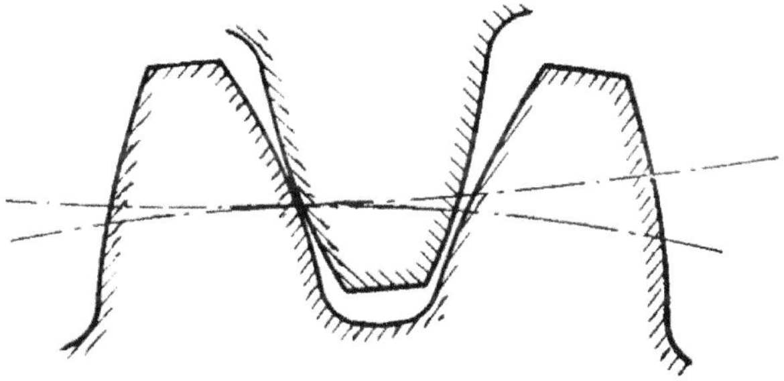

Fig. 75 – Circular Arc Form

Objection to Strong Mainspring

When it is said that as much power as possible be transmitted to the escapement, it might be argued that if this is the object, why not fit a stronger mainspring? We well know that with a stronger spring there is more power; more power increases friction; increased friction means greater wear, and so we go on. Therefore, it is far better to minimize friction in the train, thus enabling a weak mainspring to be fitted. Not only does this, as I have already stated, minimize wear, but it has the further advantage of being less liable to break.

The illustrations show how the epicycloidal and hypo- cycloidal curves are termed; also a correct depth with the pitch circle shown (Figs. 76, 77, 78).

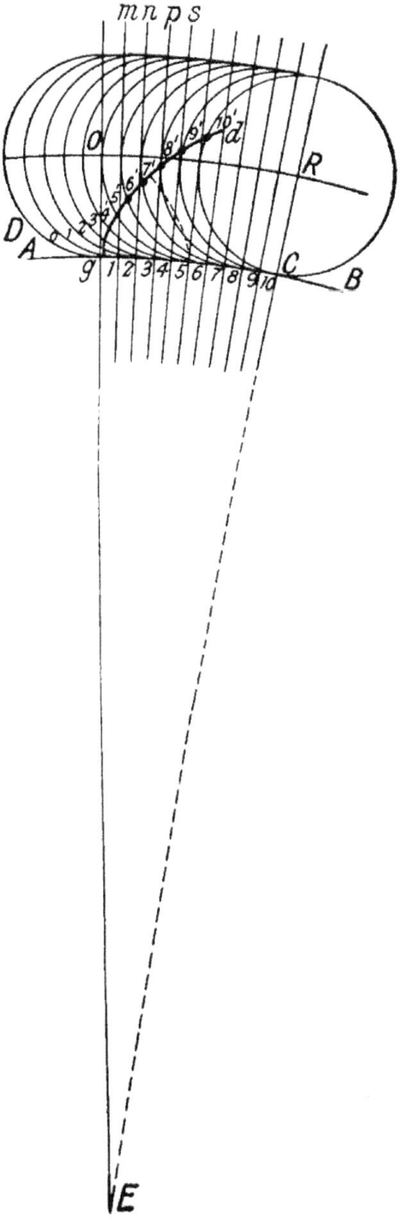

Fig. 76 – Showing Formation of the Epicycloidal Curve

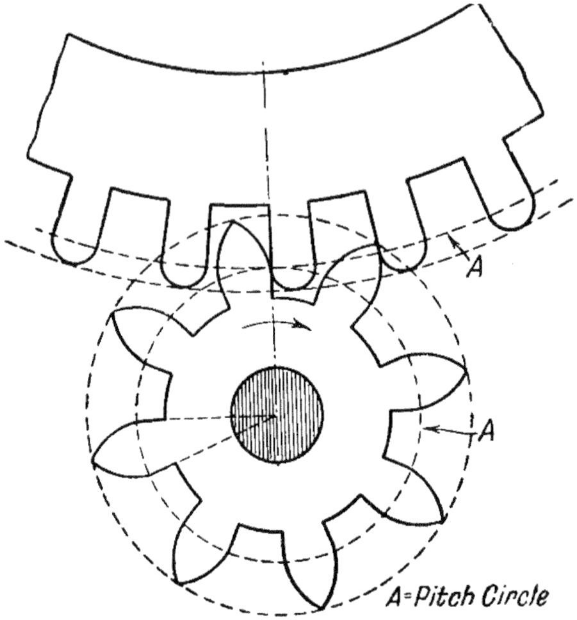

Fig. 77 – A Correct Depth

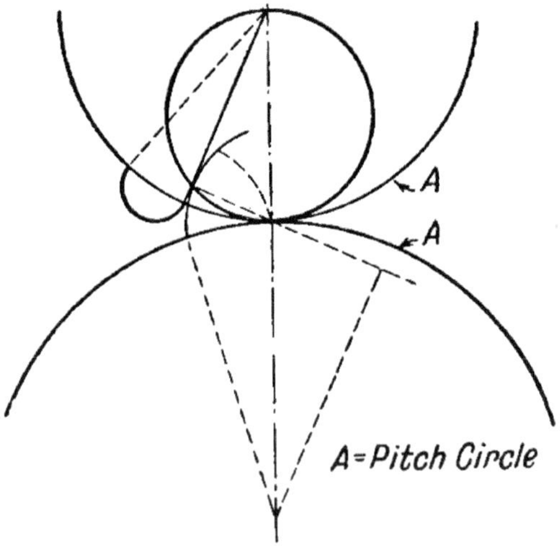

Fig. 78

Correcting Faulty Depths

Having well in mind what a correct depth is, the next question which arises is how to correct a faulty one.

As it is not possible to alter the pinion, unless it is changed altogether for another one, the wheel must receive our attention. There are some instances where it is essential to change the pinion, but we will leave that for the moment.

Replanting a Wheel

If the depth is too shallow, both of the wheel gearing with the pinion and of the pinion gearing with the next wheel, it is obvious that the wheel has been planted incorrectly. This is not always easily corrected and may mean stretching both wheels and topping in the topping tool.

Should the holes of the offending pinion be of brass, the best procedure would be to plug the holes and re-drill. Say that, for instance, the third wheel needs replanting, it is advisable, first of all, to open the hole fairly large to ensure that when the new hole is drilled in the plug there is no possibility of it breaking into the sides. The actual fitting of the plug is carried out in much the same manner as when fitting a new bouchon.

We now proceed to place the third wheel and the center wheel in the depth tool (Fig. 79) and adjust the centers so that the center wheel is gearing in the third pinion correctly. The two wheels can now be removed, but care must be taken not to disturb the depth adjusting screw on the tool.

The runners of the tool are generally so made that one end forms a male center and the other end a female, and the tool is provided with a runner which has a trumpet-shaped end; for our purpose it will be necessary to place the trumpet end runner and also one of the male center runners in position.

Fig. 79 – Depth Tool

Screw the trumpet runner firmly in position, and place the other runner loosely in the tool. Now place the trumpet end in the top center wheel hole; hold the depth tool upright, and adjust the male center runner so that it just touches the plate; then make secure.

Very lightly describe a short arc in the position you think the new hole will come. We now place the third and fourth wheels in the depth tool, adjust to the correct depth. Then, using two male center runners, place the fixed one in the fourth hole and, securing the other runner as before, make another light score which will cross the score of the center marking. At the intersection mark and drill for the third wheel pivot; use a drill smaller than the pivot, and open to size with a cutting broach, finishing off with a round broach to harden.

The lower hole can be drilled either by using the top hole as center in the uprighting tool, or by marking off, on the lower plate, with the depth tool, using the same adjustments as when marking for the upper hole.

It now only remains to chamfer the holes for the retention of oil, to finish.

In all probability it will be necessary to regild the plates, but if great care is exercised this can generally be avoided.

A Common Fault

Sometimes a faulty depth is so slight that it is difficult to detect, and this particularly applies to the instance of a badly proportioned wheel and pinion. A watch may stop and you know that it is through a faulty depth; there is plenty of power, everything is perfectly free, the escapement is correct, but directly the case is opened the watch starts off again and the cause of the stoppage is obviously very light and the mere jar of opening the case is sufficient to start it off again.

The trouble can generally be located at the fourth wheel and escape pinion depth. I do not know why it is, but manufacturers of the mass-produced watches seem to overlook this all-important depth.

The slightest obstruction here will cause a stoppage, since the power is, naturally, light. If you have your suspicions regarding this particular depth, ascertain that the wheel and pinion are of the right proportion, and to do this the sector is used (see Fig. 80).

The Sector

Invariably, the escape pinion is too large. The method of sizing is quite simple. Count the number of teeth in the fourth wheel and close the sector on to the wheel at that number. Then make the arm secure by the screw provided for that purpose. Count the leaves in the pinion and slide as far as possible into the small steel gauge at the base of the sector, and the number of the teeth should correspond with the number engraved on the scale.

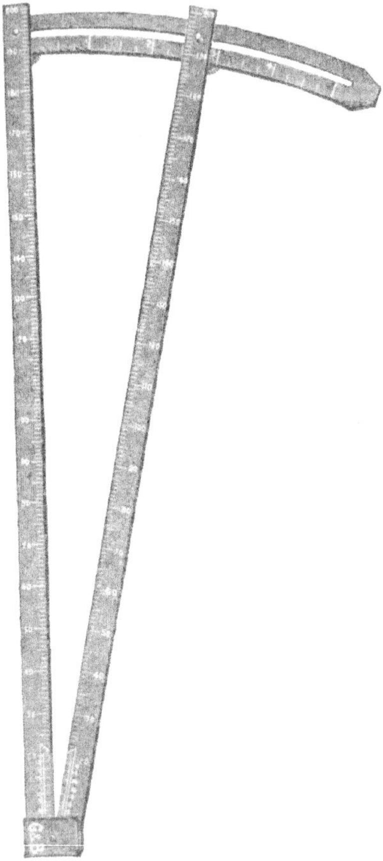

Fig. 80 – The Sector

Take care that all measurements are taken at the widest point; this especially applies to the pinion. It is possible, for instance, to gauge the pinion so that it will register considerably less than if it were so arranged that the gauge touched on the extreme ends of the leaves.

If the pinion is not correct, there is no alternative but to change it for another one. On the other hand, a doubtful depth can sometimes be corrected by slightly stretching the fourth wheel and just passing it through the topping tool. The cutter may give the teeth a better shape than hitherto.

In such a circumstance the sole object will be to re-top in order to re-shape only; therefore the cutter selected should fit the wheel exactly before the stretching commences, since we do not want to reduce the thickness of the teeth.

Should it then be found, upon testing, that the stretching and the subsequent cutting do not give the required freedom, a slightly larger cutter must be used, and the wheel re-topped, that is, provided that the teeth were too thick.

It is always much to be preferred to make one or two cuts rather than one and that one too much. We can very easily remove, but it cannot always be replaced; in this instance it would mean stretching again.

It should always be borne in mind, when using the topping tool, that it cannot correct a wheel with faulty teeth, that is, with teeth of unequal thickness. If, for instance, you come across a wheel with one of the teeth half the thickness of the others, the topping tool will not correct this; that tooth will still be half the thickness of the others after it has passed through the tool. The only way to correct such a fault is to change the wheel entirely.

The Topping Tool

I propose now to give one or two hints on the actual use of the topping tool (Fig. 81).

First select one of the brass beds of such a diameter

that it will give ample support to the wheel, but will, at the same time, be quite free of the cutter. Generally, it is a little smaller than the root circle of the wheel.

We next select a cutter; if you propose just to pass the wheel through for re-shaping, the cutter should be the same thickness the space between the teeth, as already explained. Should the wheel be altogether too large, proceed exactly the same, and select a cutter that just fits and make several cuts to reduce the diameter. If, on the other hand it is required to make the teeth a little thinner, a cutter that is slightly wider than the space between the teeth should be used. Here, again, carry out the thinning operation gradually; it may be necessary to change the cutter two or three times before the desired result is obtained.

Fig. 81 – Topping Tool

Having selected the cutter, it is now placed in the tool. Some topping tools are so arranged that the guide is on each of the cutters, and on others the guide is effected by a separate piece. In either case the cutter is placed so that the thinnest end comes against the fixed end of the guide, and, as the guide enters the tooth space, it presents the thin end of the cutter first.

Now carefully make the machine revolve, and adjust the guide by means of the screw provided for that purpose, so that the spring-piece, upon which no cutting edge is made, will come exactly in the center of the space of the succeeding tooth. This will have the effect of moving the wheel round one tooth, and it will be in the required position for the next cut.

This adjustment is most important, and great care must be exercised, otherwise there will be a risk of damaging the wheel.

On the tool another guide is attached to ensure that the cutter is at right angles to the wheel, and this is generally a hook-shaped piece with a sharpened end. This guide can be swung forward when required; the point of the guide should coincide with the center of the broadest part of the cutter.

If you find that this is not correct, an adjusting screw is fitted for the purpose of rectifying. The cutter is now practically ready for operating, and the wheel should be adjusted between the centers in the tool so that it rests lightly on the brass bed; then secure the lower runner, applying a little pressure to the upper runner to bind the wheel slightly, and make secure.

The wheel should be quite free, but not as free as when running in the frame of a watch.

The light pressure of the wheel on the bed and the slight binding of the pivots will just give it that friction to hold it in position whilst being cut.

Finally, before the actual cutting takes place, bring another guide into position to check that the wheel is at the correct height, that is, in line with the center of the cutter, otherwise a full cut will not be made.

To take an exaggerated case, the upper part of the wheel will be cut, but the lower part quite free.

Here, again, there is a screw to adjust for height. When all is ready, carefully lower the cutter to engage with the wheel, and see that the guide part only engages first. You will notice that there is an adjusting screw which determines the depth the cutter can intersect the wheel; this should be adjusted so that the guide just touches the bottom of the space between the teeth.

Slowly make the cutter revolve, and when you are sure that all is in order, proceed to cut all the teeth, just applying a slight pressure on to the handle of the tool to keep the cutter well in contact with the wheel. You will quickly become aware when all the teeth have received their cut, by the freedom of the cutter.

I would like to emphasize here the absolute necessity for carrying out this work carefully. It is quite a simple matter for teeth to be cut out of upright, etc., but if all the adjustments enumerated have been attended to, there is no fear of damage.

It is always advisable, after each cut, to remove the wheel and try the depth with the pinion before proceeding either to lower the cutter farther into the wheel or to change the cutter for a wider one, as the case may be.

After the wheel has been topped, it will be noticed that the cutter has thrown up a series of burrs; these can be removed with a glass brush. If the wheel is gilt, care must be taken not to mark it unnecessarily, but should the finish be of the circular grain type, then use the glass brush in the direction of the grain.

Wheel Stretchers

Sometimes, if the depth is shallow, or you are at all doubtful about the depth altogether, and feel that the teeth are not of a good shape, it is better slightly to stretch the wheel before re-cutting. There are many ways of carrying out this work, and I am of the opinion that the best is to use the simple tool here illustrated (Fig. 82). The wheel is placed in position between the stakes and the top stake or punch is tapped with a hammer, much in the same manner as when riveting. The wheel is made to revolve with the fingers during this process. The tool is shown with the punch held open to show the guide pin, which is solid with the stake and runs in the hole of the punch.

Here, again, caution is necessary. The taps should be light and frequent, and the wheel made to revolve fairly quickly, so as to ensure so far as possible an equal stretching, and, at the same time, marking the wheel as little as possible.

There is another tool by means of which the wheel is made larger by rolling. The wheel is placed between two slightly, rounded steel wheels, one of these wheels being made to revolve with the fingers, the other hand being used to guide the wheel which is being stretched. Pressure is applied by means of a screw which binds the two steel wheels together.

I find from experience that the wheel so treated is rather inclined to show a mark which is difficult to remove, but this system has the advantage should you wish to stretch the wheel only; to correct a shallow depth, it will not be necessary to pass the wheel through the topping tool, since the position of the wheel or rollers can be so arranged by applying the pressure at the base of the teeth, and not actually interfering with the shape of the teeth themselves; furthermore, the stretching is constant for the whole of the wheel.

Fig. 82 – Wheel Stretcher

Generally speaking, however, it is much to be preferred to stretch the whole of the wheel and to pass it through the machine afterwards to ensure that it is perfectly round.

Should it be found that one part of the wheel only is at fault, it is still advisable to stretch the whole wheel and re-cut.

CHAPTER 6

THE LEVER ESCAPEMENT

To proceed with the examination of the movement. It is usual to examine the escapement (see Fig. 83) after the hands and dial have been removed and before the movement has been taken to pieces. But, for convenience, we took the movement to pieces in a previous chapter, so we must assume, again for convenience that that work has yet to be done.

The lever escapement was invented by Thomas Mudge, an Englishman, born 1715, and died 1794. The original escapement was made with a double roller; there was, however, no draw to the lever. The knife-edged guard pin touched the knife-edged safety roller; it was not, therefore, entirely a detached escapement. Some interesting examples of the lever escapement are to be seen with elaborate devices to minimize this roller friction, but it was not until some years after its introduction that the real cause of the trouble was eliminated, when the pallets were so designed that they were drawn into the escape wheel and thus made free of the balance. This is attributed to Josiah Emery. By virtue of the "draw," the guard pin is held away from the safety roller, and the balance is free to vibrate, the only interference being when the ruby pin engages with the lever notch. The lever escapement is thus known as the "detached lever."

To Remove Balance Spring

For the present we will ignore the balance spring.

I propose to deal with that separately, so the balance spring can be removed.

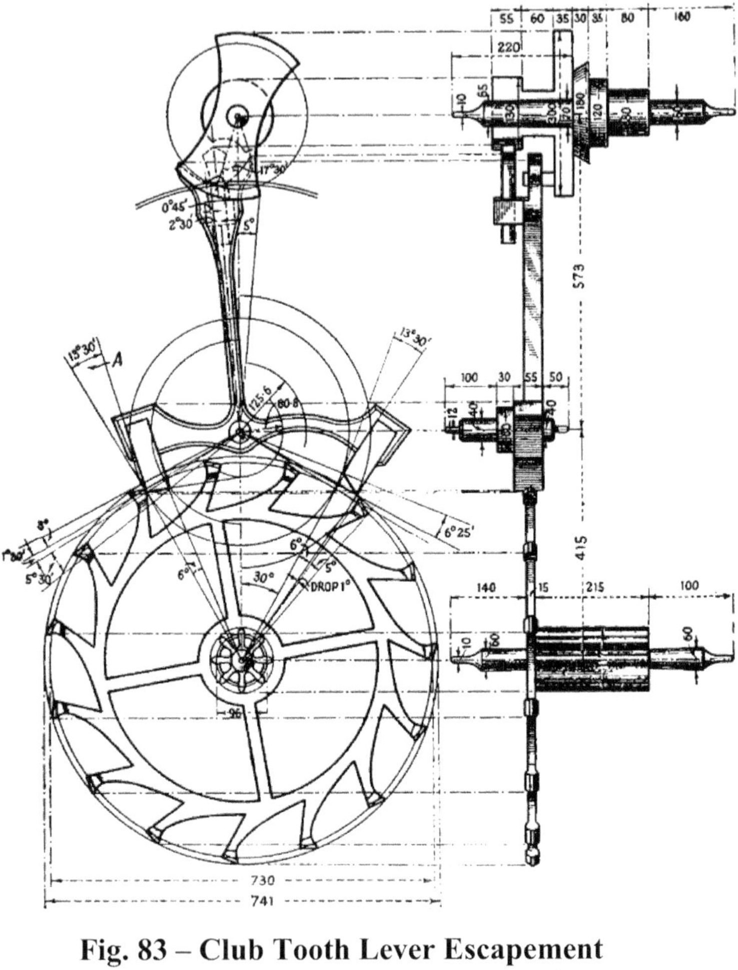

Fig. 83 – Club Tooth Lever Escapement
Measurements are 30 times actual size.

The best method of removing the spring is to insert into the slot of the balance spring collet a flat piece of steel, similar to an oiler. Hold the balance firmly in one hand and with the oiler in the other, give the oiler a steady anti-clockwise twist, and at the same time pull upward. Such a procedure will remove the tightest collet and there will be no fear of damaging the spring (see Fig. 84). Should, however, the slot of the balance spring collet be too wide, then the same shaped tool, only a little wider blade, must be used. Place the blade under the collet so far as possible, and give a steady twist (Fig. 85). Some watches are met with in which the collet is of the solid steel type; generally fine quality English watches are so fitted. In such cases, hold the collet with a pair of stout brass or nickel tweezers, and then give the balance itself a slight twist, first one way and then the other. At the same time slightly pull the balance away.

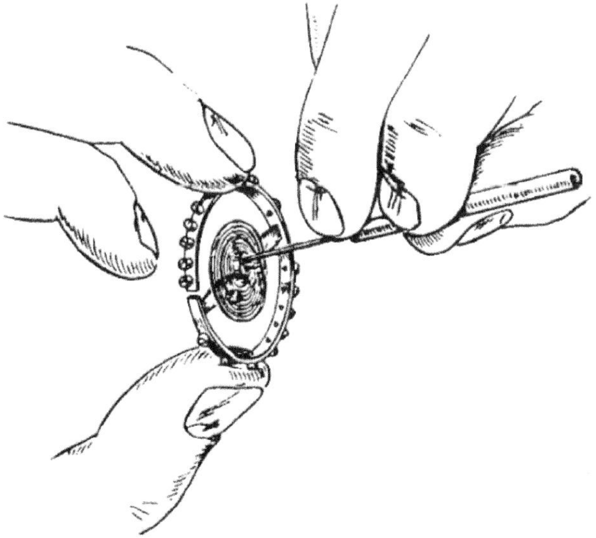

Fig. 84 – To Remove Balance Spring

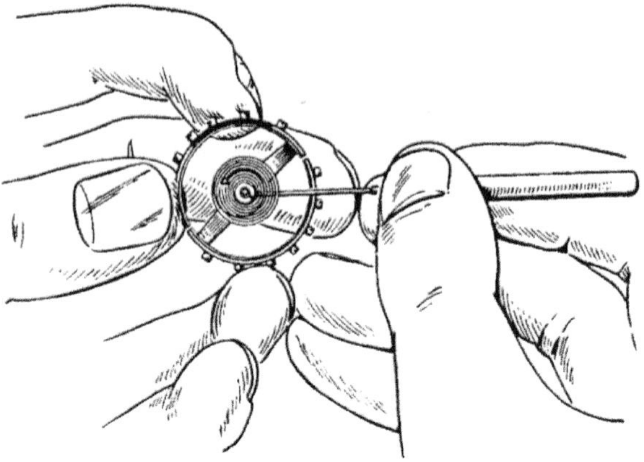

Fig. 85 – Removing Balance Spring by Placing Lever Under the Collet

Do not be hasty when removing the balance spring from the balance; even if it takes a minute or two to remove the spring satisfactorily, it is quicker than fitting a new spring owing to impatience. A word of advice is necessary here. Where possible, always take the precaution of removing the balance spring stud from the balance cock before taking the balance cock off. In some cases this is not possible, and the cock must be removed with the balance and spring attached. There is a risk of distorting the balance spring and care should be taken to bring the balance down on to the board as quickly as possible. Having removed the balance spring, replace the balance in the watch. We will not proceed with the examination of the escapements.

End Shake

First of all see that the balance has end shake; it does not require much, not as much as, say, the train wheels, but it must be perfectly free. A very good test, and it also tells us if the pivots are free in their holes, is to replace the movement in its case. Then hold the watch flat and close to the ear, move the head to one side, and then fairly sharply jerk it to the other side. In so doing you should be able to hear the ends of the balance pivots knocking against their respective end-stones. Further, should the balance be inclined to stick on one side you will be able to detect which is the faulty pivot, or, maybe, faulty jewel hole or end-stone. You should be able to hear a definite metallic knock. With some of the very small movements this test may not be possible, but from 8-1/2 lignes upwards it is practicable.

Another test is, when the watch is assembled and going, apply a little pressure to the top balance end-stone with a pointed peg-wood. If a very light pressure stops the balance, then we can be sure the end-shake is too close; if on the other hand it requires some considerable pressure to stop the balance, then the end-shake is in excess. Each individual watch must be judged as regards the pressure, a thin balance cock not requiring so much as a stout one, etc.

Detecting Machine

A useful instrument used in Switzerland is a form of sound amplifier to detect escapement faults. The Swiss pay great attention to the aural test. It is practically impossible to test some of the small baguette movements aurally unless an instrument is used. The method adopted is as follows: the movement is placed on the diaphragm of a microphone of a form of wireless set, and with the aid of earphones the actions of the movement can be listened to. The movement is placed in various positions during the test. The modern watch-timing machine could be put to the same use.

The Locking

As the movement we are examining is a Swiss

straight line lever (Fig. 83), it will be necessary to remove the balance and cock before we can proceed further. Take the power off the train first by letting down the mainspring.

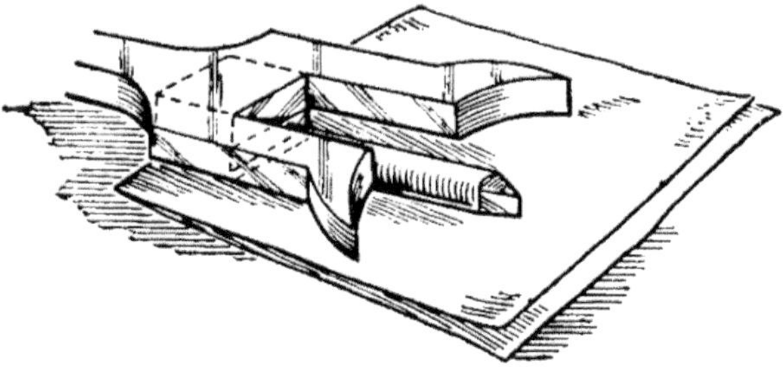

Fig. 86 – Showing Piece of Folded Paper Under Lever Notch

We next wedge the lever, this can be effected in most watches by cutting a small piece of paper and folding it in two, place the folded end under the lever notch and the springiness of the paper so folded will bind the lever the correct amount. A piece of notepaper will do for some movements, whilst for others, of the smaller sizes, tissue paper is sufficient (Fig. 86). With a fine pointer, such as an oiler, apply a little force to the escape wheel, and with another pointer move the lever over until a tooth of the escape wheel unlocks. Directly the tooth is on the impulse face of the pallet stone remove the pointer from the lever but continue to apply force to the escape wheel. This will cause the lever to move, and the escape wheel tooth will slide up the face of the pallet and eventually drop off. The escape wheel will then be arrested by a tooth dropping on to the locking face of the other pallet, ease the force on the escape wheel, but still keep it in the forward position, and it is at this precise moment that we shall be able to determine that the locking is safe and correct. To be correct the locking should be approximately 1.5°; Fig. 87 shows the correct amount. It is not practicable to measure the depth of the locking, so study Fig. 87 carefully. As a further help, the amount of locking is usually equal to the thickness of the balance spring. We then move the lever back, still with force on the escape wheel as before, and when a tooth drops off and the wheel is again arrested by the other pallet stone, examine that locking and in this manner continue until all fifteen teeth have been tested on each pallet stone. It does not matter which stone is tested first. Say the entry or straight pallet stone is the first, then when the tooth drops off that pallet the exit or bent pallet stone will arrest the wheel and the tooth on that pallet is examined.

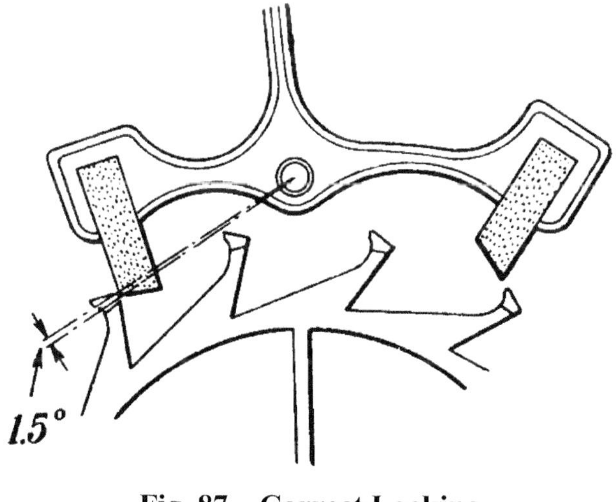

Fig. 87 – Correct Locking

To Correct the Locking

Before proceeding further with the other tests we will talk for a moment about correcting, assuming that the locking was not correct. If the escape tooth does not drop on to the locking face and mislocks, it may mean that the stone will have to be drawn out. Care, however, must be taken before either stone is altered, as we must bear in mind that if, for instance, the entry pallet mislocks and the exit pallet is too deep, to make the entry pallet deeper will also make the exit pallet deeper still. So in such an instance it will be necessary to draw the entry pallet and push the exit pallet in. On the other hand, if the entry pallet is too deep and the exit also is deep, altering the entry pallet will connect the exit pallet. So it is advisable to study the escapement well before making any alteration.

To Move the Pallet Stones

Exposed pallet stones, such as are generally met with in Swiss and American watches, are moved quite easily. Place the pallets upside down (i.e. with the shellac uppermost) on a bluing pan and place on the pan a small piece of shellac. Hold the pan over the flame of a spirit lamp and when the spare piece of shellac is soft we know that the pallet stones can be moved. This piece of shellac serves a double purpose; we are sure, if the shellac is examined frequently and touched with a pointer, that the shellac of the pallets will not burn and lose its adhesive qualities; further, some pallet stones are cleaned free of all shellac on both top and under surfaces, relying upon the small amount of shellac on the sides of the stones to hold them in position, and in these circumstances the shellac cannot be seen. When the stones are ready to be moved, remove the bluing pan from the flame and place it on a piece of metal on the bench; now with a pair of tweezers hold the lever, still on the pan and in the same position, and with another pair of tweezers, previously slightly warmed, move the pallet stone or stones as required. Remove the pallets from the pan and the shellac will set immediately. We can now test in the movement to see if our alteration is correct.

Impulse

Before we proceed further, test to see that the impulse acts correctly. Wind the mainspring up a little. Move the lever carefully until a tooth has unlocked and then suddenly let the lever go; it should flick over smartly to the banking on the other side. Try both pallets. We are sure then that the balance will receive impulse correctly.

The Draw

Remove the paper wedge and leave the mainspring wound up a little. With the pointer, move the lever away from the banking pin until it is just about to unlock a tooth of the escape wheel. Do not move it so far that the tooth is released. It should still be on the locking face; then withdraw the pointer suddenly. If the draw is correct the lever will return smartly to the banking pin; try on both sides. This action is due to the fact that the pallet stones are set back at an angle of approximately 14° from a radial line drawn from the escape wheel center (see illustration Fig. 88).

It was the lack of this property that held Mudge's escapement back for so many years. It will be appreciated that the draw is very important, for without it the guard pin is liable to rub on the safety roller and good timekeeping in these circumstances would be impossible. The absence of draw is more detrimental to a portable timepiece—particularly to a wrist-watch. Such watches are subjected to frequent concussions, and were it not for the draw, the guard would continually rub the safety roller. I have not yet met a case where the draw was in excess, so we need only concern ourselves with the want of it.

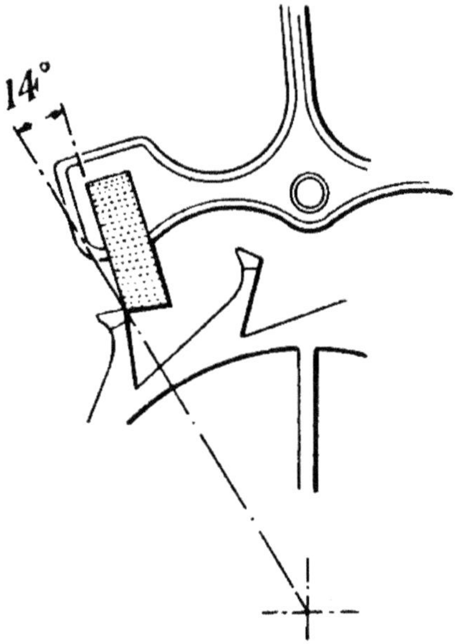

Fig. 88 – Showing the "Draw"

The Correct the Draw

Remove the pallets from the movement and place them on the bluing pan, again with a piece of shellac as a guide. When the shellac is soft enough, remove from the flame and place on the bench as before. Hold the lever with one pair of tweezers and with another pair of tweezers or a pointer push the stone to one side as indicated (Fig. 89). If the exit stone is at fault, the stone is moved in the same direction as the entry stone.

The illustration also shows, in dotted lines, the narrower pallet stone. Hold in this position and blow on to the pallets so that the shellac shall set. If this procedure is not followed, there is a risk of the stone returning to its original position, the amount of movement necessary to correct it being so slight. Usually the pallet stones do not fit their slots in the lever so tight that they will not move to one side a little, and it is only a very little movement that is required. If care is exercised during this operation the locking will not be upset. Should, however, you find that it is not possible to move the pallet stone sufficiently, a new and slightly narrower stone must be fitted. In the majority of instances it is not practicable to open the slot into which the pallet stone fits.

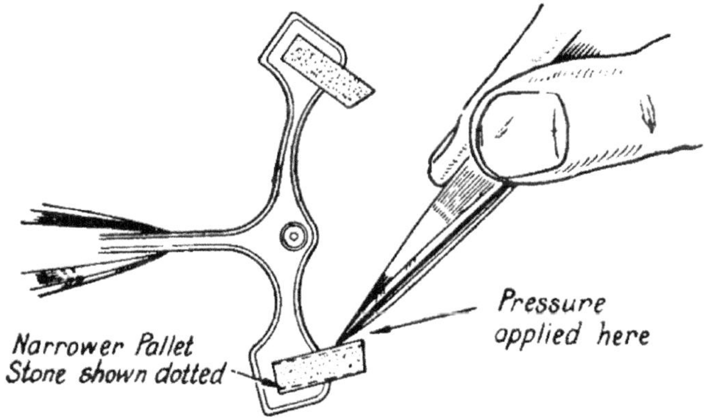

Fig. 89 – To Correct Want of Draw

Run to the Banking

This test is sometimes confused with the shake on the banking; run to the banking is quite a distinct function and we shall come to the shake next.

Wedge the lever again and wind the mainspring up a little. Move the lever away from the banking pin, with the pointer, until a tooth of the escape wheel drops off the pallet, and then note very carefully the amount of movement necessary to give to the lever to bring it up to the banking pin (Fig. 90).

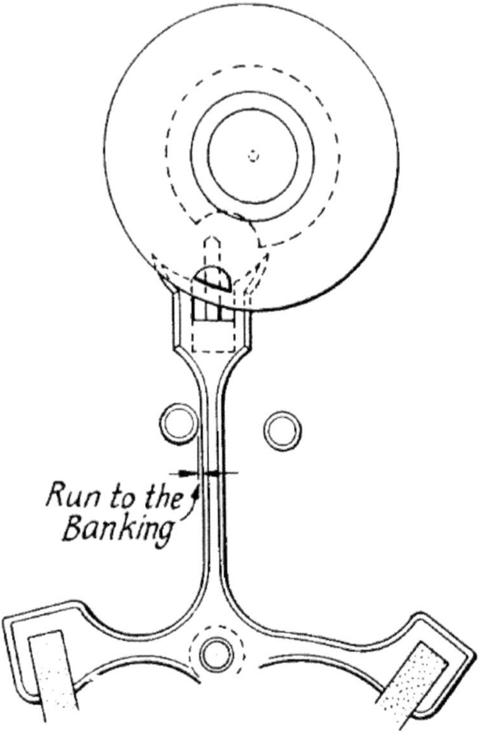

Fig. 90 – Showing the "Run to the Banking"

The movement of the lever, after the locking, to the banking pin is the run to the banking. This movement should be equal on both banking pins. The actual amount of movement necessary to be correct is equal to approximately 2° of movement of the lever, i.e. when the tooth is locked and the run completed the pallet stone will intersect the escape wheel by about 4°. The amount of run depends to a great extent upon the quality of the escapement. A cheap escapement requires more run to be safe. In any case, the run is a necessary evil; it is the amount of freedom required to keep the guard pin away from the safety roller. It is an evil in the sense that the more run there is the deeper the intersection, and consequently the greater the work imposed upon the balance to unlock, and this can impair the action or the arc of vibration of the balance. A poor action, as we all know, spells poor timekeeping.

To Correct the Run to the Banking

This is effected by opening or closing the banking pins. If the run is too little then the pins must be opened. When the bankings are pins and not solid parts of the movement, this is quite simple, taking care to see that they are parallel, otherwise the run will vary with the position of the movement. For instance, if they are V-shaped, the run may be correct when in the dial down position, but would be excessive when in the dial up position. In the case of the solid bankings, if more run is required, a thin shaving of the metal can be removed with a fairly stout watch screwdriver. Sharpen the blade on the Arkansas stone to a fine cutting edge; a gentle press downwards on each banking is all that is required. If the run is excessive, the correction is not quite so simple; should the run be much in excess there may be sufficient room to drill two holes and fit banking pins. Another method is to cut a slot by the side of each banking and then close the post so left inwards a little, with the blade of a screwdriver.

Shake on the Banking

Remove the wedge from under the lever and place the balance in position in the movement. Lead the balance round so that the ruby pin is out of the notch, hold the balance thus. With a pair of tweezers or the pointer, try the shake of the lever on the banking, or as some prefer to call it, the shake on the roller, i.e., the amount of freedom the guard pin allows the lever before it is stopped by the banking pin on one side and the safety roller on the other. It should be equal on both sides.

To Correct Shake on the Banking

The only way to correct the shake is by shortening or making longer the guard pin. If the shake is not sufficient, and it should be equal to the amount of movement of the run to the banking, the guard pin must be made shorter. This can be effected by stoning away with the Arkansas slip, retaining the original shape of the end, which should be V-shaped. If we find there is too much shake, then draw the guard pin out a little; if this is not possible, a new pin must he fitted.

Bear in mind that the guard pin is not a functional part of the escapement. The watch will work without it, but it will not, however, withstand jerks, and it is, as its name implies, a guard, so the functional parts of the escapement must not be altered to suit the guard pin; in other words, do not open the banking pins to correct the shake on the banking.

The Angle

The test to find if the lever is in angle is as follows. Wedge the lever a little tighter than before, place the balance in position and make this to bind also, so that when the balance is moved it will stay where put. To do this, place a bristle from the watch brush under the foot of the balance cock at the back, so that it makes the cock tilt and gives no end shake to the balance. Wind the mainspring up a little. Now move the balance round slowly and with exceeding care. When a tooth drops on to the locking face continue to lead the balance round until the ruby pin is free of the lever notch. Note carefully the amount of movement of the lever after the tooth is locked, to the position where the ruby pin is free of the lever notch. Make a mental note of the amount of movement you were able to detect, or if there was no movement at all. Then reverse the balance and make the same observations on the other side.

For the angle to be correct the amount of movement on each side should be equal; if there is no movement on one side then there should be no movement on the other.

If, however, the movement is unequal or there is none on one side, and some on the other, then the lever is out of angle.

To Correct the Angle

What we shall have to do is to bend the lever. To take a definite example, say there was an appreciable movement when the lever was moved towards the entry pallet and no movement at all when moved towards the exit pallet, then the lever must be bent towards the exit pallet, and by so doing we shall experience a little movement on both sides.

If the pallets are made of a soft metal such as brass, use the tool here illustrated (Fig. 91), and bend the lever with the tweezers. The illustration is self-explanatory. Should the lever be made of a hard metal (steel) we shall peen the lever as illustrated (Fig. 92). If either of these methods is adopted there is no fear of breaking the lever.

Fig. 91 – Tool to Correct the Angle of the Lever

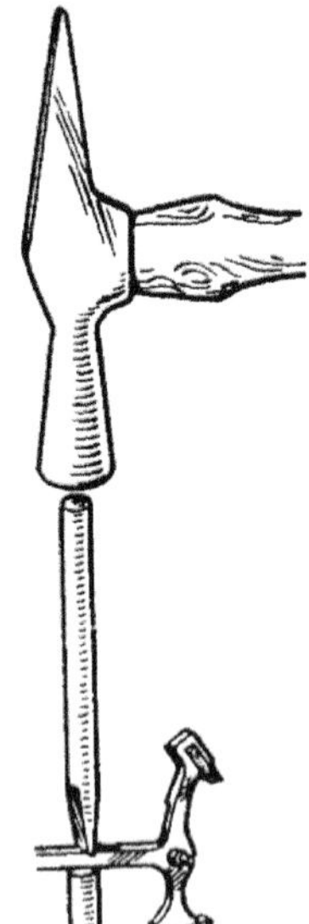

Fig. 92 – Peening the Lever to Correct the Angle

Length of Lever

To find if the lever is of the correct length leave the balance and lever wedged. Move the balance carefully until a tooth of the escape wheel drops on to the pallet stone, and then take particular note of the amount of movement of the lever afterwards. For the escapement to be absolutely correct there should be no movement at all, but such a condition only refers to a very fine quality escapement, with close-fitting jewel holes, etc. For ordinary work a small movement is permissible, but if the movement is excessive, i.e. the ruby pin takes the lever almost over to the banking pin, then the lever is too long. It is important that the angle should be correct before we decide about the length of the lever.

If the lever is too short it will be noticed that it is necessary to move the balance an excessive amount before the wheel is unlocked. Instead of the ruby pin impinging on the side of the notch it will travel further and operate on a part of the lever horn. This is to cite an extreme case.

To Correct Length of Lever

In the case of the lever that is too long, remove the guard pin first and select a piece of mild steel rod the diameter of which coincides with the curve of the horns of the lever. The English escapement makers used the tool illustrated in Fig. 18, and it is used to polish the horns of the lever. The illustration depicts the application, and it is not possible to use this tool for the lever we have in hand, unless we remove the pallet stones and the pallet staff. Quite a good job can be made if we hold the lever between the first finger and thumb so that the notch only projects. Charge the steel rod with oilstone dust and oil, rest the hand with the lever on the edge of the bench, and draw the rod up and down between the lever horns. At the same time twist the rod and in this manner reduce the length of the lever (Fig. 93). If the lever is made of soft metal, such as brass or bronze, a burnisher, the correct size and shape, sharpened on a dry, medium carborundum-stone, is efficient. Test to see if the lever is of the correct length, and if so, clean off the oilstone, charge with diamantine, and polish in a similar manner to that employed when reducing the lever of the English watch. Should the lever be too short, then we must stretch it, and this can be done with the peen of the hammer, or a punch is used in a similar manner to that employed when bending the lever; the punch should be of chisel shape, but with a flat end, and we operate on the underside of the lever.

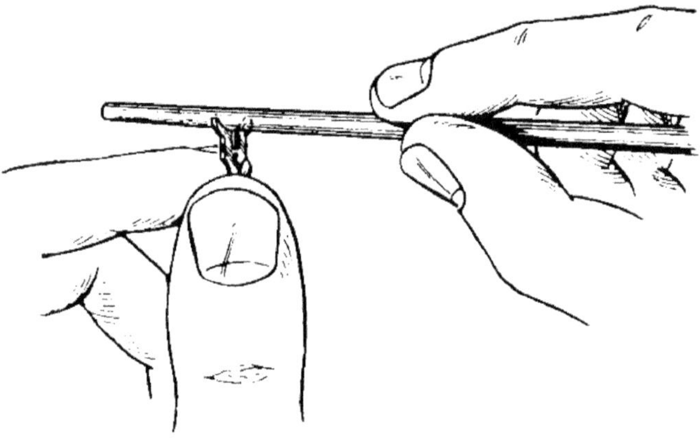

Fig. 93 – Method of Holding Lever When Shortening by Hand

Guard Pin

An important test to ensure that the guard pin functions correctly is, with the lever and balance in position, to hold the lever over so that the guard pin presses fairly hard against the safety roller and whilst in this position lead the balance round so that the ruby pin enters the notch. It should enter the notch quite freely; there must be no indication of it rubbing the horn of the lever but should enter so that it impinges cleanly on the side of the notch it is to move to unlock the escape wheel. If the ruby pin does rub and the guard pin is of the correct length, it may be necessary to polish out the horns of the lever, virtually shortening the lever, but not to touch more than possible the length of the notch; that is, the active length of the lever. In an extreme case it may be necessary to change the safety roller for a slightly larger one, in which case it would be necessary to make the guard pin shorter.

Inside and Outside Shake

This test determines if the escape wheel is of the correct size. Remove the balance and wedge the lever, and wind the mainspring up a little. Move the lever with the pointer so that a tooth of the escape wheel is just about to drop off. It will be found that if the tooth is on the entry pallet the tooth on the *outside* of the exit pallet will, if the escape wheel is moved, butt against the back of that pallet, and in this manner the wheel is arrested between two teeth of the escape wheel, and the amount of shake or play the wheel has is important (Fig. 94).

The shake just referred to is the outside shake. Now move the lever over to the other side in a similar manner so that the tooth escapes and then move the lever back just a shade. This will lock three teeth between the pallet stones; try the shake here—known as the inside shake (Fig. 95) —it should be the same as the outside shake, to be correct.

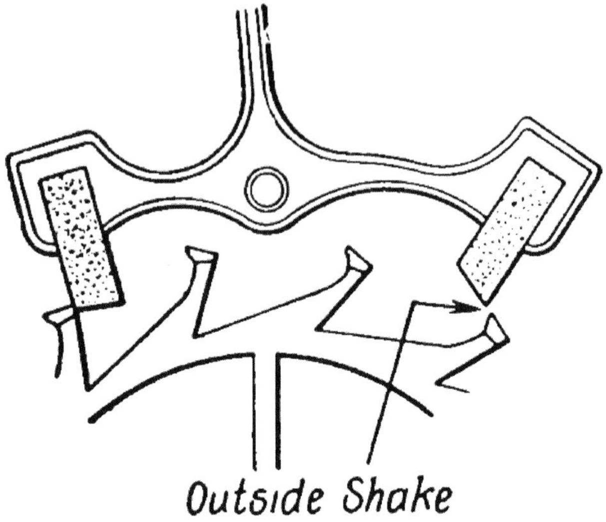

Fig. 94 – Outside Shake

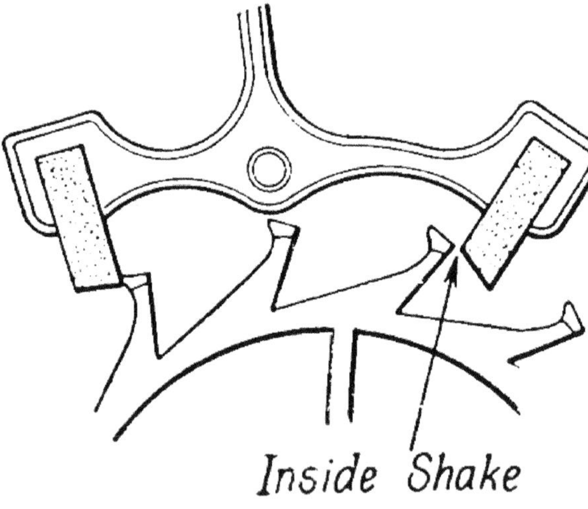

Fig. 95 – Inside Shake

To Correct Inside and Outside Shake

If there is no inside shake and an excessive outside shake it denotes that the escape wheel is too large.

Should there be no outside shake and an excess of inside shake then the wheel is too small. Conversely, should there be no inside shakes and excessive outside shake, the wheel is too large. In both instances, to correct, the escape wheel must be changed for one that is smaller or larger in diameter, as the case may be.

Ruby or Impulse Pin

The ruby pin should be exactly upright; if it leans to one side there is a risk of it binding in the notch when the watch is in various positions. Should the ruby pin lean backwards or forwards the intersection in the lever notch will vary with changes in position of the watch.

The ruby pin should fit the notch freely. There must be no indication of binding at all. At the same time there must not be any excess of side shake, otherwise power is lost and the action of the balance will be impaired.

To Open the Notch

If the ruby pin is tight in the notch or the notch appears to be rough, proceed as follows. Take a piece of watch mainspring about three inches long and one-eighth wide, well soften it and drill a hole through each end (Fig. 96), bend a piece of brass wire to form a handle and also to hold the spring taut. Cross cut the surface of the spring with a fairly coarse emery buff, charge with oilstone dust and oil and polish the sides of the notch. To finish, clean off the oilstone, and rebuff, charge with diamantine and polish. During polishing, the spring will give just sufficiently to round the surface treated; this is desirable as a large surface is then not presented to the ruby pin. The best way to hold the lever is between the first finger and thumb, with the notch projecting. Let the notch rest on a piece of soft wood held in the vice.

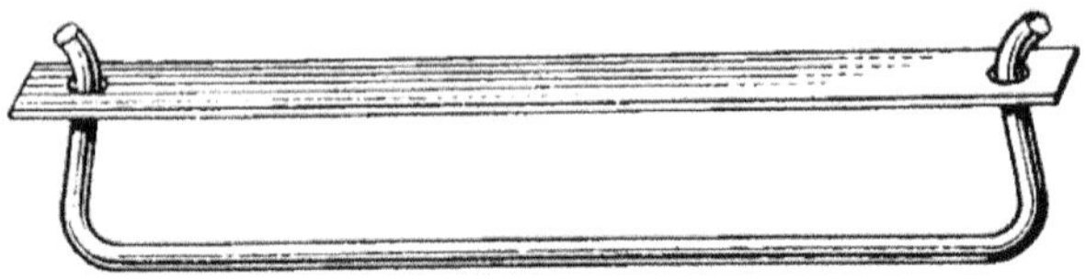

Fig. 96 – Lever Notch Opening Tool

To Set the Ruby Pin

One method is to secure the ruby pin whilst the roller is still on the balance. Remove the balance spring, place the balance on the bluing pan, roller downwards, apply a very small piece of shellac on the end of the ruby pin from the back, and hold over the flame of a spirit lamp. Observe the shellac closely, and directly it becomes soft touch with the pointer, and when it runs and so covers the top of the ruby pin and part of the roller, remove the balance quickly. It is perfectly safe so to treat the balance. Shellac melts long before steel changes color.

To set a new ruby pin it is better to remove the roller from the balance staff. File a long taper on a piece of brass wire and place the roller there. Screw the wire in the pin tongs so that about two inches of the wire projects, leaving the roller about half an inch away from the end. Apply heat to the wire at the end near the pin tongs in the flame of a spirit lamp. The heat will run along to the roller. When the roller is hot apply a small piece of shellac to the topside, at the ruby pin hole (Fig. 97).

A convenient method to transfer the shellac is to crush a piece on the bench and then pick up a small piece with the moistened end of a pointer; the heat of the roller will take it from the pointer.

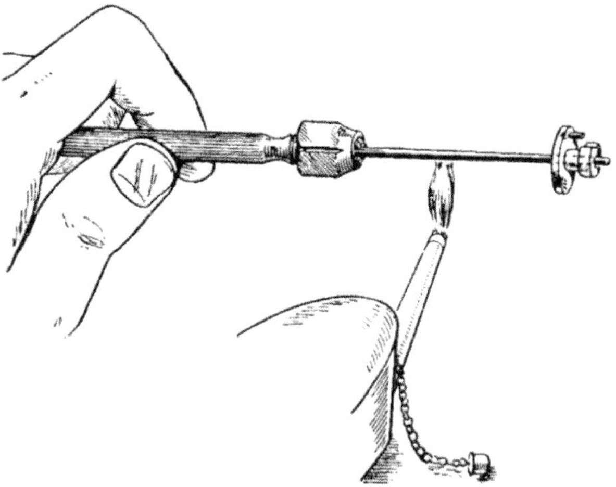

Fig. 97 – Setting Ruby (or Impulse) Pin

Hold the wire in the flame again and place the ruby pin in position from the underside. When the shellac is soft enough the ruby pin will push through the hole. Hold the wire in the flame a little longer so that the shellac becomes quite liquid, and then draw the ruby pin in and out so that the shellac finds its way inside the hole. We are sure then of a rigid pin. To finish off, heat again; make sure that the pin is upright and that the shellac flows over the end of the ruby pin in the roller. All traces of shellac are removed from that part of the ruby pin which projects, i.e. the acting portion. The shellac comes away freely if a piece of brass wire filed as the blade of a screwdriver is used.

If the ruby pin is out of upright it is sometimes possible to bring it up by heating a piece of iron, similar to a polisher, and holding this against the pin, sufficient heat is applied to soften the shellac and so enable the pin to be moved.

To Set Pallet Stones

If you are fitting new stones (or resetting) place the pallets on the bluing pan, adjust the stone (or stones) in position, apply a small piece of shellac with the pointer or tweezers on the end of the stone, warm over the flame of a spirit lamp, allow the shellac to become quite soft, almost liquid. Remove the pan from the flame and place on a piece of metal on the bench; hold the lever with a pair of tweezers and with another pair of tweezers draw the stone in and out so as to work the shellac along the sides of the stone. Finally, replace on the pan over the flame to make the shellac flood over. In a fine quality escapement, the shellac is cleaned off both the top and bottom surfaces of the stone, and it is made secure by the good fit of the stone and the shellac, the width of the slot being equal, or almost equal, to the width of the stone. In any case, sufficient shellac will find its way there to secure the stone. In ordinary work we rely upon the plate so formed by the shellac on the underside and also the shellac at the sides. With both methods all trace of shellac is removed from the top side and that part of the stone which projects. The shellac is easily removed with the sharpened blade of a watch screwdriver; it will chip off cleanly.

To Oil the Escapement

When oiling the lever escapement the greatest care must be exercised to ensure that the top pallet pivot is not over-oiled, this especially applying to the straight line lever. If this pivot is over-oiled the oil will spread and cling to the lever itself, and will have a serious retarding effect.

The pallet stones are best oiled as follows. With a little power on the train and an escape wheel tooth on the entry pallet stone, place a very little oil on that stone.

Now move the lever and make four or five teeth escape. It is not advisable to use the oiler for this purpose unless it is well cleaned in pith, otherwise there is the risk of oiling the ruby pin.

The balance pivots are oiled before the balance is placed in position. Apply an oiler full (a fine watch oiler) of oil to each jewel hole, and the balance pivot will carry the oil to where it is wanted. Some watchmakers advocate using a feeler to work the oil through to the end stone. I have never found this necessary.

The ruby pin should not be oiled.

Beat

The lever escapement is in beat if the balance does not set, i.e. you are unable to stop the balance, which is when the watch is fully assembled and wound. Such a condition is, however, not always possible. Some of the lower grade escapements do set, and that being so, the balance should set equally on both sides. To test for beat, stop the balance with the tweezers, lead the balance round until a tooth unlocks, and by arresting the balance either between the screws or by the arm, observe if the balance will travel on the return journey without your assistance. Still controlling the balance thus see if the same condition applies to the other side. If it does, the balance does not set and the escapement is in beat. Should, however, it set on one side and not on the other the escapement is out of beat. Also, should it set on both sides and it is found necessary actually to move the balance through a greater arc on one side than the other to unlock, then the escapement is out of beat. To correct, move the balance spring collet on the balance staff. See Beat in Chapter 8, cylinder escapement.

CHAPTER 7

THE BALANCE AND BALANCE SPRING

Now we come to that portion of the watch which has received, in all probability, more study and attention than the rest of the watch put together: the balance and spring.

Practically every year we find that some new field has been opened; either in the composition of the balance itself or its spring, and in the method of its application or manufacture. That the balance and spring are important is beyond doubt, and too much care and attention cannot be paid to these pieces. I do not propose to go into the molecular composition but to deal with them as at the repairer's bench.

Rust

In the first place, both the balance and the spring must be entirely free from rust and this more particularly applies to the spring. Rust can in a great many cases be removed from the balance, but should the spring show the slightest sign of rust it must be discarded and a new one fitted if anything like accurate performance is to be expected from the watch. These remarks apply to the steel balance spring.

If the balance shows signs of rust—I refer to a compensation steel and brass one—first remove all the screws and place them for convenience in the lid of a small round box such as an ordinary pill box, or, as these boxes are known in the trade, escapement box.

Draw a line on the lid to represent the arm of the balance and pierce small holes to correspond with the holes in the balance, and as the screws are removed place them in the holes in their respective positions. Such a procedure will, ultimately, save a great deal of time.

Now remove all rust from the steel parts of the balance with oilstone dust and oil. If the rust is on the inside of the rim, work the polisher along the length of the balance arm, leaving a straight grain finish as originally.

Generally, a piece of peg wood charged with oilstone dust and oil answers well, finishing off with dry oilstone dust to give it the bright effect. If the underside needs attention, this is best effected by using the underhand polishing system, leaving a circular grain as the final finish. In this instance, of course, the balance staff must first be removed. The top, or face, of the balance is rather a longer operation.

With the staff removed, shellac the balance to a small brass plate and proceed to polish underhand on ground glass charged with oilstone dust and oil, and give the final finish by polishing on a zinc block charged with diamantine.

In both these latter instances, such a procedure is only justified if the quality of the movement calls for it. In the case of the lower grade balance the rust can be removed and the balance polished without removing the staff. To do this, place the balance on cork held in a vice when treating the underside and work with the iron polisher charged with oilstone dust, leaving a circular grain as well as possible. The top is best polished by either shellacking the balance to a wax chuck in the lathe or polishing underhand on a block with a large hole in it to receive the balance staff. This will give freedom for the movement during the underhand polishing. This method, however, is not always convenient unless the balance is small.

In the case of polishing in the lathe the polisher is held flat against the balance, and by making the balance revolve slowly, the polisher is worked backwards and forwards quickly to break the grain as much as possible.

To Fit New Balance

When fitting a new cut balance you will find that they are sold uncut. The method of cutting is quite simple. First mark on the side of the balance with a pair of dividers the position of the cut (see Fig. 98).

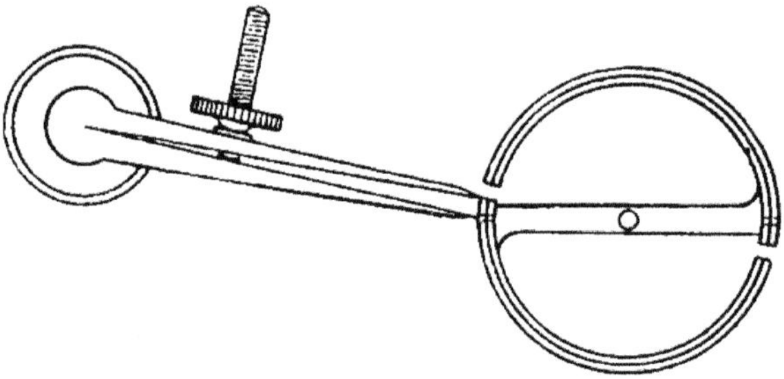

Fig. 98 – Balance—To Determine Cut

Measure from the quarter screw near the arm and then mark on the other side to ensure the cut being exactly opposite or, in other words, the length of the free arms to be of equal length. This is most important, otherwise the balance will be out of poise in temperature.

Having marked the balance, hold it securely in the vice with wood chops to cut. Cut with a screw head slotting file, making the cut towards the center of the balance.

The amount of the balance to be cut away is determined by the thickness of the balance itself. It is only necessary to give sufficient freedom to allow the arm to pass inwards freely.

The ends are finished with a fine file and Arkansas slip; just touch the four edges of each end with the Arkansas slip to ensure that no burrs are left. For the weight of the balance to be correct it should run to half time, i.e. when the balance, after fitting to the staff, etc., is placed in the movement and the mainspring wound, start the balance vibrating. It will continue so to do, and the time registered by the hands should be equal to half that shown when the balance spring is fitted. For instance, after one hour's running, mean time, the hands will show half-an-hour.

Truing Balance

Now rivet to staff in position. You may find after the cutting that the arms are inclined to spring outwards a little and the balance will, consequently, be out of truth. In such circumstances remove all screws for the purpose of truing the balance.

The actual truing itself can generally be effected by manipulation with the fingers, using the finger nails as the fulcrum on which to bend the balance.

Should it be necessary to use pliers, the pattern shown in Fig. 99 is useful. The ends are of soft brass and will not mark the metal work. You will sometimes find, and this even in quite good quality watches, a mark has been made on the arm of the balance, in order to make it run true, owing to the fact, it would appear, that the hole for the staff had not been placed in the correct position.

Fig. 99 – Balance Pliers

I mention this to show that many devices are used even by the best manufacturers to obtain the desired result.

After the balance has been made true and tested on the poising tool and put in poise, if it is found wanting, place in the calipers and give a spin. Pass the balance, still revolving, through the flame of a spirit lamp, several times, quickly. Do not hold in the flame long enough for the steel part to change color, but, at the same time, sufficient heat must be applied to allow for the expansion and subsequent contraction of the rim.

Now, remove the balance from the calipers and allow to cool, then try again on the poising tool and, should it be found that the changes in temperature throw the balance out of poise, there is no alternative but to change the balance for another. There must be some small flaw in the manufacture, such as the annealing or the fusing of the two metals together. It is gratifying to note that this fault is not often present. Unfortunately, however, it is not possible, either in the first place to detect it before cutting, or to correct it after it has been discovered.

Method of Manufacture

Just a few words here on the manufacture of the compensating balance will not be out of place, and it will help you to realize the general weaknesses, etc., of the balance.

In the first place, a round piece of steel, a little smaller than the finished balance is to be, is drilled through the center. This disc is placed on an arbor and turned perfectly true both in the round and on the flats. The disc is then removed from the arbor and the hole is filled with graphite. The steel disc is then placed in a crucible and brass is fused to its edges and the underside. The top is left as free as possible in order that the same hole can be used for turning.

The disc, with the brass adhering, is then removed from the crucible and the brass from the underside filed off. The edges are carefully hammered to harden. The disc is then replaced on the arbor and turned perfectly true, the flats being just skimmed again to ensure flatness.

The thickness of the brass in the finished balance is three as compared to two of steel, so the final reduction of the brass should be left until the balance is nearer completion.

The disc is then mounted in the mandrel and the center turned out, leaving the correct proportion of steel on the side which will form the rim. The depth of the cut is determined by the thickness of the arm of the balance, which is generally equal to the steel in the rim. It now remains for the arms to be pierced out and the balance is nearly complete.

Holes are drilled into the side and tapped; the distances apart are measured in a tool on a similar principle to the counting plate of a wheel cutting engine. It is essential that the holes should be so drilled to ensure that when a pair of screws are moved during the temperature adjustments the balance will still be in poise.

The balance is now polished, the top as explained, and the sides by placing on an arbor and holding the polisher flat on a T-rest which has, in the first place, been secured so that it is absolutely square with the balance.

By just moving the flat polisher backwards and forwards and at the same time tilting it until it just touches the balance edge, a perfectly flat surface is ensured. The polisher itself is of tin and charged with either crocus or rouge. The inside of the balance, that is the part turned out, is polished out with a large soft iron polisher which just fits into the recess, the balance being held in the mandrel and shellacked on to a plate and made to revolve quickly during this process.

First clean with oilstone dust and oil and, finally, with dry oilstone dust.

The underside of the balance is finished as already described. The screws are then made, usually of gold, and, in some cases, of platinum. The making of screws for balances, however, was in England quite a separate trade, as, indeed, was the making of the balance itself.

The Swiss Method

The procedure in the escapement making factories of Switzerland is similar, with the exception, of course, that machines carry out the hand method I have described. For instance, the cutting out of the center and the truing of the edge are done in an automatic capstan lathe and the piercing of the arm is stamped out, etc. The illustration (Fig. 100) showing the various stages of manufacture of the balance, is from models of a Guillaume balance kindly lent me by Paul Ditisheim.

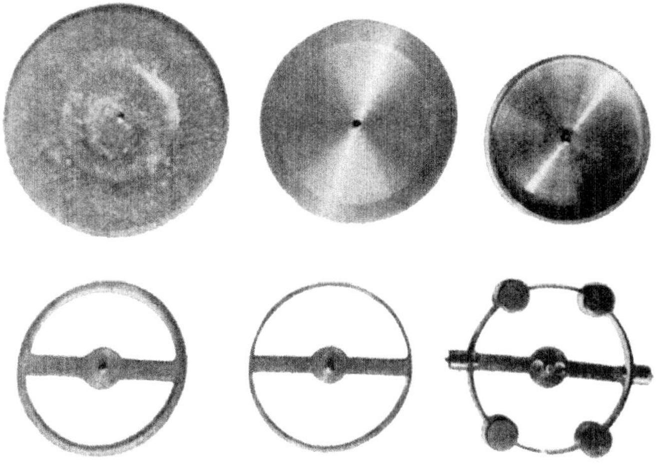

Fig. 100 – Stages of Manufacture of the Balance

Out of Poise

Generally speaking, the balance should be in absolute poise if the watch is to function satisfactorily. With some of the plain balances (not compensated), where steel balance springs are used, it is permissible to throw the balance out of poisc to thc cxtcnt of 1-1/2 to 2 minutes per day fast in the pendant up position.

The object of this is to give a crude form of compensation. It is calculated that a watch fitted with the steel balance spring loses approximately one minute per day for a rise of temperature of 10° F.

The temperature in wear is about 90° F, which is a change of, say, 30° F from the normal temperature of a room, therefore the watch has passed through a variation in temperature to the extent of 30° F, which is equal approximately to 3 min. of time. As the average person wears his watch two-thirds of the day it would have a tendency to lose 2 min. during wear, so the balance is thrown out of poise to correct this.

Very crude, you will say, but, at the same time, it is effective.

Timing in Reverse

There is, however, a condition which must be watched and that is, the balance must not vibrate more than one complete turn, otherwise it will register the reverse result, that is, lose pendant up. This can, however, be provided for by making the balance heavy at the top instead of at the bottom, but this "timing in reverse," as it is known, is not desirable, since, if the vibration of the watch falls off to under one turn, our adjustment will be wrong.

Invar and Elinvar

The better plan with the plain balance watch is to fit either an Invar (nickel steel) or Elinvar balance spring, which is a harder substance than Invar, and is, on this account, to be preferred. Elinvar contains 33% nickel, 61% iron, 4% chromium, and a small percentage of tungsten, manganese, silicon, and carbon.

These springs are very satisfactory and are used extensively today in some of the lower grade watches in fact, many with this form of spring have been submitted to the various trials, including Kew, and have obtained remarkably high positions.

Invar alloyed springs are soft, which not only makes them difficult to handle but does not allow the balance to vibrate well when the oil of the watch is becoming thick. There does not seem to be any life or assistance in the spring itself; it lacks elasticity. The Elinvar spring, however, overcomes this drawback to a very great extent and I understand that experiments are still being carried out to make these springs harder. It is also claimed for these springs that they are rustless and non-magnetic, or more correctly, they *retain* little magnetism; they are, however, influenced while in the magnetic field.

Guillaume Balance

There is a balance I would like to talk about which has been most successful at the trials both here at Teddington (Fig. 100) and at the Continental tests. I refer to the Guillaume balance already mentioned, invented by Dr. C. E. Guillaume, of Paris. Invar, which is an alloy of 64% steel and 36% nickel, commonly known as nickel steel, was first discovered by Dr. Guillaume. His investigation brought to light the fact that the alloy of nickel and steel in these proportions was practically unaffected by changes of temperature. The expansion or contraction is negligible. In the place of steel, Dr. Guillaume used what he named Anibal, 42% nickel, for the manufacture of the compensation balance with results we all know so well.

It is interesting to note, upon consulting the records of the Kew trials of recent years, the astounding number of watches fitted with the Guillaume balance that have been placed well in these trials. One great advantage of the Guillaume balance is that the middle temperature error is very much reduced.

Poising the Balance

With the exception of the case already explained, it is essential that the balance should be in absolute poise and to do this effectively it is best carried out in the following manner. The poising tool shown in Fig. 101 will be found very useful for our purpose. The balance, without its spring, but with the roller in the correct position, is placed on the tool and the heaviest point is noted.

Fig. 101 – Poising Tool

The object to be achieved is that the balance should have no heavy point; in other words, it should remain in any position where placed. You will find from experience that this can present difficulties. I refer more particularly to the compensation balance. It is not always advisable to poise the balance by means of the quarter screws, because it is the acme of perfection to leave all four quarter screws at the same distance from the rim of the balance, so the temperature screws must receive our attention.

We will assume for a moment that our balance has a decided heavy point. Remove the balance from the tool and, with the slotting file, deepen the slot of the screw which was at the lowest point. In this manner the balance will be lightened, and, at the same time, it will not be defaced.

When poising the balance of a watch from which a very fine rate is required (i.e. five positions and three temperatures, and positions in temperature) it is advisable to remove the roller before poising. When the balance is in poise, replace the roller; it will be found that the balance will not then be in perfect poise. To correct, reduce the weight of the roller by chamfering the underside near the ruby pin. This procedure will remove a slight positional error when timing in positions in temperature. If the balance is poised in the usual manner, it must be out of poise, however slight, when tested for changes of temperature. We have, in effect, poised the roller separately.

We often meet with balances with the screws showing rough file marks, but in good work this is not permissible. I know that with some of the lower grade mass-produced watches such methods are resorted to in the factories and, in these circumstances, there is no harm in carrying out the work as it has been done hitherto.

The American System

The Americans lighten the balance screws by recessing the underside of the screw in the following manner. A set of rose cutters (see Fig. 101A) are fixed tightly in the box containing them. It is not necessary to remove the cutter to use. Select a cutter of the correct diameter and with a hole that will take the thread of the screw freely and at the same time with no undue side shake. Place the screw in position (Fig. 101B) and work with the screwdriver to cut the recess as indicated in Fig. 101C.

The Swiss System

The Swiss achieve the same object by chamfering the end of the balance screw. As this mutilates the screw, more or less, it should only be used on the lower grades of watches. You will, however, find that quite good grades of watches have so been treated and obviously by the manufacturers. Fig. 102 is self-explanatory.

Fig. 101A – Rose Cutters for Balance Screws

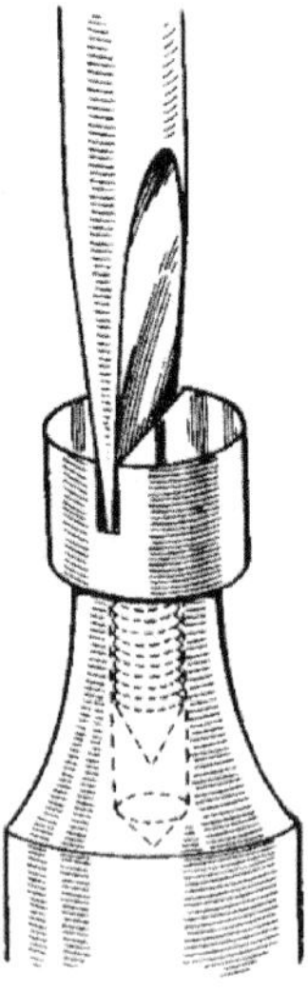

Fig. 101B – Showing Method of Cutting Recess in Balance Screw

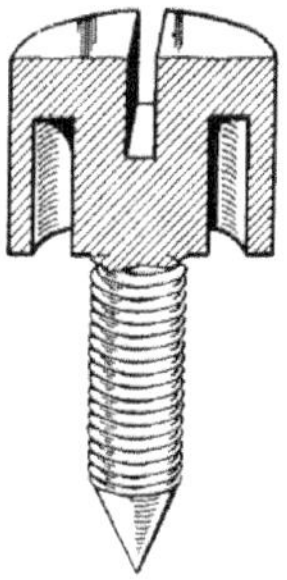

Fig. 101C – Balance Screw Showing Recess Cut

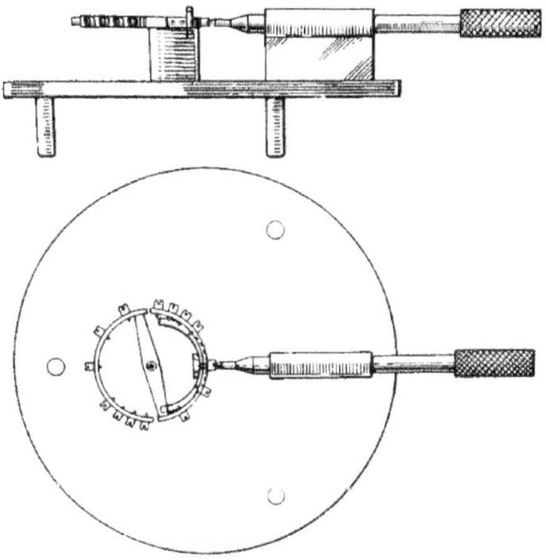

Fig. 102 – Tool to Chamfer the Head of Balance Screws

Another Method

There is another method of testing the poise of the balance, and that is by placing it in the calipers, but not tightly, and with the rounded part of the tweezers stroking the side of the calipers, which has notches cut on its edge which will have the effect of making the balance revolve and enable the heavy point to be detected. I prefer, however, the poising tool, as explained, as I consider it is much more accurate.

The Neutral Point

In the case of an ordinary steel and brass balance the center bar is, of course, made of steel. In heat this expands and the linear expansion has the effect of taking the two quarter screws, at least, farther from the center, and the one or two screws next to them to a lesser degree; there is, however, a point which is neutral, and this point is static.

It is, therefore, not advisable to move these screws during the temperature adjustments. For example, in heat, the free ends of the balance bend inwards, and this makes the balance virtually smaller, with the result that it will gain and so compensate for the loss of elasticity of the balance spring, with its attendant loss of time. If the watch is gaining in heat the screws at the free end need to be moved nearer to the fixed end to make it lose. You will see that if the screws inside the neutral point are moved towards the neutral point it will have little or no effect; in fact, if they were moved towards the center arm, i.e. away from the cut end, it would have the tendency to make the watch lose. It therefore follows that, if the watch has been adjusted for temperatures, the screws at the neutral point should be altered for mean time adjustments, as they remain at the same distance from the center of the balance during changes in temperature.

This point, however, varies with different balances, and it would not be practicable for the man at the bench to determine the neutral point in all the various balances that pass through his hands before he was able to make a mean time alteration.

The usual procedure is to bring the watch to within, say, two or three seconds in the 24 hours before the temperature tests start, and make the final adjustment to obtain this result by means of the quarter screws: and if, after the temperature adjustment has been made, it is found necessary to alter for mean time, the amount the screws will have to be withdrawn or run in, as the case might be, will have little or no effect on the temperature adjustment. Now, since the Guillaume balance is made with Anibal to replace steel, this center bar is not materially affected and, consequently, there is practically no neutral point, or, to put it another way, the neutral point is at the end of the arm.

Middle Temperature Error

The middle temperature error is the error between the temperatures. If a cut brass and steel balance is adjusted for 42° F and 90° F an error will show at 60° F. There is no adjustment for this middle or secondary error. Forms of auxiliary compensation are made, but they are delicate and costly to manufacture. The Guillaume balance has the advantage of reducing the middle temperature error. The reason for this is that the moment of the balance alters in temperatures at the same rate as the balance spring loses its elasticity, therefore the error of the balance spring is practically compensated for at most temperatures.

Zinc Balance

Experiments are still being carried out in connection with the compensation of the balance spring and the latest one is a balance made of zinc.

The balance is uncut and the arm is rolled lengthwise, as it were, and owing to the peculiar properties of such treatment to zinc the balance becomes slightly oval in heat and, as the balance is fitted with screws—as in the ordinary cut balance—adjustment is possible. Such a balance is fitted with Elinvar balance spring and the adjustment necessary is very slight.

Paul Ditisheim overcame the difficulty of the small adjustment necessary when fitting the Elinvar balance spring by the addition of segments of the compensation balance to a non-cut balance.

It must always be borne in mind that Invar and Elinvar are not without a temperature error; in fact, some tests have shown that these metals can show a plus error in heat.

For those interested in this fascinating subject there are many exhaustive works published.

Uncut, Monometal, or Plain Balance

Having spoken of the cut or compensation balance, we must now talk of the plain balance type. This form of balance with Elinvar or beryllium balance spring is no doubt the balance of the future. There are many points in its favor—

1. Excellent results as regards rating.
2. More robust than the cut balance.
3. Non-magnetic, or practically so.
4. Non-rustable.
5. Middle temperature error considerably reduced.
6. Less costly to produce.

Such balances arc made of brass, nickel, Invar, and in some instances one of the beryllium alloys when used with the Nivarox balance spring.

Beryllium Alloy

Of the metals for the balance spring beryllium alloy is the newest comer. This spring is sold under the trade name of Nivarox, and is an alloy of iron, nickel and a small percentage of beryllium and other metals. It is, I believe, manufactured under patent rights. This metal has all the attributes just mentioned, with the additional advantage of being harder than Elinvar; in fact it can be made as hard as hardened and tempered steel. There are other beryllium alloys available, such as beryllium copper; but the modulus of elasticity in heat is not constant. With Nivarox, however, the modulus of elasticity is practically constant in heat, and it is therefore one of the most valuable contributions to horology in recent years.

Beryllium itself is a light, brittle metal obtained by electrolysis from the mineral beryl, which is of the emerald family. The following is taken from *Agenda Horologer*, 1938.

Choosing the Hairspring to Match the Balance

Perhaps it is due to the increasing variety of hairsprings that are offered to watch producers that some confusion now arises in the choice of the hairspring to match the balance, and *vice versa*.

The compensating qualities of the oscillating system, balance and hairspring, should be judged by the two following standards: thermal coefficient and secondary error (also called residual compensation error) or Dent's anomaly, or again "variations of proportionality."

The watch is observed in the horizontal position in three temperatures, generally 32°, 18°, and 2° C. The difference between extreme temperatures is 30° or 15° above and below the 18° of the room temperature.

The thermal coefficient or variation per degree Celsius is equal to—

$$\frac{daily\ rate\ in\ the\ oven\ -\ daily\ rate\ in\ icebox}{differences\ in\ temperature}$$

This coefficient is theoretical; in reality, the watch does not vary regularly by *x* seconds, degree by degree. In other words, the variations are not proportional to the variations in temperature. There exist variations of proportionality or secondary errors.

Secondary Error

Observations and calculations of secondary error vary between observatory practice, official timing bureau, and the manufacturer. We take the method that we recommended when attempting to determine the compensating qualities of an oscillatory system.

The daily rates consist of five periods of three days each at temperatures of 32°, 18°, and 2° C. The first daily interval of each period is omitted in our calculations.

Two secondary errors have been calculated, one starting from 32° to 2° and the other starting from 2° to 32°. The mean value is the aggregate secondary error. This method, which requires fifteen days' observation, is only justified in common practice when it is necessary to judge, as we wish to, the quality of a hairspring or of a balance.

The calculation of the thermal coefficient gives us—

$$\frac{mean\ daily\ rate: at\ 32° - daily\ rate\ at\ 2°}{difference\ in\ temperature}$$

A third standard, the restarting rate, gives us indications as to the stability of an oscillating system. In the case of a hairspring complete with a mono-metallic balance, it will be, in particular, the stability of the hairspring that will be revealed by this figure.

The restarting rate is the difference between the two extreme periods.

The algebraic calculations given in these few examples are explained in the paper, "A Few Indications on the Observation in Watch Rating," by Paul Berner. See *Agenda Horologer*, 1936.

It is known that if we couple a mono-metallic balance (brass) with a steel spring, the watch will lose about 10 seconds in 24 hours per degree of elevation in temperature. This is explained by the rise in temperature lowering the elasticity of the spring. The fault can be corrected by using a steel-brass bi metallic balance which corrects or more or less cancels out the effect on the spring. We say then that the balance is compensating, and it does in fact compensate the effect on the spring of a change in temperature.

A non-cut mono-metallic balance is a ring of metal which, speaking generally from the point of view of regulation, may be considered stable; that is, not subject to any appreciable influence under change of temperature. In that case the steel spring cannot be used. A special alloy is necessary.

Two groups are generally known today: the iron-nickel alloys of Dr. Charles Ed. Guillaume (Elinvar, Par-Elinvar) and the alloys iron-nickel-beryllium of

Mr. R. Straumann (Nivarox).

Much is demanded of a hairspring. The ideal balance spring must have no less than seven qualities—and no flaw.

1. Low thermal coefficient.
2. Low secondary error.
3. Low absorbance of the balance oscillation.
4. Stable physical properties.
5. Practically insensitive to magnetism.
6. Non-rustable.
7. High elasticity for ease in manipulation.

Examining the more important types of progress in horology for the last fifty years, we believe it is with the hairspring that the biggest strides have been made.

Cause of Temperature Error

The major cause of the error in temperatures of the steel balance spring is due to its loss of elasticity in heat with the attendant losing in rate of the watch.

In 1773, Ferdinand Berthoud, the eminent French horologist, calculated that a watch fitted with a steel spring passing from 32° F to 92° F lost in twenty-four hours: 62 seconds due to expansion of the balance, 312 seconds due to the loss of elasticity, and 19 seconds due to elongation of the spring.

It has since been pointed out by T. D. Wright that the error due to elongation is not correct. No doubt an error of 6 minutes 33 seconds did exist, but the 19 seconds must be placed, between the expansion of the balance and the loss of elasticity. T. D. Wright pointed out that the thickness and the width also increase in the same proportion as the length, and if these dimensions only were considered, not taking into account the loss due to loss of elasticity, the watch would gain in heat. It will be appreciated that if an Elinvar or Nivarox balance spring is fitted to a balance made of Invar we should have little or no temperature error, but there are other considerations.

Invar has a slight positive error for temperature, i.e. it expands in heat, therefore the balance will get larger and the watch will lose. Certain alloys of Elinvar and beryllium have a positive error in heat and the metal of the balance can so be alloyed that one balances the other, and then we may get a balance and spring with no temperature error. There is every indication that research in this direction is nearing the point where the almost perfect compensation will be obtained with the monometal balance. Such progress makes a poor case for the cut balance and steel spring. I am, however, the first to admit that for appearance a good quality of cut balance and a well-polished and blued steel balance spring is to be preferred; it is something to admire; but for results it must be admitted that the subject of the foregoing leaves nothing to be desired.

Fitting the Balance Spring

I propose to deal with the fitting and adjusting of the balance spring as experienced by the man at the bench. Many books have been written and lectures delivered on this subject, principally the theoretical side. We will take, for instance, the Breguet or overcoil balance spring, so called after the inventor, Abraham Louis Breguet, born 1747 and died in 1823.

To Pin the Collet

The spring is fitted to the collet first, before the overcoil is made, and to do this easily, proceed as follows. Break away from the center of the spring sufficient to allow the balance spring collet freedom to the extent of the distance between two coils. A tool which is very useful for this purpose is an ordinary sewing needle with half the eye stoned away; this leaves a two-pronged fork. If the balance spring is held with a pair of fairly strong tweezers just above the point you wish to sever, and the small fork placed over the spring and given one or two backward and forward twists, you will find that the spring will break easily. The needle is best handled if held in some small holder such as a length of clock bouchon wire.

Now, with the aid of the small tool just mentioned, bend a piece of spring inwards, practically at right-angles. Make this piece straight and the length of this straight piece should be a little longer than the length of the hole in the collet. Before pinning in it is advisable to prepare the pin first. The spring is, no doubt, longer than is necessary, so a short piece can be broken from the outer coil, which we proceed to flatten.

File a long, tapering, brass pin to fit the hole in the collet. Burnish the pin and, with an Arkansas slip, stone away on one side to the extent of about one-third. Then place the piece of balance spring in the collet and fit the flattened pin in, flat side towards the spring. Make sure the pin fits tightly and, with a sharp knife, just mark the pin at the point the superfluous piece is to be cut off, also the other end, which will give us the length for the pin.

Carefully withdraw the pin and, by holding it flat side downwards on the boxwood filing block, cut away the portion not required, with a knife.

If the edge of the knife is placed in the nick made and a little downward pressure is applied, the pin will sever cleanly. With the Arkansas slip, make the end flat and just trim the burrs from the sides.

Now, with the knife, partly cut through the other mark, but make sure not to sever. The nick so made will enable the pin to be placed in position quite easily and then broken off, leaving the short piece in position.

Method of Holding Collet

The most convenient method of holding the collet is to place it on the tool as shown in Fig. 102A. The actual portion where the collet is held is left rough from the file—draw filed—to prevent it turning. The tool should be hardened and tempered.

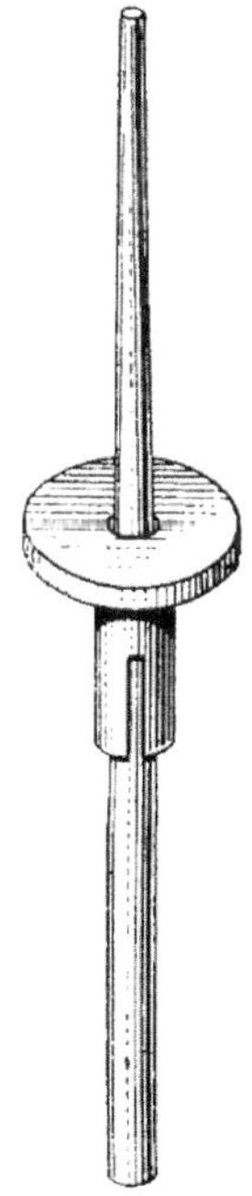

Fig. 102A – Tool for Holding Balance Spring Collet

A small round table is made so that it can be worked up and down on the rod and an old enamel watch seconds dial is shellacked to the top to make the spring more visible. This table is useful when truing the spring round the collet. We are now ready to pin.

Place the collet on the rod and bring the table up to it, then place the spring in the hole and push the pin partly home and break off. By not securing tightly, at first, it will enable us to move the spring to get it flat. The pin will turn in the hole and, when you are satisfied that the spring is perfectly flat, push the pin home tightly either with a fine joint pusher or a pair of stout tweezers.

Make sure the spring is held absolutely firmly in the hole, as any movement here will be disastrous to good time-keeping. The extent the spring should enter the collet hole is shown in Fig. 103, and if this advice is carried out, it will be found that the truing of the center will not be such a trying business as if the spring came gradually away from the collet.

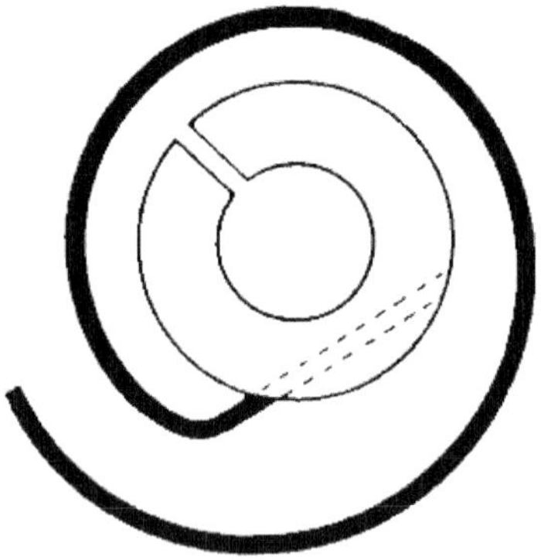

Fig. 103 – Balance Spring Pinning to Collet

Theoretical Terminal

Some of the watches which have passed through Kew and have obtained exceptionally high marks are so arranged that the inner pinning of the balance spring is made to conform to the theoretically inner terminal curve.

Such forms of pinning are admirable, but I do not think that they will concern the average man at the bench. If he is able to fit a balance spring that runs absolutely flat and true in the center I do not think he need bother about the inner terminal curves unless he is interested in this ultra-form of time-keeping. The commercial world does not, fortunately, call for this form of watchmaking. For those interested, however, the same Lossier curve (Fig. 107) can be used.

Break Down to Size

As I have said, balance springs are usually supplied larger than required and, before we finally true up in the center, it will be convenient to make the spring as small as possible. It will not, then, be inclined to move about when spun on an arbor.

I should mention here that it is always advisable to remove two screws from the balance before sending to the tool shop for the new balance spring or even selecting one from your own stock. You then have some scope. If there are any quarter screws, it is also advisable to see that they are screwed in to a reasonable position. If the balance is loaded with timing collets, remove them. That is, of course, if the balance has removable screws.

Now place the spring on the balance and count. The tool shown in Fig. 104 is very useful, is accurate, and saves considerable time. It is generally fitted with three balances vibrating 16,200, 18,000, and 21,600. If this tool is used, the spring can be broken down very nearly to size

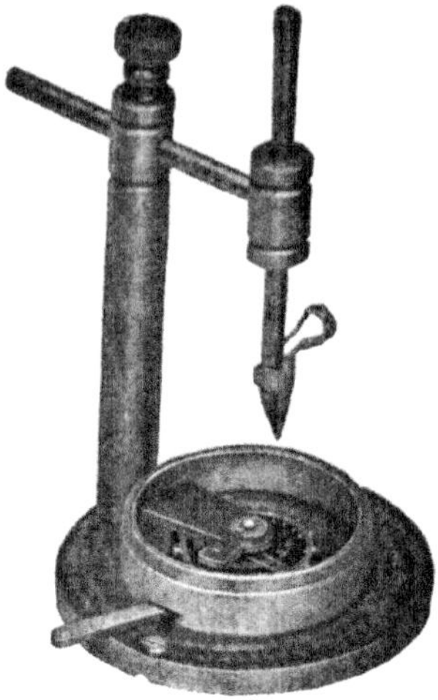

Fig. 104 – Balance Counting Tool

Remember, in the case of a watch with an index, to hold the spring in the tool at the point where the index pins operate, or, in other words, to make an allowance for the length of the spring between the pins and the stud.

If a balance counting tool is not available, then hold the balance spring with a pair of tweezers in such a manner that the bottom balance pivot just touches the glass of a watch fitted with a seconds hand. Next, give the hand holding the tweezers a slight twist, which will cause the balance to vibrate. The arc of the vibration should be slight, say an eighth of a turn. Then count the vibrations by noting the arm of the balance as it swings towards you. While this is proceeding, keep an eye on the seconds hand of the watch. You will find that it is possible to observe both at the same time. Say it is an 1,800 train with which you are dealing, then there are 300 vibrations to the minute, and as you are counting the alternate vibrations, that is 150 swings of the arc towards you.

In the initial stage, count for half a minute only, that is 75 alternate vibrations. As you get nearer to the correct size, count 150 alternate vibrations to the minute.

To True the Spring

Having out the spring down to the correct size we can now proceed to make quite true and flat.

Place the spring on an arbor (the brass ferrule and arbor answer well) and spin in the calipers, manipulating until there is no jerky movement whatsoever; just an even flow, as it were. Practice alone can teach how to do this. It should be aimed at that as few bends as possible be made and these of the very slightest and as gradual as possible; the final touch can be given when the spring is on the balance and the balance spun in the calipers.

A balance spring well fitted has the effect, when vibrating in the watch, of the fourth or fifth coil from the center remaining absolutely stationary, whilst the other coils are expanding and contracting evenly.

To Make the Overcoil

Having made the spring quite true and flat, we can now pull up the overcoil. There are many methods adopted to do this; special tools and tweezers exist by the dozen and each man has his own particular fad, but it can be accepted that the less the spring is bent or pulled about, the better.

Some advocate a sharp bracket bend and special tweezers are made that will carry out this work in two operations. I do not advocate this procedure; if the spring is quite soft and you have the means of hardening and tempering after the overcoil has been made, all well and good; or if the spring is made of some soft metal, such as Invar or Elinvar, this practice could be adopted. But, in the average workshop, such facilities are not available. The Americans use this form of overcoil considerably, and in a factory where there are many springs of exactly the same size to be fitted, elaborate measures can be indulged in. But, in the case of a workshop, where all and sundry pass, other means must be adopted.

Further, the results at the trials show that the watches placed high are not fitted with balance springs having sharp bracket overcoils, but with gradual curves.

Lay the spring flat on a piece of white paper on the bench. To form the overcoil it is usual to use about 3/4 of a complete coil. Use fairly stout tweezers as it is necessary to grip the spring firmly, and narrow-pointed tweezers would cause the spring to slip and even to snap out, which would mark the spring. This applies more to steel springs than to, say, Elinvar. Keep the tweezers upright with the points just touching the paper. With one pair of tweezers grip the spring at a point a little beyond the 3/4 point, and with the other pair of tweezers hold the extreme end of the spring. Hold the first pair of tweezers quite still and firmly and the other pair lift straight up, considerably higher than the height of the overcoil is to be; this is to ensure that the "bracket" will be sufficiently high.

The actual height of the overcoil is controlled by the distance between the balance and the balance cock, and when we have decided upon the height we can start to bend the upstanding piece of spring down. The bracket or elbow occupies about 45°. So at the 3/4 (or 270°) point grip the spring with a stout pair of tweezers and with the other tweezers grip the spring at the 45°

from the 3/4 point, hold the left-hand tweezers very firmly and bend the spring down a little with the right-hand tweezers (top illustration. Fig, 105). Then move the left-hand tweezers to approximately 35° from the 3/4 point (on the original commencement of the overcoil) and the right-hand tweezers about 25° further along (as bottom illustration, Fig. 105) and give another bend down. We shall now have an elbow bent up, occupying approximately 45°. The piece of spring still to be manipulated will need to be made parallel, and this is effected by bending the spring sideways. Up to now we have bent the width of the spring edgewise as it were.

To do this effectively the bends are small and frequent; for instance, hold one pair of tweezers firmly and the other pair lightly and so run the last-mentioned tweezers along the spring, swaying them towards you to bring the spring up, and away from you to bend down, and at the same time nipping the spring frequently as each bend is made. By so doing we shall make no violent bends. Sharp bends are to be avoided at all costs; they are dangerous. Slight fractures may also occur; this more particularly applies to steel.

Between the last bending down point and the end of the spring, the major portion of the flattening of the overcoil or making the overcoil parallel takes place. It should be done gradually (see Fig. 106).

Theoretical Curve

Much depends on the shape of the curve of the over or upper coil itself, and this, in conjunction with the pinning in at the collet, is responsible for the accurate timing in positions.

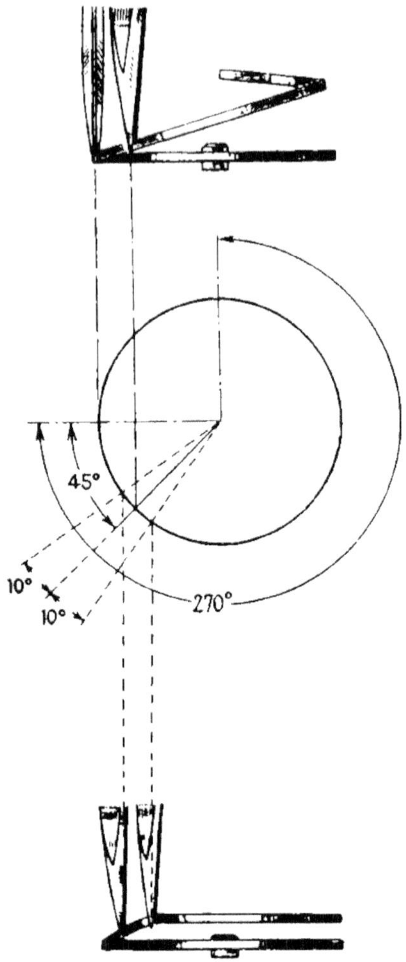

Fig. 105 – Making the Elbow or Bracket of the Overcoil

Top – The overcoil having been pulled up the right-hand tweezers are moved as indicated, to commence the bend down. Left-hand tweezers at 270° point and right-hand tweezers at 45° from that point.

Bottom – Left-hand tweezers moved to approximately 35° point and the right-hand tweezers to approximately 25° from that point.

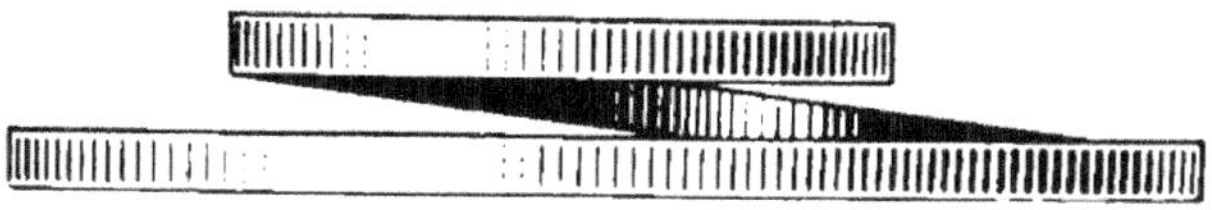

Fig. 106 – Balance Spring Curve to Overcoil

The actual shape or curve is to a certain extent governed by existing conditions; for instance, the index pin, the measurement from the center of the balance hole to the center of the space between the pins is a definite condition and the curve of the spring must be made to comply with it.

Certain stipulations are made in theory but, unfortunately, they cannot always be carried out absolutely accurately in practice; we can get very near, which is most helpful in obtaining our object. The object, of course, to be aimed at is that the long and the short arcs of the vibration of the balance should be of the same duration, in other words they should be isochronous.

If we wish to fit a theoretically correct overcoil, draw the overcoil first on paper. Assuming that the distance from the center of the balance jewel hole to the center of the apace between the index pins is 20.100 mm, then the shape of the curve will be as shown in Fig. 107. This curve is known as the Lossier, named after the mathematician who invented it, to the formula of M. Phillips; the radius of the spring is determined as follows—

Lossier lays down the following stipulation to obtain the correct curve: an arc of a circle with a radius of .67 of the radius of the entire spring, and of the arc so formed 83 degrees are used, and this to extend from the index pins or, in other words, the acting part of the spring. From the point so determined to the exterior coil of the balance spring is bisected and a curve is drawn from this point to connect the outer coil with the segment of 83°.

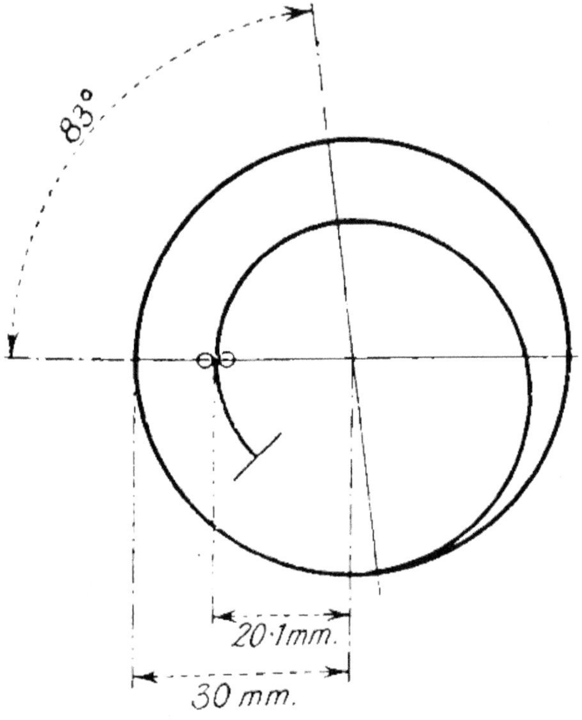

Fig. 107 – Lossier's Overcoil Made to Phillips Formula

The illustration depicting a balance spring for a watch with the index pins 20.100 mm. from the center is, of course, an enlargement and is drawn for the purpose of demonstration.

As our measurement is 20.100 mm, we arrive at the radius of the balance spring thus:

$$\frac{100}{67} \times 20.10 = 30 = \textit{the radius of the spring}$$

It will be seen that, for all practical purposes, the radius of the first arc described is two-thirds of the radius of the outer coil of the balance spring. Some of the Continental books on springing have many illustrations of theoretical curves, giving many sizes, and it is convenient, if you have such a book, to use it, but should you not be so provided, it is quite a simple matter to draw a sheet of curves, making them the sizes you are likely to require.

We now proceed to manipulate the spring to this curve; all bends must be carried out gradually. Before actually forming the curve, the spring is manipulated to conform to the curve of the outer coil of the balance spring for 22°, and from this point we begin to bend the spring inwards to the shape as just described, as shown in Fig. 107A.

The tweezers to be used are shown in Fig. 108, and about four pairs with different sized curves will be found sufficient for most overcoils. During the bending of the curve, frequently hold the spring over the drawing to ensure that the curve is shaping well.

The Swiss Method

In one of the Swiss schools I visited, a large drawing of the spring is placed on a table and the actual balance spring placed on a glass slide, the image being projected on to the drawing and enlarged to the size of the drawing, so that progress of the curve can be observed to a very close degree of accuracy.

The same device was used in connection with illustrating the wheel and pinion depths, etc.; a very useful instrument for a school or large factory.

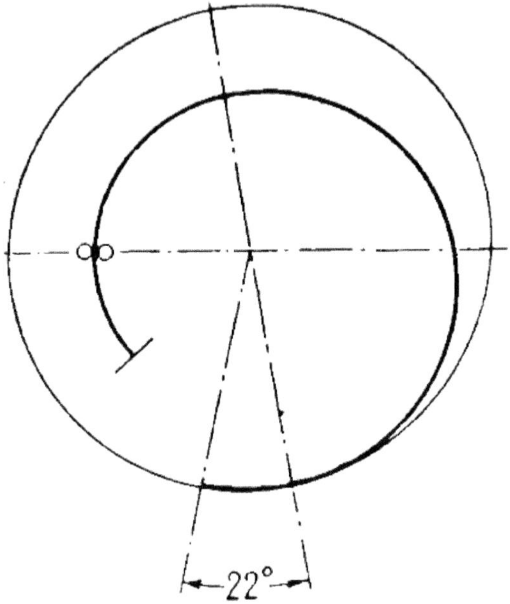

Fig. 107A – Showing 22°, the Amount the Overcoil Follows the Outer Convolution Before the Curve Bends Inwards

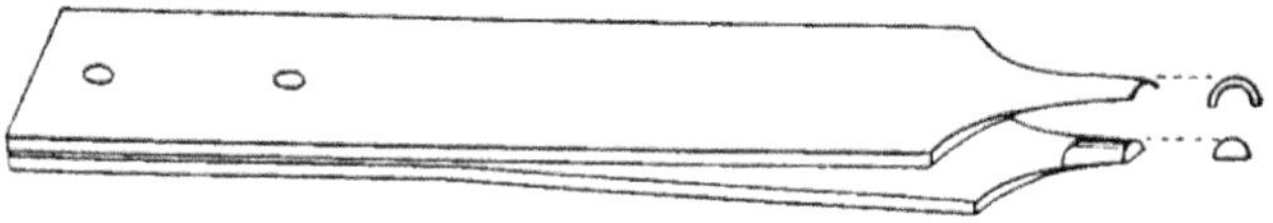

Fig. 108 – Balance Spring Tweezers

Another Curve

The curve illustrated in Fig. 109 is useful when converting a flat sprung watch into a Breguet spring. By using such a curve it is unnecessary to alter the position of the index pins, or the balance spring stud. If the index pins were to operate on the horizontal line (Fig. 109), then the curve would comply with Phillips' conditions, and is known as the Phillips curve.

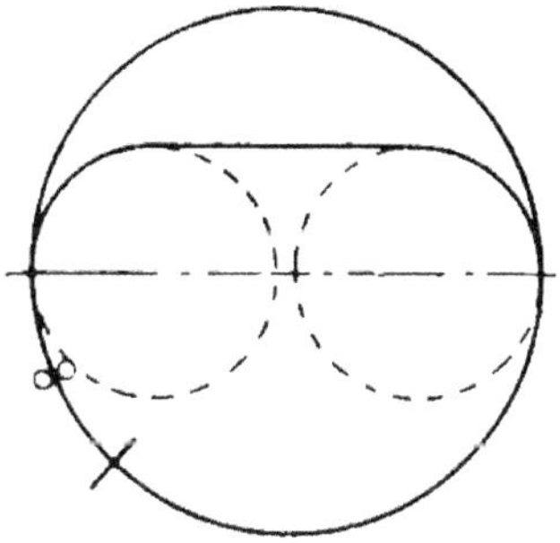

Fig. 109 – Curve Used When Converting a Flat Spring Watch to a Breguet

Unfortunately, moving the index to + would cause the balance spring to buckle, because the overcoil of the spring is not concentric with the index center at that point. For all practical purposes, I think the position of the index pins as shown in Fig. 109 has no detrimental effect on the rating.

Memorize the Curve

Now the fitting of a theoretically correct curve calls for a good deal of time, and unless the watch is a pocket or larger model from which a very close rate of time-keeping is expected, it may not be worth our while to take this trouble of drawing the curve, etc., but it is always worthwhile having in your mind's eye the shape of a theoretically correct curve and making your spring as near as possible.

It must be remembered that these curves are made to correct errors amounting to a few seconds in the various positions, and, when dealing with wrist-watches especially, if the error is within, say, 2 minutes per week, the piece can be considered to be going well. In Switzerland, however, the curve of the overcoil of even some of the smallest wrist-watches is made accurately; when we consider that the curve made is perhaps used on many thousands of watches of the same size it is well worth the time taken in the planning. It must, however, be said that, based on experience gained from rating considerable numbers of wrist-watches, the best results are obtained from those fitted with the Breguet balance spring.

The wrist-watch cannot, in the fullest meaning of the word, be regarded as a "rated" watch. Such a watch—considered not necessarily as a watch, but rather from the manner in which it is worn—calls for the same scrupulous care as, say, a deck watch. But—memorize the theoretical curve of the overcoil, and make the spring as near it as possible.

Two exactly similar watches, with exactly similar curves to the overcoil, would not rate the same. Slight alterations would be necessary to suit the individual requirements of each watch.

To Pin to the Stud

Having made the overcoil it now remains to pin in to the stud and to do this well make a pin first in a similar manner to the one used for the collet. The pin in this instance is not cut short and both ends should be stoned flat. To pin up, place the stud on the balance cock, the balance (with the spring in position) in the movement, with the balance cock screwed down, now lead the balance round; the end to be pinned to the stud should enter the hole in the stud without any assistance other than perhaps a very slight lift due to the weight of the spring itself bearing down.

The extreme end of the spring must be manipulated until the above conditions are possible. We shall then be sure in the first place that the spring is central, and, secondly, that there is no side pressure of the spring on the balance pivots.

In the instances where there is an index, the spring must maintain the same shape, no matter in what position the index is placed; in other words, that portion of the spring upon which the index pins operate should be in circle with the balance jewel hole, since the index is usually concentric with the jewel hole. If the conditions mentioned have been adhered to this will be so.

Make sure the pin is pressed well home; I cannot emphasize too strongly the absolute necessity for both the pins—the collet and the stud pins—to fit well, and to hold the spring firmly, there must be no movement of the spring whatsoever at these two points. The same observation applies to the index pins themselves.

The flat-sided pins prevent undue distortion, and in some watches you will find that to achieve this object more or less elaborate precautions are taken.

In some you will find a form of clamp or grip is utilized, not only at the stud but also at the collet.

When pinning up the spring to the stud it should be observed that the pinning of the spring at the collet should be in the position as illustrated (Fig. 110).

The spring comes away from the collet at right-angles to a line drawn parallel to the pendant up position. It was discovered by Jules Grossman that if this condition is observed the best results are obtained in the positions when dealing with ordinary inner terminal, that is not employing the terminal inner curve; that is, the pendant up, right, and left. It will be found, however, that the pendant down position will show considerable variation, up to 30 seconds in 24 hours—provided the pendant up position is nil—but as the watch is not worn in this (the pendant down) position, we need not worry about it. Advantage can, however, be taken of this peculiarity to overcome positional errors.

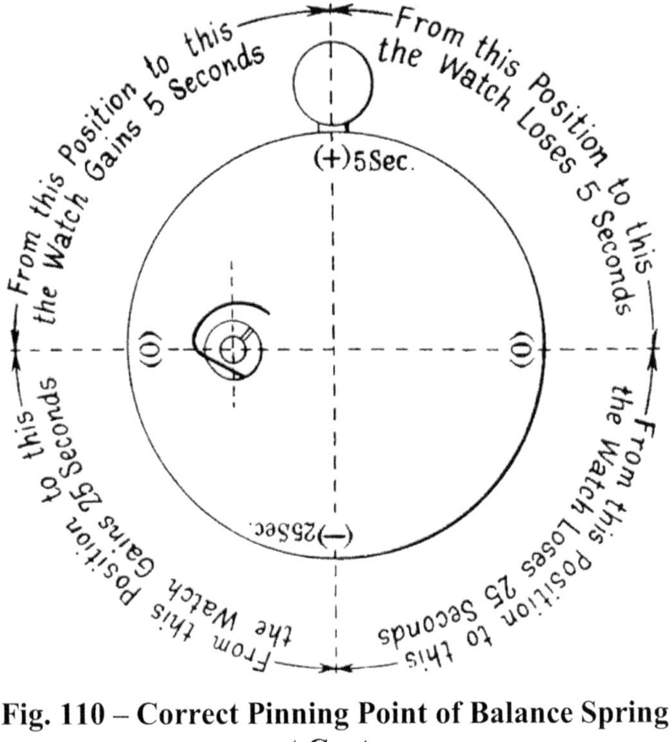

Fig. 110 – Correct Pinning Point of Balance Spring at Center

For pocket watches the correct pinning point is as illustrated (Fig. 110) and for wrist-watches the same conditions prevail when the watch is pendant down. Wrist-watches are usually worn on the left wrist, and when the arm is loose at the side the button (or pendant) is in the downwards position.

A watch correctly pinned is + pendant up ± pendant right ± pendant left and – pendant down. If we find that the watch we are adjusting has an excessive + error pendant up some of this error can be absorbed in the other two vertical positions. As the point of attachment is moved upwards away from the original "correct" pinning point so we move the + point round. In fact, if the pinning point is moved half way round, so that the spring develops downwards, we shall then have reversed the error, i.e. + pendant up to – pendant up, so there is a point between these two which can be utilized to correct our error.

By turning the sketch (Fig. 110) round, it will be seen clearly what effect the change in position of the pinning point has.

To Find the Correct Pinning Point

To find the correct pinning point for a particular watch, first observe where the center of the spring develops from; draw an imaginary line parallel with the pendant, cutting through the center of the balance and then a line at right angles to that, again cutting the center of the balance, then turn the watch round so that the center of the spring develops up on the last mentioned line, and call that position pendant up (or pendant down if a wrist-watch; we shall however refer only to pendant up, for convenience). It is more convenient to use the dial as an indication of the pendant; say the watch has: been turned to comply with the foregoing and we find that 9 o/c is pendant up, then 6 o/c will be pendant right, and 12 o/c pendant left. During the tests in the vertical positions thus, we find that pendant up is + in excess of what is required, then move the watch round so that the spring develops up above the line, which makes the pendant up then read as 8 o/c, and continue that until the result + pendant up ± pendant right and ± pendant left is obtained or as near as is possible. Then observe when the watch is turned to its true pendant up position where the pinning point is, and calculate how much must be cut away from the center to satisfy this condition.

When fitting the spring in the first place, it is not practicable to pin in at the correct point and also to form the overcoil correctly. It is far simpler to adopt the method just discussed. When fitting a steel spring to a cut balance, as much as 3/4 of a turn can be cut away from the center without upsetting the temperature adjustment.

In the case of the Elinvar and beryllium balance springs this query does not arise, but it will be necessary to retime to mean time in any case, as cutting away the spring will make the watch gain, and the balance must be made heavier.

The foregoing refers to fine timing; low-grade watches are not expected to have three vertical position adjustments, and watches that are expected to respond to these adjustments have balances fitted with screws and the screws are utilized to bring the watch to mean time. It is not advisable to alter the length of the balance spring, as by so doing we shall upset the curve of the overcoil. Generally speaking, two positions only are required of a wrist-watch, dial up and pendant down. The correct pinning point can account for 30 seconds, and as regards one vertical position this equally applies to the flat balance spring.

Other Positional Adjustments

We have discussed the theoretically correct curve and also the correct pinning point. We now come to what may be called the less permanent forms of adjustment, less permanent because the adjustment is lost, or partly so, when the balance is removed from the watch, or due to wear, or not as efficient as the oil becomes thick. The two systems just discussed are permanent provided that ordinary care is exercised during overhauling.

Index Pins

Considerable adjustment is possible by manipulation of the index pins. Incidentally, this form of adjustment is resorted to, in a mild form, by some of the best Swiss springers and adjusters.

If a watch is, say, losing pendant up, and shows a small gaining rate dial up, to correct this, open the index pins a little and make the balance spring bear against one pin. When dial up, the arc of vibration of the balance is at its greatest (long arcs) and the balance spring opens to its greatest extent; in these circumstances the balance spring will leave the curb pin and we shall say for the moment loses dial up. When the watch is in the vertical position the arc of vibration is not so great (short arcs) and the spring is not so inclined to leave the pin and the watch will therefore gain.

By comparison we have made the vertical position + (Fig. 111), the watch being brought to mean time by altering the weight of the balance. It is possible to adjust the balance spring and index pins to make a difference of 90 seconds and over in 24 hours. This would be in the nature of an extreme case, the pins would have to be fairly wide, and the spring made to bear or hug one pin to such an extent that when in the short arcs it would not leave the pin at all or, maybe, only during a very small period of the vibration. It will be seen that this form of adjustment offers considerable scope, but it has this disadvantage: when the balance and spring are detached from the cock the adjustment is lost; further, when carried to excess, the adjustment is not so effective when the oil thickens and the vibration of the balance is decreased. This form of adjustment is only suitable for one vertical position, and is suitable for flat and overcoil springs. It has the decided advantage that it is not necessary to remove the balance from the movement.

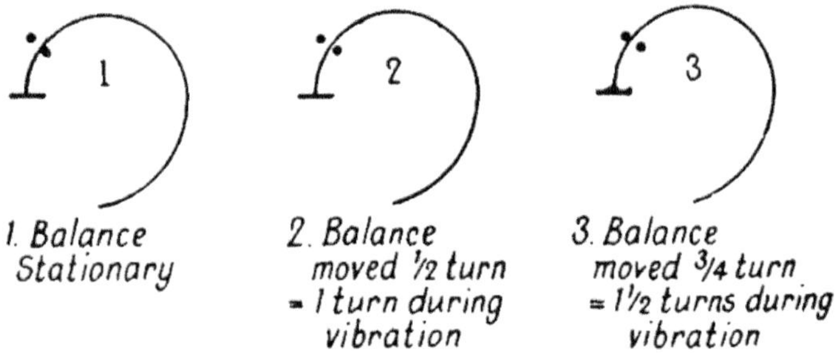

Fig. 111 – Indicating Position of Balance Spring with Relation to Curb or Index Pins
(1) The spring is hard on the pin. (2) Just about to leave the pin. (3) Just about to touch the other pin. An adjustment such as this can account for 45 seconds fast in the short arcs.

Positional Adjustment by Poise of the Balance

Another method is to throw the balance out of poise. Again, if the watch is slow pendant up the balance is made heavier at the lowest point when the balance is at rest in the vertical position. Adjustment can be made in this manner to the extent of 3 to 4 minutes in 24 hours. There are, however, certain conditions to comply with; if the vibration of the balance is much over one turn the reverse part of the balance must be made the heavier, and this is sometimes referred to as "timing in reverse." It is natural to be slow in the vertical position, but occasionally we find a watch fast, and this may be due to the conditions now being discussed being in existence perhaps accidentally, although some adjustments have not been made. In these circumstances, to correct, reverse the adjustments made to make the watch fast in the vertical position.

In practice it is sometimes found that to correct a small error the foregoing does not apply. I have dealt with watches vibrating 1-1/2 to 1-3/4 turns and with the lowest point heavy, making them gain in the vertical position. Should the error be great however, the top would have to be the heavy part. The disadvantage of this adjustment is that the result varies with the condition of the oil, more especially with the timing in reverse, since as the vibration of the balance slackens you could even have the watch losing as much as you made it gain. This adjustment is only applicable to one vertical position.

Positional Adjustment by Altering Shape of Balance Pivots

This form of adjustment is sometimes resorted to by the best Swiss springers and is in the nature of a fake. The results are not long-lived, as we shall see.

To make the watch gain in the vertical position we make it lose when horizontal, by making the ends of the balance pivots more flat (Fig. 112). The friction is increased when dial up with its attendant losing, when compared with the vertical position. To be more correct, the amount of frictional resistance is unaltered, but it acts at a larger radius, therefore its moment is greater. This adjustment is suitable for the three vertical position adjustment but has the disadvantage that as the pivots wear, the adjustment is lost or partly so. Another system of a similar nature, which is permanent, is to change the jewel holes. To make the watch gain when vertical, reduce the diameter of the staff pivots and fit smaller jewel holes.

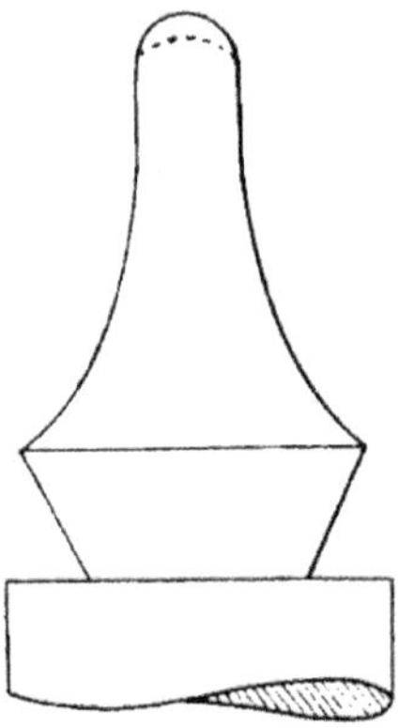

Fig. 112
Dotted line indicates flattened balance pivot to make the horizontal position slow and consequently the vertical position fast by comparison.

The friction of the balance pivots is reduced when in the vertical position and we have the comparison of fast pendant up; it is also true that the friction is reduced when in the horizontal position, but not to the same extent. This adjustment is suitable for the three vertical position adjustment.

Positional Adjustment by Altering Shape of Curve

Another and permanent positional adjustment is to alter the shape of the overcoil. To make the watch gain pendant up the overcoil is re-shaped as indicated by dotted fine in Fig. 113. The extent of the re-shaping depends upon the error to be corrected. To achieve the same result the whole overcoil could be made smaller, or, as the Americans put it, the overcoil is moved nearer to the balance staff. What we really do is to stiffen the overcoil. There are certain objections to this form of adjustment, however—

1. We alter the theoretically correct curve and by so doing may create greater errors in the other vertical positions if the watch is to be adjusted in the three vertical positions.
2. The correct pinning point will be altered, necessitating re-pinning at the center.

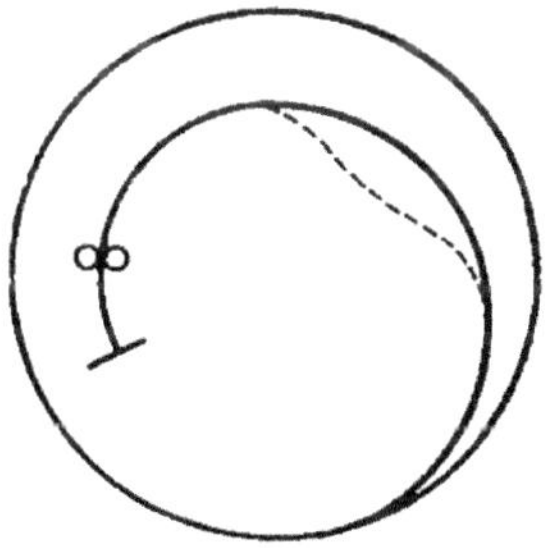

Fig. 113 – Balance Spring—Correction to Overcoil

The Ideal Index Pins

The ideal condition of the index pins is to be close. There should be no perceptible play, but the spring must be free so that when the index is moved there is no fear of the pins causing the spring to buckle. A good test is to lift the spring just a little at the index pins and it should return quite freely, then lower the spring and again it should return. We are sure then that should the watch be jerked there is no fear of the spring sticking between the pins.

The pins should be parallel, the rate will then not vary in the dial up and dial down positions. As we have seen, however, the ideal is not always practicable.

Final Words About Positional Adjustment

Before attempting to adjust a watch in positions see that the movement is in as near a perfect condition as possible.

The mainspring must be sufficiently strong to ensure that the balance vibrates at least 1-1/2 turns. It is not suggested that a stronger mainspring only should be fitted to achieve that end, but should the train be perfectly free, good and correct depths, jewel holes perfect, escapement correct, etc., and still not a good action, then change the mainspring for a stronger one.

We have discussed seven methods of positional adjustment. There are others; but these seven are the most practicable. It remains for you to select the method (or a combination of methods) that best suits your purpose.

Temperature Adjustments of the Cut or Compensating Balance

These observations do not apply to the monometal balances. Should watches so provided show a temperature error there is no adjustment. Paul Ditisheim, as we have seen, overcame this difficulty, but this appears to be the chief system. If the watch loses in heat, the weight is increased at the free ends of the balance; conversely, if the watch gains, in heat, weight is taken from the free end. Watches are usually tested and adjusted for temperatures of 32° F in an ice-box or refrigerator and 90° F in an oven. Watches and clocks, used in aviation are adjusted for temperatures of

–4° F +85° F, and special attention is given to the oil used, more generous tolerances, as regards fitting, etc.

To revert to our adjustment of the cut balance. The temperature screws from the quarter screws—or if there are no quarter screws, the position where they should be—are the effective ones, and the screws which make the most difference are the ones at the extreme end, the free end. So if the error to be corrected is slight (a very accurate adjustment is possible with the temperature adjustment) then the screws near the quarter screws are manipulated. If the watch registers a considerable losing error in heat it may be necessary to move all possible weight to the free end, and even then the weight may not be sufficient. In these circumstances the free end screws (that is the one at each end) are changed for screws of platinum. It may even be necessary to change two screws at each end for platinum.

When platinum screws are substituted for either brass or gold screws it will be necessary to lighten the balance to bring to time, and then we operate on that part of the balance nearest the arm. A very useful little tool to maintain the original weight of the balance is a balance or scale here illustrated (Fig. 114).

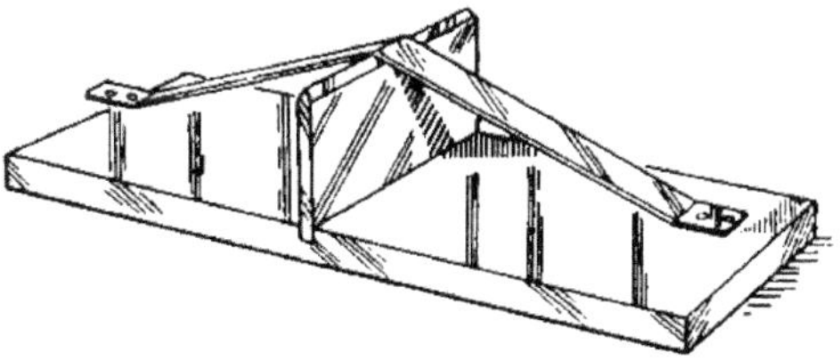

Fig. 114 – Balances for Weighing Balance Screws

A piece of brass 1/2 in. × 1 in. and 2mm. thick forms the base. A piece of steel 1/2 in. wide and about 1/2 in. high and 0.5 mm. thick is slotted into the base.

The top edge of the steel piece is filed to a V shape to form a knife edge. We know procure a piece of watch mainspring about 0.25 mm. thick, 3 in. long and 3 mm. wide. Soften the ends and the center of this piece of spring, make a nick in the center with a slotting file and bend as indicated. Drill two holes at each end and bend the ends up so that they are parallel with the base. Carefully make it balance by filing as required. To use the scale, place one of the pair of screws that are to be changed on one end of the scale, then select another screw from the balance to make the scale balance. Remove the screw to be changed from the scale and put in its place the new screw; on the other end of the scale add timing washers or it may be necessary to add another screw from the balance, so that an equal balance of the scale is obtained. Remove the new screw and replace the original free end screw. We now reduce the head of the screw on the other end of the scale until the scales are made to balance; the added weights are not removed during this balancing. We have lightened the screw by an amount equal to the added weight. If it was necessary to add a screw to make the new screw balance, then we remove a screw from the balance. In either case the same weight is removed from both limbs of the balance, not only to keep it in poise but also that the required weight shall be removed and so keep the watch to mean time. To do this accurately, use the reduced screw on one side of the scale and take the screw that pairs with it, and reduce this screw to balance with the other. If an entire screw was used then select its pair. See that it balances with the other and leave both screws off the balance.

When timing in positions in the oven, you may find that its rate is not as good as when tested in the same positions out of the oven, and this may be due to the fact that the change in temperature throws the balance out of poise. There is no remedy for this; the balance must be changed. Before taking this drastic step it is advisable to test the watch again, first in normal temperature and then again, always in the same position, in the oven. Such an error may be due to a flaw in the metals of the balance, a fracture, or faulty fusing of the brass to the steel, or the new screws fitted not the same weight.

A Useful Table

A useful table in "*Formulaire Technique*" is well worth quoting; it tabulates the number of times the error of a watch must be multiplied in order to find the error for 24 hours.

H. Min.	Multipl.	H. Min.	Multipl.	H. Min.	Multipl.	H. Min.	Multipl.	H. Min.	Multipl.
0 15	96·—								
0 30	48·—	10 —	2·4	20 —	1·2	30 —	0·8	40 —	0·6
0 45	32·—	10 30	2·286	20 30	1·171	30 30	0·787	40 30	0·59
1 —	24·—	11 —	2·18	21 —	1·142	31 —	0·774	41 —	0·585
1 30	16·—	11 30	2·087	21 30	1·112	31 30	0·762	41 30	0·578
2 —	12·—	12 —	2·—	22 —	1·09	32 —	0·75	42 —	0·57
2 30	9·6	12 30	1·92	22 30	1·066	32 30	0·738	42 30	0·556
3 —	8·—	13 —	1·846	23 —	1·043	33 —	0·727	43 —	0·555
3 30	6·857	13 30	1·778	23 30	1·021	33 30	0·716	43 30	0·552
4 —	6·—	14 —	1·72	24 —	1·—	34 —	0·706	44 —	0·545
4 30	5·33	14 30	1·655	24 30	0·98	34 30	0·696	44 30	0·539
5 —	4·8	15 —	1·6	25 —	0·96	35 —	0·686	45 —	0·533
5 30	4·364	15 30	1·548	25 30	0·941	35 30	0·676	45 30	0·527
6 —	4·—	16 —	1·5	26 —	0·923	36 —	0·666	46 —	0·522
6 30	3·692	16 30	1·454	26 30	0·906	36 30	0·657	46 30	0·516
7 —	3·43	17 —	1·412	27 —	0·889	37 —	0·649	47 —	0·510
7 30	3·2	17 30	1·371	27 30	0·873	37 30	0·64	47 30	0·505
8 —	3·—	18 —	1·33	28 —	0·857	38 —	0·632	48 —	0·5
8 30	2·823	18 30	1·297	28 30	0·842	38 30	0·623	48 30	0·495
9 —	2·67	19 —	1·263	29 —	0·828	39 —	0·615	49 —	0·489
9 30	2·526	19 30	1·231	29 30	0·814	39 30	0·607	49 30	0·485

For instance, if after running a watch for 7-1/2 hours there is an error of 3 minutes, then 3 multiplied by 3.2 equals 9 minutes 36 seconds in 24 hours.

The Ligne System

For some reason, and it is difficult to find why, an obsolete French method of measurement has been adopted to determine the size or diameter of the watch movement.

Chas. Frodsham, in his book, published in 1862, entitled *The Elements of Watch and Clock Making*, states that no attempt had been made to establish a system of measurement which has some relation to a standard measure, both as regards the size of the movement itself and matters such as the pitch of the threads of screws, etc. That observation was made in 1862, and we are in the same position today. Attempts have been made to standardize measurements, but they do not seem to have met with much success. I can see no reason why the millimeter should not be adopted with reference to the diameter and the height of movements.

We have become accustomed to recognize the size of movements at sight, such as a nine-ligne movement, etc. It would not take very much practice, however, to refer in terms of millimeters.

You will sometimes find the Swiss tabulate a movement a certain size, and when checked with a ligne gauge find it is another. The reason for this is that the actual size of the movement should be taken from the size of the bottom plate and not include the flange which projects and is made simply as a means of resting the movement in the case.

Some factories, however, measure their movements to include this flange. An interesting point to note is that the Geneva factories, that is, the makers of the finer quality movements, do not recognize fractions of sizes. Such sizes as 7-3/4 and 8-1/2, etc., are foreign to them; their movements would be 7 and 8 ligne, etc.

The Geneva manufacturers rather look with disdain upon fractions of sizes. The ligne system, however, is generally adopted in this country and abroad. One or two makers here in England do, however still recognize the Lancashire gauge system of sizes.

Chas. Frodsham, in his book (page 15), says:

"I found no small difficulty in giving a value to the old Lancashire movement gauge, for, although I conversed upon the subject with some of the oldest men in the trade, they only treated it as a tool, without regard to any standard of measurement whatever."

"I at length, however, unraveled its meaning. The Lancashire movement gauge, then, is a 3-in. rule subdivided duodecimally: a watch whose movement is 1 in. in diameter is said to be 0 size, and the second inch is subdivided into 30 equal parts or sizes, so that each size is one-thirtieth of an inch."

"Now, although the old duodecimal division was evidently the principle adopted, yet this term would not, by its name, determine the size of the watch, because (the first inch in all cases being dropped) the technical size refers only to the size of the plate, or that upon which the movement is constructed, and not the brass edge or dial plate for which five sizes are added for what is termed the fall; that is, for room to allow the works to open and shut in the case. An English 16 size watch is, therefore, 1 in. + 16/30 + 5/30 = 1.7 in. which shows little connection in point of measure with the technical size of the diameter of the watch."

This measurement does not affect us very much today, but it is interesting.

Below is a table showing the ligne compared with the millimeter, from "*Formulaire Technique.*"

lig.	mm.	lig.	mm.	lig.	mm.	lig.	mm.	lig.	mm.
1	2·256	7	15·791	13	29·326	19	42·861	25	56·396
2	4·512	8	18·047	14	31·582	20	45·117	26	58·652
3	6·767	9	20·302	15	33·837	21	47·372	27	60·907
4	9·023	10	22·558	16	36·093	22	49·628	28	63·163
5	11·279	11	24·814	17	38·349	23	51·884	29	65·419
6	13·535	12	27·070	18	40·605	24	54·140	30	67·675

The old French ligne table is here shown—

OLD FRENCH MEASURES

1 douziéme or point	= 0·0074
12 douziéme or points	= 1 ligne = 0·0888 in.
12 lignes or lines	= 1 pouce = 1·0657 in.
12 pouces or inches	= 1 pied or foot = 12·7892 in.
Old French foot	= 324·7 mm.
	= 1·06576 English feet
English foot	= 304·8 mm.

The heights of movements are referred to as twelves, such as seven twelves (which is very flat); sixteen twelves is the average thickness of a watch movement. The twelves in this case refer to douziémes and will read seven douziémes thick, or sixteen douziémes thick, or high, as the case may be.

CHAPTER 8

VARIOUS FORMS OF ESCAPEMENT

The cylinder or horizontal escapement is now practically obsolete. It is still, however, manufactured and used in some of the very cheapest watches, but, generally speaking, we can say it is dead. Watches with this escapement still pass through the workshop and are likely to for many years to come (Fig. 115).

THE CYLINDER ESCAPEMENT

The cylinder escapement was invented by George Graham (born 1674, died 1751) and is, in reality, the dead-beat escapement embracing one tooth only, which also was invented by Graham; at the time of its introduction it was a great step forward in the art of accurate time-keeping. Saunier has pointed out in comparatively recent years that the cylinder escapement has natural compensating properties. In heat, when the watch loses, owing to the loss of the elasticity of the balance spring, the oil becomes thin and therefore does not have the retarding effect it would do when the oil is thicker in cold or a more moderate temperature; then the watch would have the tendency to gain: a very crude form of compensation and, as we all know from experience, not very satisfactory. To express a personal view, I will say that I should prefer one of the old well-made horizontal watches to one of the new poorly-made levers. I fear that such watches are made just to sell only, with no pretense of an improved timepiece. They are troublesome to repair, of no service to the wearer, and will certainly give a bad reputation to the vendor and the watch trade in general; in short, most unsatisfactory watches.

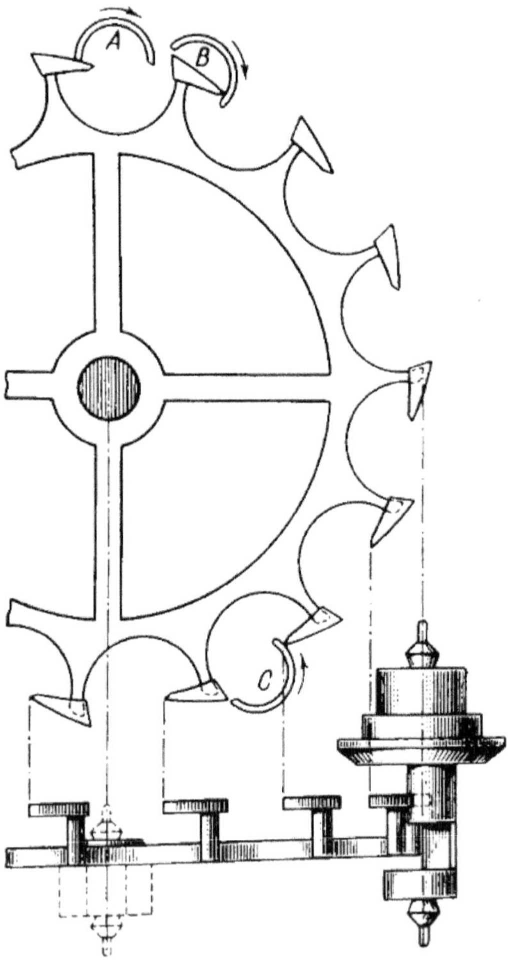

Fig. 115 – Cylinder or Horizontal Escapement A = Showing Impulse, B = Inside locking, C = Outside locking

To Examine

The action of the cylinder escapement is quite simple. With the balance in position, but with no balance spring, proceed as follows to examine. Apply a little power to the train and move the balance round until a tooth escapes, then immediately reverse the direction of the balance. The amount it is necessary to move before the escape wheel commences to move again is the depth of the locking.

The extent of this movement or locking should be from 3° to 5°; generally there are three dots on the balance to denote the 5° on each side of the center dot, and one dot as center on the lower plate. Sometimes the lower plate is so marked and in these circumstances only one dot is placed on the balance. Usually these markings cannot be relied upon; the balance may have had a new cylinder and the cylinder not placed in exactly the same position as originally, but in any case the distance as shown will be an indication of the movement necessary for the locking to be correct

To Correct

If the depth is not correct, it can be adjusted by means of the chariot on the lower plate, which, if moved, carries with it the balance cock and so keeps the balance upright.

As this adjustment is a free one, there is no form of screw arrangement. It is advisable to make a light mark across from the chariot to the plate as a guide to the amount of movement made. (See Fig. 116.)

Next, see that the teeth enter the cylinder quite freely; sometimes it is found that the edge of the cylinder rubs the base of the escape wheel. It will be noticed that in these circumstances the wheel will have a tendency either to hesitate or reverse. This is due to the cylinder being too low and the remedy is to raise it. If it is much too low it may be necessary to fit a new and longer lower plug and reduce the length of the upper one.

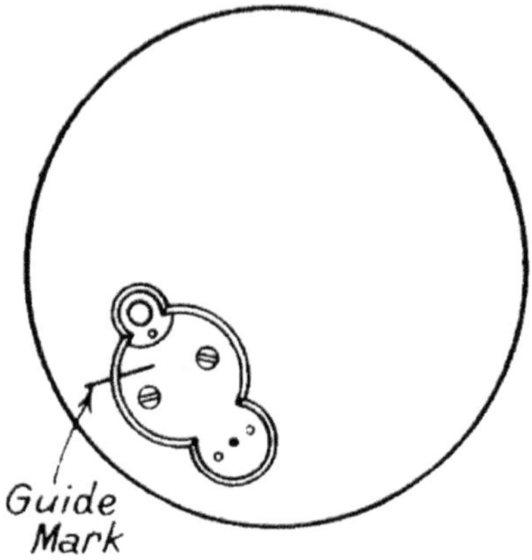

Fig. 116 – Chariot of Cylinder Escapement

It is advisable to burnish the lips of the cylinder with a small oval burnisher (the part upon which the teeth operate when giving impulse to the balance). Do not burnish flat but give the edges a rounded finish more inclined to be oval if anything. Also, burnish the edges of the teeth themselves, that is, the part that is in actual operation.

The Mainspring

The cylinder watch does not require a strong mainspring, and sometimes a better result can be obtained by changing the mainspring for a weaker one.

The balance of the cylinder escapement should not vibrate more than three-quarters of a turn; if in excess of this, there is a fear of knocking the banking.

Beat

This escapement is in beat when the balance will not set, i.e. you are unable to stop the balance, that is, of course, when the watch is wound.

If, however, the escapement has the tendency to set, as it often does, it is in beat when the balance has to be moved an equal amount on each side to unlock.

A useful method to determine easily in which direction to move the balance spring to correct for beat is to note mentally the direction in which it is necessary to move the balance most to unlock after setting. If, for instance, the balance must be moved more in the direction to unpin the balance spring, then the collet must be moved in the opposite direction. So we can say, in effect, "run the spring in"; this may seem a little childish, but, by the time the stud has been removed from the balance cock and the cock removed from the movement, a doubt can easily arise in your mind as to which direction to move the spring. This also applies to the lever escapement.

Never attempt to alter the position of the collet whilst the balance is in position; I know this is sometimes practiced, but it is dangerous and may prove a waste of time turning in a new cylinder or staff; this method is equally injurious to the chronometer, lever, and duplex escapements.

Another objection to such a practice is that altering the position of the collet has the tendency to make it out of flat, therefore, before replacing the balance in the watch again, make quite sure the collet is pressed home.

Oiling

Now, as regards oiling the cylinder escapement, all that is required, other than the usual oiling of the pivots, is to place just a little oil on the top of every other tooth of the escape wheel. The oil will find its way to the acting surfaces; the edges of the teeth.

Some watchmakers place oil in the cylinder itself, but I find that, owing to that property, capillary attraction, the oil has the tendency to remain at the base of the cylinder and little or none finds its way to the acting surfaces.

THE CHRONOMETER

This escapement as we know it here in England refers to the detent or Full Chronometer, as used in ships' chronometers (Fig. 117).

On the Continent it refers to any escapement capable of giving accurate time, usually the lever. Lexicographically, of course, it means "a time-measuring instrument." As this escapement is a book unto itself, I will treat with it briefly but sufficiently, however, for the average watchmaker.

It was invented in its present form by Thomas Earnshaw, born 1749, and died 1829. John Arnold's escapement is similar in its action, but the shape of the escape wheel teeth is different and the action of the escape wheel is away from the foot of the detent and not towards it, as is Earnshaw's.

To Examine

Now for a general examination. The balance and the escape wheel pivots should fit particularly well; a certain margin is permissible with the cylinder and to a lesser degree with the lever, but with the chronometer and the duplex there must be little or no side shake; the actions and clearances are fine and any side shake would make for faulty functioning.

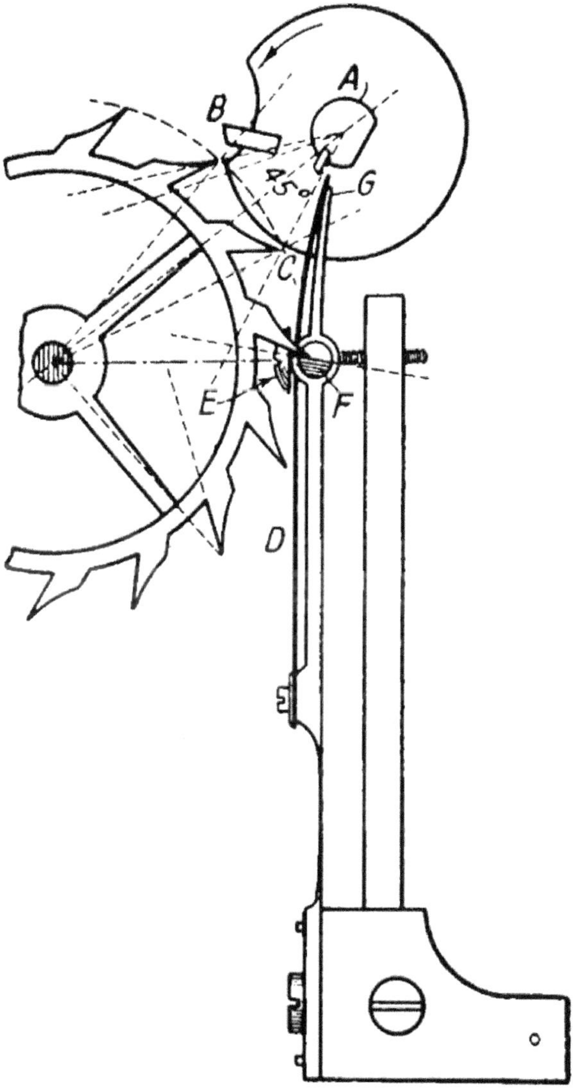

Fig. 117 – The Chronometer Escapement
A = Discharge Roller, B = Impulse Pallet, C = Showing "Light", D = Gold Spring
E = Banking Screw, F = Locking Pallet, G = Detent Horn

First of all, we must remove the balance spring, and it is most important that the escape wheel be fixed before the balance cock is removed. Sometimes, a screw with half a head is so placed that by giving the screw a half turn the head will arrest the escape wheel. If there is no such provision, very carefully arrest the wheel itself, or if more convenient the fourth wheel, with a chip of peg wood.

Every care must be exercised to ensure that the escape wheel is not in any way forced, especially forward. The detent is very delicate and can quite easily be irreparably damaged.

We now unscrew the stud screw to release the balance spring, then remove the balance cock, then, holding the balance by the upper portion of the staff with a pair of tweezers, lift gently upwards and so away from the movement. I give this in detail because incalculable damage can so easily be done if the chronometer is dealt with thoughtlessly or hastily.

Now remove the balance spring, replace the balance and remove the train obstruction.

The Detent Horn

With the power of the mainspring on, slowly lead the balance round until the discharging pallet on the lower roller of the balance staff has come into contact with the gold spring.

Arrange so that the direction of the movement will lift the gold spring and not unlock the escape wheel, in other words, the "dead" beat.

Continue to move the balance until the gold spring has been fully lifted and dropped off; note the distance or arc it has been necessary to traverse the balance from the moment of contact with the spring until it drops off. Then reverse the direction of the movement of the balance and continue to make it rotate until a tooth of the escape wheel has been unlocked and the tooth has given impulse to the impulse pallet and dropped off. The distance it has been necessary to move the balance in each direction should be the same. If it is not so, an adjustment must be made to the detent horn; it must be bent until correct.

The Drop

Now move the balance until the escape wheel is just about to unlock and note very carefully the amount of drop of the escape wheel tooth on to the impulse pallet; it should be equal for all the teeth. The drop should be sufficient to ensure that the tooth lands safely on the impulse pallet, usually about 5° of the arc of vibration of the balance. If there is not sufficient, the discharge roller must be twisted on the staff a little towards the impulse pallet in order to allow it to be in position before the escape wheel is released by the discharge pallet.

Should, on the other hand, the drop be excessive, the discharge pallet must, of course, be moved away from the impulse pallet.

Length of Gold Spring

To ensure the gold spring is of the correct length, move the balance until the discharging pallet has lifted the detent to a distance equal to the depth the locking pallet had intersected the escape wheel when at rest; the gold spring should now drop off, i.e. lead the balance round until the escape wheel is unlocked. Note the amount necessary to move the balance, the balance should traverse the same distance to release the gold spring on the other side, the "dead beat." If it is found necessary to shorten, carry out this operation with great care and slope off from the inside or the part that rests on the detent horn. Should it be necessary to lengthen, the hole in the gold spring, which is usually elongated, can generally be drawn sufficiently to rectify this.

The "Lights"

We now examine to see that the distances between the escape wheel teeth and the edge of the impulse roller are correct; they should be equal on both sides of the pallet. If they are not correct, an adjustment can be made by the detent itself; you will notice that the hole in the detent is elongated for this purpose. If the distance or "lights" is excessive, there is a risk of "tripping" and the impulse pallet must be brought into position to ensure that the tooth will give the impulse safely, and to do this the pallet is drawn by heating the roller to soften the shellac which holds it in position.

Detent Spring

The detent spring should be sufficiently set on so that if the banking screw were removed, it would spring forward to the rim of the escape wheel, and this strength ensures the detent returning smartly to the banking screw, making a safe locking.

The strength of the detent spring, quite apart from the amount it is set on, is determined by its actual thickness. This is a matter of judgment. It should be as weak as possible, that is, consistent with strength; undue stiffness of this spring obviously interferes with the vibration of the balance, and we must always remember that the balance is the time-keeper, and the less interference it has the better.

Beat

The escapement is in beat, if, when the balance is

at rest, the discharge pallet is touching the gold spring on the inside. This, however, is not always possible; the object is that the escape wheel be released if the balance is moved an equal amount to either side from the point at rest.

Move the balance until the gold spring drops off the discharge pallet, in the "dead beat" direction, then release the balance and the escapement should start. Now move the balance in the opposite direction until a tooth of the escape wheel has unlocked and the detent returned to its banking screw, then release the balance when the escapement should start off.

Draw

The locking stone on the detent is held in position by a gold half round pin and the stone is set at an angle from a line drawn from the center of the escape wheel; this constitutes the draw, similar to the escape wheel and pallet draw of the lever escapement. In this case the angle of draw is about 5°.

Oiling

Just a word about oiling; the balance and escape holes are oiled in the ordinary way, otherwise the escapement does not require oil.

A chronometer escapement maker friend of mine says that if, after the chronometer has been running some time, he finds that its action is falling off, he just greases a piece of peg wood (made chisel shape) with oil, and touches each of the escape wheel teeth; he maintains that the result is remarkable. It must be remembered that one of the virtues of this escapement is that it is frictionless, the pivots always excluded, and therefore should not require oil. When I say frictionless, that is, detrimental friction; the locking, the impulse blow, and unlocking function are all forms of friction and will not, or perhaps I should say should not, with advantage, be minimized by the application of oil.

For pocket use, the chronometer has the disadvantage that it is liable to trip, i.e. if the balance receives an extra impetus and it vibrates more than say 1-3/4 turns, it can unlock the escape wheel then and thus register fast time, and this tripping can last for many seconds.

THE DUPLEX

As some watches are still in circulation with the duplex escapement, we will just give this a cursory examination (Fig. 118). Like the cylinder, the duplex is a frictional rest escapement, but in a lesser degree.

In the first place, the balance and escape wheel holes must fit their pivots exceptionally well, and there must be no side shake. It is better to remove the balance spring before proceeding, and, as with a chronometer, the train should be arrested by wedging with a chip of peg wood before the balance is removed.

To Examine

Now, with the balance in position without its spring and the power of the mainspring on, lead the balance round carefully until one of the long or locking teeth is about to leave the notch in the ruby roller. Continue the motion of the balance and note the amount of drop of the upright or impulse tooth on to the impulse pallet, also see that the contact is safe; try this with all the teeth. The amount of movement of the escape wheel from the moment the locking tooth leaves the notch in the ruby roller until the impulse tooth falls on to the impulse pallet should be from 6° to 10° of the arc descr-

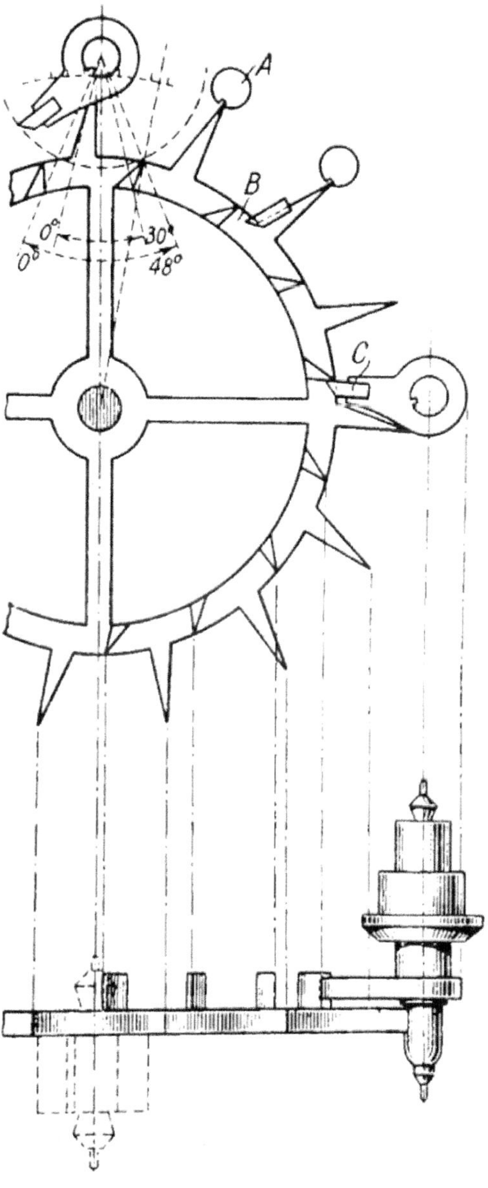

Fig. 118 – Duplex Escapement
A = Ruby Roller, B = Showing drop of escape wheel on to impulse pallet, C = Impulse Pallet

ibed by the balance, according to the condition of the escapement. If it is in a really first-class condition, both as regards proportions and wear, 6° to 7° is sufficient. To adjust tills, the impulse pallet is twisted on the staff.

Generally speaking, the duplex is far superior to the cylinder, but as it is more delicate and the pivots of the escapement must fit accurately, it is more costly to manufacture and, although it is capable of a much finer performance than the cylinder, the cylinder has been (and still is) made in much greater quantities on account of its sturdiness and cheapness. Furthermore, the duplex has the disadvantage of "tripping" and "setting" when used as a portable timepiece. Many devices have been introduced to correct this drawback, but when compared with the lever escapement the duplex is obsolete.

Beat

The escapement is in beat if, when the balance is at rest and with the power off, the notch in the ruby roller is in such a position as to embrace one of the locking teeth; in other words, it should be pointing directly to the line of center of the locking tooth. This is sometimes not exactly correct. The angle of the teeth may call for the position of the tooth to be just clear of the notch, in order that it is in the "line of centers" of the joining, the escape wheel axis and the balance axis.

If this condition is observed we are then assured that the least possible movement of the balance will start the escapement off and so obviate setting as much as possible.

Oiling

As regards oiling, the pivots are oiled as usual and just a spot of oil is applied to the notch in the ruby roller.

The impulse does not require oil, and the locking teeth will take all the oil that is necessary from the notch.

It is always advisable to make sure that the tips of the locking teeth are smooth, and to see that during cleaning the notch is perfectly free from thickened oil. To ensure this sharpen a piece of peg wood chisel shape, dip this end in benzine and work up and down in the notch.

CHAPTER 9

COMPLICATED WORK

In dealing with complicated work, a very big field is opened, and it would be practically impossible to describe the many varieties of design and methods used in achieving the same object.

I propose, therefore, to take an example of each watch. The governing principles will be the same in all types, and it will be necessary for each individual watch to be studied before being taken to pieces to observe the function of the various pieces.

Men who are used to complicated work more or less build the movement up, as it were, after repairs and cleaning. By this I mean that a certain piece is wanted, and, when found, is placed in position, then, maybe, a spring is required to operate on that piece, and so on until the movement is complete.

When taking complicated watches to pieces it is advisable, and will ultimately save time, if all springs, screws, etc., which are used to hold pieces in position are kept with their respective pieces. Generally, the screws are of varying lengths, and if this rule is not observed, much time can be wasted and probably damage done.

If the fundamental principles are understood and a general survey made as suggested, little difficulty will be experienced when assembling.

THE CHRONOGRAPH

The chronograph, as its name implies, is a writer or recorder of time; we associate it with the stop and fly back mechanism (Fig. 119).

Its Action

The action is quite simple, and the model illustrated shows a wheel attached to the extended pivot of the fourth wheel. This wheel, therefore, revolves once in 60 sec., and, in turn, gears into a similar wheel which is carried on an arm. As this arm is pivoted, it can be moved so that the wheel on it is always in gear with the continually rotating one on the fourth wheel, and at the same time connects with the center chronograph wheel to which the center seconds hand is fitted.

Fig. 119 – Chronograph

The action of moving this arm is effected by the castle wheel, and as the arm is held close to the blocks on the castle wheel by a spring it will be understood that the arm can be made to lift out or drop in as the sections are made to revolve by the moving of the castle wheel.

The minute recording action in this instance is effected by a finger piece attached to the underside of the center chronograph wheel; this moves the minute recording wheel forward one tooth at each revolution. Now fitted on to the center chronograph and minute recording wheels is a heart-shaped piece, and a lever, which is governed by the castle wheel, can be made to bear on this heart-shaped piece by means of a stiff spring, which will make both these wheels revolve smartly to a definite position, known as zero.

Starting from the zero position, the first movement to push the castle wheel forward will lift the levers from the heart pieces and will, at the same time, bring the wheel on its arm into gear with the center chronograph wheel. It will also lift the lever which has been resting on the edge of the center chronograph wheel, and the object of this lever is to hold the wheel steady, as we shall see.

The chronograph hand is now revolving and another move forward of the castle wheel will throw the wheel on its arm out of gear with the center chronograph wheel. The chronograph hand will have immediately stopped, and, at the same time, the lever already referred to will have been brought into action, thus holding the center chronograph wheel firmly. A slight jar might move the hand if it were not for this lever. In some of the cheaper chronographs you will find that this lever is dispensed with. The object of the light friction spring is to ensure that the center seconds hand shall not register the jumping movement due to the back lash of the chronograph wheels. The next movement of the castle wheel will allow the return levers to fall smartly on to the heart pieces as already explained.

To Clean

When cleaning the chronograph it is advisable to clean the fine teeth of the chronograph train with a glass brush.

Ordinary cleaning in benzine and brushing does not seem searching enough. The wheels are held with the teeth uppermost between the first finger and thumb of the left hand and with the glass brush in the right hand the teeth are gently stroked until quite bright.

Oiling

Now, as regards oiling, there is divided opinion; a manufacturer of chronograph watches in Switzerland advocates that the lower pivot of the center chronograph wheel should not be oiled (this is the pivot that works in the brass bouchon in the hollow center pinion). It is claimed that the friction is negligible and that the oil becomes dry and gathers the dust, doing more harm than good. Personally, I prefer to apply a little oil, and in some years of experience have found no detrimental effects. The other pivots of the chronograph work can be oiled with safety; it is only the long pivot which is debatable. Slightly oil or merely grease the heart pieces. A mere suspicion of oil should be applied to the block on the jumper spring of the minute recording wheel; I have found chronographs actually stop for the want of oil here.

General Adjustments

The adjustments to be observed are the depth of the wheel gearing with the center chronograph wheel and the changeover of the minute recorder.

A screw with an eccentric head determines the depth of the two wheels and can be adjusted to the required position; the shape of the teeth of the chronograph wheels is not conventional, but just pointed shape, and no hard and fast rule can be laid down determining a correct depth. A free depth is assured with the minimum of back lash if a "light" can be observed between the teeth when they are in mesh.

Examine carefully to see that the minute counter arm on the center chronograph wheel is free of the preceding tooth of the minute counter wheel. This can be adjusted by the manipulation of the jumper spring, which places the wheel in the required position; this spring has an elongated hole for that purpose.

It is advisable when testing the chronograph watch to run it with the chronograph on for at least 24 hours.

THE SPLIT-SECONDS CHRONOGRAPH

This is the ordinary chronograph movement (Fig. 120) with the addition of the mechanism to operate a second chronograph hand.

The action is that, when the chronograph is started, the two hands revolve at the same time, and the hands are so adjusted that by a quick glance the second hand is not visible.

By depressing the split seconds push piece, the one hand will stop, and upon depressing again the hand will catch the other up and travel with it.

Its Action

The mechanism is quite simple and acts in this manner. Working over and in conjunction with the center chronograph wheel is another wheel (without teeth) and attached to this wheel is a short arm to which is fitted a small ruby roller or wheel. A light spring bears on this arm and holds it against a heart piece which is fixed to the center chronograph wheel, so that, in its normal state, the two wheels rotate together just by virtue of the light spring holding the ruby roller to the heart piece (at the apex).

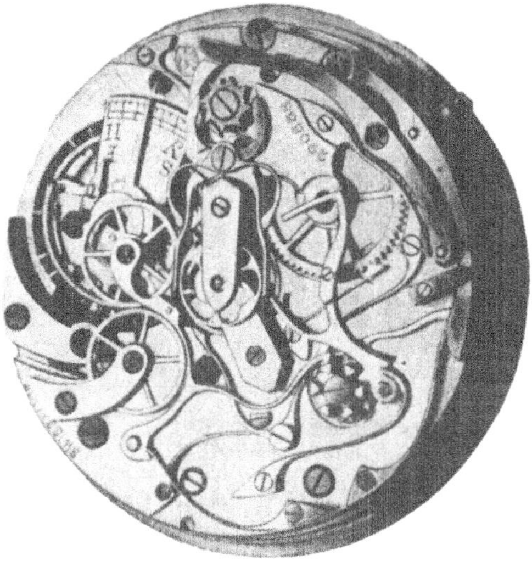

Fig. 120 – Split-Seconds Chronograph

If the split wheel is held the center chronograph wheel will still continue to rotate, lifting the ruby roller up and down in so doing; and if the split wheel is released, the ruby roller will slide down the heart piece and return to its zero which is the apex of the heart.

The method of arresting the split wheel is by means of double levers operating on a separate castle wheel and having a scissor-like appearance; the wheel is held by its edge with the two levers.

Oiling

Now, as regards oiling, it is most essential that no

oil be applied to the ruby roller or to the split seconds wheel pivots; there is no doubt that the friction of this split seconds wheel is negligible, but still more important is the fact that the power at our disposal to return the split hand to its zero position is so slight that oil would retard it and make the return sluggish.

I have seen instances where, owing to oil, it has not been possible to make the split hand return until the split action button has been depressed several times.

As regards the general adjustment, it is precisely the same as the ordinary chronograph, with the addition that the split hand must return to the other hand as smartly as that hand returns to its zero when the lever is brought on to the heart piece.

INDEPENDENT SECONDS

This type of movement (Fig. 121) is now practically obsolete, but a few still pass through the workshop for repair. In the majority of cases the independent seconds hand operates from the center.

There are two distinct trains, and if the movement is of the keyless type the backward motion of the button winds one train and the forward motion the other.

If a key wind movement, there are, of course, two winding squares. The independent seconds train is dependent upon the escapement of the other train for its motion.

The independent seconds train terminates in a pinion with just a pin attached to it in the place of a wheel, and this pinion is arrested and released by the leaves of the escape pinion of the going train into which it intersects, much in the same manner as if it were a one- and, in some cases, two-toothed wheel.

The movement is oiled in the usual manner, and it

is not necessary to oil the flirt pin of the independent train; this is generally made of gold.

Fig. 121 – Independent Seconds

The independent hand usually registers seconds and, for some special purposes, two seconds.

THE QUARTER REPEATER

The quarter repeating movement here illustrated (Fig. 122) is the type in general use today. It is fitted with the usual "all or nothing" piece, which does not allow the watch to strike at all until the slide is pressed quite home and the correct number of hours and quarters thus gathered up.

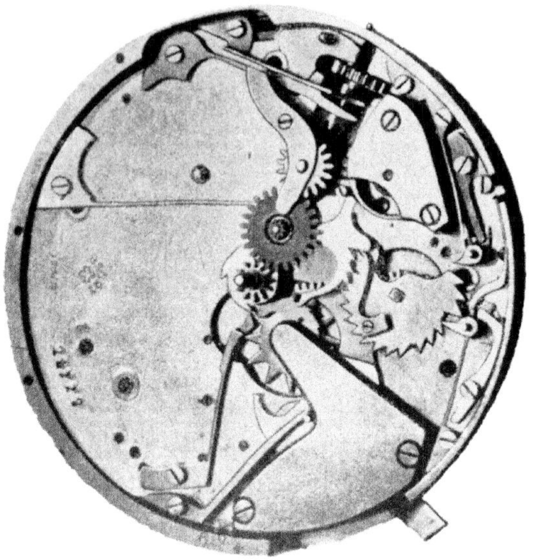

Fig. 122 – Quarter Repeater

As the term implies, all the hours, etc., are struck or nothing. In some of the older type of repeating watches it is possible, by slightly drawing the slide or, in the instance of the pump action, slightly depressing the pump, to strike as many hours as you wish, providing, of course, that they were of a lesser number than indicated by the watch.

To Set Up the Mainspring

When assembling, the repeating mainspring is set up and the best manner to do this is to place the hour rack in position and wind the mainspring to the full extent, then let the train run down two complete turns of the hour rack. Then arrest it and place the slide rack in position It the repeating mainspring is now wound by means of the slide to its full extent, that is to enable 12 hours and also the three "ting-tangs" of the three quarters, the greatest amount of work the mainspring will be called upon to do can now be tested.

The mainspring should not pull on the hook and, at the same time, there should be sufficient force to strike all the hours and to gather the rack up after it has fallen the full amount.

Some repeaters are so arranged that the mainspring can be set up after assembling; the barrel is free to move, and the upper side forms a ratchet wheel and is held in position by a screw, the head of which is cut so that by giving the screw a slight turn it releases the barrel and allows of its adjustment.

Another method sometimes met with is a stiff click and spring combined. By this means, the repeating work can be assembled and the mainspring set up afterwards.

The object to be aimed at is that the blows struck should be of equal speed, whether a small number or a big number of hours are to be struck.

Oiling

As regards oiling, very little oil indeed should be applied to all the actions of the repeating train; an excess is inclined to creep, leaving the acting surfaces dry, thus defeating the object.

Accurate Register

The correct position to place the minute hand to ensure that the watch will strike the correct quarter immediately after the quarter and not "very near" is, before the going train is wound, to wedge the escape wheel to prevent any possible movement of the train. Then draw the repeating slide back as far as it will go and hold or wedge, if it is possible, in that position. Now, if the hands are set in the usual manner, you will hear a slight click at each quarter, and this will indicate the exact position the minute hand should point to, having regard, of course, to the correct quarter to be struck. In these circumstances, the hand must be placed in position at the quarters; if the hour mark is used the rack will have fallen to the lowest point of the snail, and it will not be possible to move the hands forward until the rack has been gathered up.

MINUTE REPEATER

The mechanism of the minute repeater (Fig. 123) is the same as that of the quarter repeater, but has the addition of the minute rack and also the four minute snails, each with 14 steps attached to the cannon pinion.

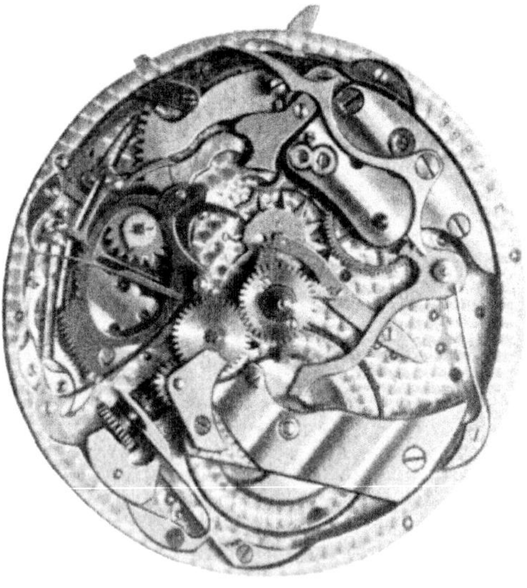

Fig. 123 – Minute Repeater

Upon drawing the slide to make the watch strike, the hours are determined by the hour snail and the quarters by the quarter snail and the minutes by the snails already referred to. Fitted to the underside of the minute snail is a piece which, by means of a long lever, is thrown forward when one minute only in to be struck. This piece is called the surprise piece and its object is to ensure that the minute rack does not drop down to the lowest point and 14 minutes struck instead of one. Also so that the rack cannot jam should the rack be made to drop between the 14th and 15th minutes. The observation as regards the adjustment of the mainspring applies equally to the minute as to the quarter repeater; the piece should be made to strike 12 hours, the three quarters, and 14 minutes to ensure all is in order.

Oiling

As regards oiling, it is not necessary to oil the surprise piece on the cannon pinion, but the surprise piece lever that works on the edge of the surprise piece should be greased with thick oil. It is not advisable to apply oil or grease to the case slide.

The minute hand is placed in position in a similar manner to the quarter repeater with the exception that, instead of the quarter rack dropping off the snail at each quarter and giving a click, the adjustment is taken from the minute rack dropping off the steps on the minute snail. This method of placing the minute hand in position is even more important with the minute repeater than with the quarter repeater, and the best position on which to place the minute hand is between the three and eight minutes past the hour.

TRIPLE COMPLICATION

This, as its name implies, is the minute repeater with the addition of the chronograph, sometimes split-seconds chronograph, and calendar work (Figs. 124 & 125).

Fig. 124 – Showing Under Dial of Triple Complicated Watch

Fig. 125 – Dial of Triple Complicated Watch

Usually the arrangement is for the chronograph work to be at the back of the watch, with the repeating work under the dial as usual and the calendar work on a separate plate over the repeating work.

As regards the general adjustment, the points already referred to under their respective headings should be noted. The calendar work is generally the perpetual type, and care must be taken when assembling to see that the month hand is placed in the correct year.

I need hardly mention here that watches of this description call for the greatest skill and care, and, unless the workman is fully proficient with the other forms of complicated work, he should not undertake the repair of the triple complicated watch first. Even experienced men find these watches tedious, and their repair calls for the close and undivided attention of the watchmaker.

It would be futile to attempt to describe in detail the repair of the complicated watch; not only would it make difficult reading, but I am convinced no good purpose would be served. It is important that the work should be entrusted only to an experienced man: a man who has had sufficient experience to recognize his limitations and his ability to undertake such work with confidence.

Every man must make a start, it is true, but commence on the less complicated work, master that, and then proceed.

CHAPTER 10

A METHOD OF CLEANING THE WATCH

There are many methods of procedure when cleaning a watch. Some advocate drying the pieces in boxwood dust after they leave the benzine, others not using benzine at all. The method I propose to give is the one generally adopted in the best workshops both here in England and in Switzerland. Watch-cleaning machines are used in England today. They are an innovation from America and have received much attention in books recently published, so I do not feel it necessary to discuss this system here. We will assume that the movement has been repaired and it is now only necessary to clean and re-assemble. Remove all springs and end pieces, etc., from the bottom plate, dip a watch brush (kept especially for this purpose) in the benzine and well brush the plate, then place the plate in the benzine bath for a minute or two, remove and dry off the superfluous benzine with a clean, soft, linen cloth kept specially for that purpose. The other pieces removed from the plate can now be placed in the bath.

The Use of Tissue Paper

Hold the plate by its edges with a piece of best silver tissue paper (which is free from fluff) and with a soft brush proceed to finish the cleaning. If the movement is gilt give the brush a circular motion—this leaves a non-scratched appearance—occasionally breathing on the plate to moisten slightly. If the movement is of the silvered or nickel variety brush in the direction of the grain or damascene finish of the plates, etc. When both sides of the plate and edges are clean and bright, peg well all sinks and recesses, surfaces of all jewel holes, also the countersunk parts of the jewels. This last is very important as it is the reservoir or store place for the fresh oil. See that the acting surfaces of the jewel holes are bright and free from congealed oil. Now sharpen the peg wood to a fairly long point and peg well all the pivot holes from both sides, do not leave off until the peg, after insertion, is perfectly clean. I mention a long point because if a short point is used there is a risk that all parts of the hole will not be cleaned. Place the plate and all parts after cleaning under a glass cover.

To Handle Small Pieces

Now remove the small pieces from the bath and put the train including the barrel—the mainspring having been removed—and also the other bars and bridges, removing first all endstones, into the benzine, after well brushing with the benzine brush.

It is not necessary to dry small pieces with the cloth, neither need they be held in the fingers. Hold them with the tweezers down on the board paper and brush well until bright. Such pieces as the small intermediate wheels can be treated in this manner as well as all screws and small bridges, making sure both sides are clean and that the slots of the screws are free from dust. It is advisable now to replace the parts removed from the bottom plate, as it avoids any possibility of them getting lost.

Use of the Bellows

Before parts that have been cleaned are placed under the glass shade just give them a puff with the bellows to ensure all dust is removed. Now remove the bars and bridges from the bath and proceed as with the bottom plate, replacing endstones and index, etc., as you go along.

Cleaning the Train

Remove the train from the bath and dry with the cloth. Hold the wheels in tissue paper and brush the teeth well, also the flat part of the wheel. Give the pinion itself a dabbing motion with the brush to remove all loose dust. Clean the pivots well with pith. Hold the wheel firmly in the left hand still with tissue paper; take a piece of soft pith cut flat on the end, in the right hand. Now press this pith on to the end of the pivot, twirling it between the thumb and forefinger. Continue to apply pressure so that the pith will pass beyond the pivot on to the arbor and so to the facing of the pinion. This will ensure that the pivot, arbor and facing are quite bright. The other pivot, i.e. the short arbor (if there is one, or there may be no arbor at all) is treated in the same manner. Should the pivot still be black or not bright steel color, remove the discoloration with a piece of peg wood cut chisel shape and the flat part charged with a little diamantine. Some pieces of pith are very hard, knotty as it were; I have seen such used to good purpose. Use as mentioned but first smear the end of the pith with rouge. It is not necessary to press beyond the pivot shoulder. This, however, is not always effective, in which case resort to the peg wood and diamantine. Sharpen the peg to a fair point and peg well all the leaves of the pinion until quite bright. It is advisable, with the type of wheel to which the pinion is riveted, to see that the point of the peg passes through to the other side as dust can cling here and when perfectly dry—after the benzine bath— fall into the movement should the watch get a knock when in use.

To Clean the Escapement

The escape wheel is cleaned in the same way as the other wheels, but the teeth are finally cleaned with pith. Select a soft piece, and, holding the wheel between the thumb and forefinger— in tissue—and leaving the teeth exposed. Well "brush" with the soft pith; we have in fact wiped the teeth of the escape wheel with pith. Congealed oil not already removed by the benzine brush will thus be removed. The pallets are cleaned first by holding them down on the board paper and brushing well, then holding them in a similar manner to the escape wheel, the stones projecting, and wiping the stones with soft pith. Make sure both the locking surface and impulse plane are perfectly bright. The notch is cleaned with peg wood sharpened chisel shape.

The Balance and Spring

Now for the balance: it is best to clean it first, for a reason which will be seen presently. Remove the spring and place in the bath. The balance, if it is tarnished, is cleaned by placing in a solution of cyanide of potassium for a few moments. (A piece of cyanide about the size of a lump of sugar dissolved in about two wine glasses of water gives a satisfactory solution.) Then rinse well in water. The balance is held on a piece of wire during this operation. Remove all superfluous water with an old watch brush well charged with chalk. Now place the balance in a small box of killed lime; this will ensure all traces of water being removed. If this has been done in the first place the balance will be ready to be removed by the time other parts of the watch have been cleaned. The balance should be allowed to remain in the lime for at least an hour. Having removed the balance, clean off all the lime clinging to it and buff the top edge with a buff charged with dry diamantine. The balance is now ready for the benzine bath. It need only remain here for a few moments; then remove it, dry with the cloth and carefully brush with a soft brush. Pith the staff pivots and press the pith down over the lower pivot on to the roller, so that the ruby pin is well cleaned with the pith. Remove the balance spring from the bath and place on a piece of tissue laid flat on the bench, cover it with another piece of tissue, or fold the tissue paper over it, and very lightly dab the soft watch brush on to it. Move the spring between the pieces of paper frequently until quite dry. It will be found that the spring so cleaned will be bright.

Index Pins, etc.

Sharpen a piece of peg wood chisel shape and charge with rouge, just sufficient rouge to color the peg—there should be no loose rouge—draw this up and down between the index pins to ensure they are free from grease. The banking pins—or surfaces, if of the solid type—are treated in the same manner. The mainspring need not be placed in the bath: hold it at the hook end with brass-nosed pliers and draw it almost to its full length between folds of the linen cloth.

Cleaning in Alcohol

I am indebted to Mr. Chas. Constantin of Vacheron & Constantin, Geneva, for the following method—

It is advisable when cleaning baguette and small movements to clean finally in alcohol (rectified spirits of wine). The reason is that benzine has a deleterious action on oil and, no matter how thoroughly the parts may be cleaned, there is a risk of some being left behind; in fact, owing to the oily nature of benzine, it is not possible to remove it entirely by brushing alone. With these movements, only a minute quantity of oil can be applied to the pivots, and it is most desirable to remove any danger of oil deterioration. So after cleaning in the usual manner, place such pieces as the train (barrel excepted), lower plate, cocks, and bridges, in fact all parts appertaining to the running train, in the alcohol bath.

Leave for a few moments, remove the pieces and dry by placing them *on* a soft brush and dabbing with another similar brush. Vacheron & Constantin use as the lower brush one measuring 1-1/2 in. × 4 in. long (Fig. 126); the other brush is an ordinary watch brush as we use here, i.e. about 1/2 in. × 4-1/2 in.

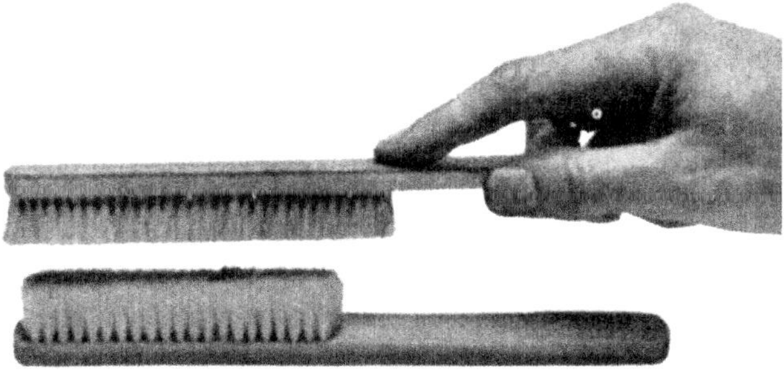

Fig. 126 – Method of Drying Small Components After Cleaning in Alcohol

It is necessary to use the peg wood again after drying, especially for the holes, to ensure that all alcohol is removed. A very important point is that these brushes must not be cleaned by using either chalk or burnt bone, but by washing with warm water and soap, drying well afterward. *These brushes must be free from dust.*

The acting portions of the pallet stones and the pivots only of the pallet staff should be dipped in the alcohol, and if the roller is on the balance staff the pivots only of the staff should be immersed, otherwise there is a risk of loosening these stones and the ruby pin owing to the action alcohol has on the shellac by which they are secured.

Cleaning the Tools

Watch brushes are best cleaned by rubbing them on burnt mutton bones, and then on wood to remove all dust. The bone from the leg is best. After all meat has been removed, place the bone in a clean red fire and leave until well burned off; upon removal it will be found to turn white. It is cleaner to use than chalk and imparts a good finish to the metal, especially gilding.

The blades of screwdrivers and the oiler are cleaned by plunging into pith. Wedge as many pieces of pith as will go into an old French clock barrel—this forms quite a good receptacle and should always be kept handy on the bench—plunge the tools mentioned frequently into this during the assembling of the watch. The tweezers are cleaned by plunging into the watch brush and then closing and drawing out, thus wiping the insides of the blades. Finally, use the bellows frequently during assembling. Before placing the pallets in position wind the movement a few clicks and whilst the train is running down puff gently with the bellows into the train; this ensures the removal of all dust.

One could go on *ad infinitum*, describing simple methods of cleaning which take much longer to describe than to accomplish; but all with the same objective, absolute cleanness.

CHAPTER 11

THE WATCHMAKER AT THE LATHE

The modem lathe is an essential part of the watchmaker's equipment today. Its many accessories and consequent usefulness make it indispensable. The purchase of a lathe is a sound investment, as it makes for greater efficiency in the man himself and at the same time adds to his earning capacity.

I have said that the turns produce the finest turning, and I still maintain that, but there are uses to which the lathe can be put for which the turns would be useless.

By using the lathe carefully it can be one of the watchmaker's greatest friends. Like many other tools it responds to careful usage. All machines are the same in this respect; they give good service in return for good treatment.

It is advisable for the watchmaker to purchase a lathe for himself. I find, generally speaking, communal tools of this description are not a success. Each man may be quite careful and conscientious, but the tool suffers from such usage. The man has not just that personal interest which makes so much difference.

Lathe work is a very wide subject, and even a volume on this interesting and important work alone could not do it justice. To understand the lathe and its uses fully is a life study in itself. The notes that follow therefore are of a necessity cursory, but we hope sufficient to stimulate the student to take further interest.

Purchasing a Lathe

When buying a lathe (it will probably be a secondhand one today) select one for which accessories and spare parts can be procured. This is not quite such a simple matter just now, but what spares are available are usually for the popular makes. That the lathe is of American or German manufacture is of no particular moment. A lathe bearing a well-known name is to be preferred. Such makes as Boley, Boley & Leinen, Lorch, Wolf Jahn, and Webster Whitcomb are amongst the most popular. It is useful to know that the accessories made by the German makers, Boley and Wolf Jahn, are invariably interchangeable. The fundamental principle of such lathes and the accessories is the same, therefore the description of one make applies to them all. Unfortunately, at the moment it is not possible to buy from a selection, but if you do have a choice, select a well-known make.

Care of the Lathe

It should be borne in mind that the lathe itself is a machine and will need attention, and like watches and clocks needs a spot of oil occasionally. Apply a little clock oil to the bearings and periodically take the head-stock to pieces and wash out with benzine to remove old oil and grit. Make sure to dry thoroughly before reassembling. See the oil channels are clean and free from oil; this ensures that the fresh oil applied is clean when it reaches the working surfaces of the various parts. Such care is well rewarded; life is added to the lathe and greater accuracy assured as the parts will not wear so quickly. One general remark here will not be out of place. Whilst all moving parts must be perfectly free, there should be no end or side shake to any of the bearings or working parts. The lathe must work in a rigid manner as it were. Some of the modern lathes are fitted with ball-bearings to the head-stock, a decided advantage, both in respect of the life of the machine and its smooth running.

The "T" Rest

I do not think I can do better than to describe the lathc and its parts by explaining the procedure of using it; making certain pieces for watches and introducing various accessories as we proceed. It will be appreciated that although perhaps the turning of a balance staff, cutting a certain wheel, or using the slide rest on a barrel cover may be explained here, the general principle of the use of the lathe equally applies when making other pieces, etc.

Fig. 127 shows the head-stock with split or wire chuck in use, the most elementary operation of the lathe and one of the most useful. You will notice that this lathe is fitted with the "tip-up" rest. This rest has decided advantages over the fixed type of rest. It can be thrown back to free the work for purposes of measurement or to remove the work for fitting, and we are sure that the rest is in the same position when returned.

It is important that the rest should be the correct distance away from the work, and that it should be the correct height. Experience will teach this—we must be comfortable at the work. With this "tip-up" rest, time is saved, as it will not be necessary to readjust it for height and distance. The same remarks apply when using the lathe as when using the turns, as regards turning, which has been fully explained elsewhere in this book.

Split Chucks

It is of vital importance when selecting a split

chuck—say to hold a piece of steel rod for roughing out a balance staff—that the rod should fit the chuck, avoiding the use of a chuck which is either too large or else too small. The rod should just fit, and this means that when in the lathe a slight screw of the draw-in spindle will be sufficient to grip the rod securely for turning. If the chuck is too large, a good deal of tightening will be necessary to secure the rod, and there is a risk of distorting the chuck; and equally if the chuck is too small, it means it must be forced open to allow the rod to enter.

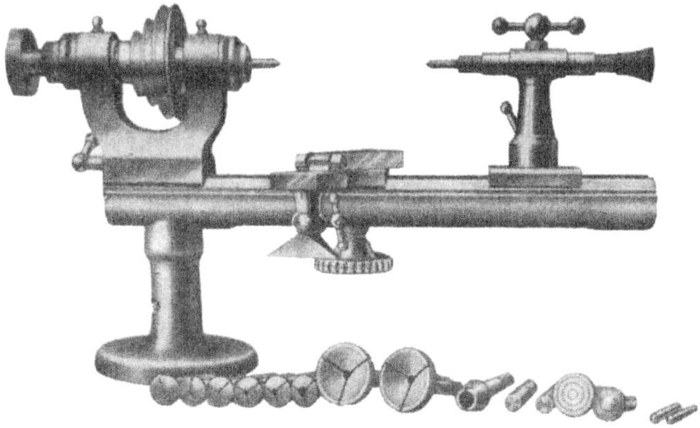

Fig. 127 – Head-Stock Showing Split Chuck in Use

Further, if the correct size chuck is not selected, the work is not so likely to run true, since the jaws of the chuck will not grip the work parallel. If the chuck is too large, for instance, it will only grip by the back part of the jaws, and pressure brought to bear on the work will, in all probability, cause it to move, since the front part of the jaws of the chuck give no support.

If the chuck is too small the jaws will grip the work

insecurely, and the same objection obtains. In these circumstances, a certain amount of wobble will be set up, although it may not be perceptible at the time of turning, but if the work is removed from the chuck and then replaced, the chances of its running true are lessened. A little time taken at this stage is time well spent; better work will result and care of the chucks is assured.

The split chuck is very useful when polishing pivots, such as the center wheel. It is more convenient than the jacot tool, although that tool provides for such pivots. When the lower pivot is to be polished, select a chuck which the pinion head fits comfortably if the pinion head is uppermost. Very little tightening of the draw-in spindle is all that will be necessary to grip, and not only will this have the effect of avoiding unfair usage of the chuck, but the leaves of the pinion will not suffer. Should the top pivot be the only means of holding, use the tail-stock as explained later.

Some men find it more convenient to use the polisher from the underside. It is argued that the work can be seen during the polishing. Personally I prefer to hold the polisher on the work and rely on the "feel" to know when the polisher is in full contact. In any case, it is a matter of personal taste and practice—the finished result is what matters. Figs. 128 and 129 show the alternative methods.

To recall the center wheel previously mentioned: the pivot is gripped by the correct-sized chuck and the other pivot; the one to be polished is supported by the runner in the tail-stock.

There are literally dozens of different split chucks for every conceivable purpose: chucks for holding balances complete with staff, staffs alone, cylinders, and so on *ad infinitum*.

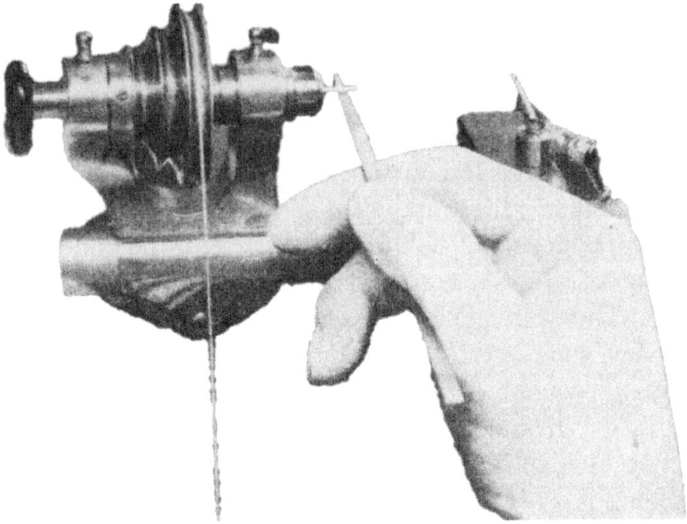

Fig. 128 – Polisher Used From Underside of Work

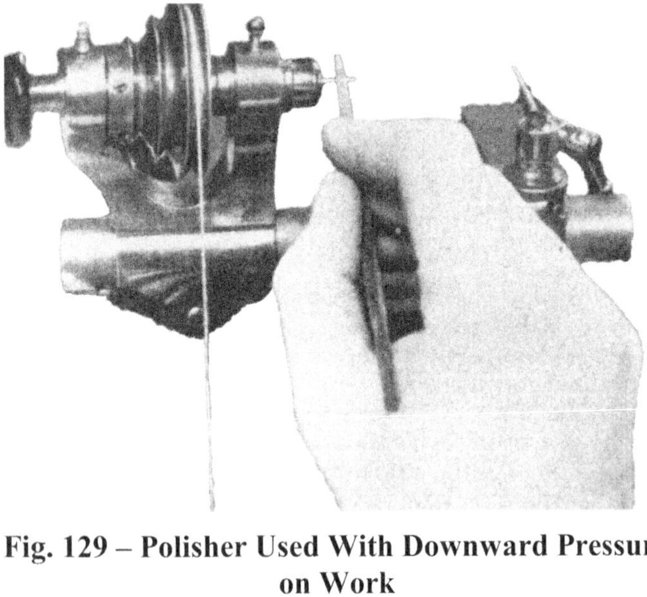

Fig. 129 – Polisher Used With Downward Pressure on Work

Step Chucks

Fig. 130 illustrates an automatic chuck to hold wheels, discs, etc. Here again, as emphasized with the split chuck, the article should just fit into one of the steps, and the closing action which is effected by screwing the chuck into the head-stock will cause it to be gripped firmly. It is important that the piece should lie flat on to thc scat of the step.

Fig. 130 – Step Chuck

These chucks are made in about six sizes, and as each chuck has about nine steps there is a big selection of sizes.

They are indispensable for such jobs as catching the center of a wheel or barrel. Say the holes of a barrel have worn wide and may be oval; after re-bushing we cannot be sure the new hole is central with the teeth of the barrel. If, therefore, the barrel is placed in a step chuck, and the hole caught true with a narrow, cutter as previously explained, when uprighting the center wheel, we are sure the hole can be made true in this manner either before or after bushing. In any case it is of vital importance that the barrel should run absolutely true in the round to ensure an equal depth with the center pinion. It would be a lengthy and troublesome business to do this and similar jobs without a step chuck.

Another step chuck illustrated here (Fig. 131) is

made to take rings and anything of a like form. The same remarks as to selection apply here. The effect when the chuck is screwed into the head-stock is to cause the steps to expand and so grip the article.

Fig. 131 – Step Chuck

The step chucks first mentioned are caused to close in when screwed and drawn into the spindle of the head-stock, by reason of the coned shapes of the spindle end and the back of the chuck, but this ring step chuck has its cone or chamfer on the outside of its stem and attached to the underside of the step part of the chuck itself; therefore the action of screwing and drawing it on to the outside rounded part of the spindle causes the steps to spread or open, and so to grip the ring-like article being worked upon.

Two step ring chucks illustrated here (Figs. 132 & 133) are made for the same purpose, but to take larger work, such as bezels, watch cases, etc., in the case of the ring type, and larger wheels and plates, etc., in the case of the disc type chuck. These two chucks are adjustable, and can be opened and closed by means of the knurled outer ring. There are many varieties of these chucks, but the two here will suffice for the purpose of illustrating.

Fig. 132

Fig. 133

Figs. 132 & 133 – Adjustable Step Chuck

Chuck for Holding Watch Buttons

The chuck shown in Fig. 134—which is self-explanatory—is useful for opening the button to fit the pendant, etc. The chucks shown in Fig. 135, which are for the same purpose, are fitted with a stop inside. There are various sizes made, and the same care must be exercised when selecting as mentioned before.

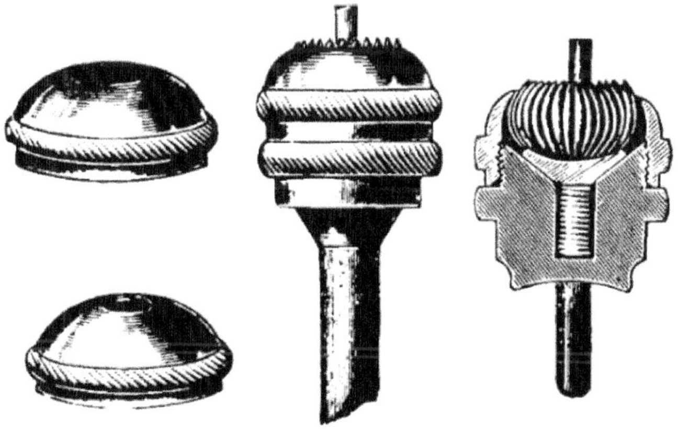

Fig. 134 – Watch Button or Crown Chuck

Fig. 135 – Watch Button or Crown Chucks

The Screw or Box Chuck

This chuck (Fig. 136) is used when the work is too large for a split chuck. If you are making a barrel arbor, for instance, the metal rod from which it is turned is a little larger than the largest part of the finished arbor. The arbor is therefore first roughed down in this screw chuck. Place the chuck in the lathe and unscrew ail eight screws so that the ends are flush with the inside of the chuck. Now give two opposite screws an equal number of turns until the distance apart of their ends is just sufficient to allow the steel rod—about 1-1/2 in. long—to pass between.

Turn the other six screws the same number of turns and place the rod in position and then screw up all eight screws so that the rod is held firmly, turning each screw as nearly as can be judged by an equal amount.

If the head is made to revolve now, the rod should revolve somewhere near truly, and by manipulating the screws it can be made to run sufficiently true for turning purposes.

Fig. 136 – Box Chuck

With the T-rest in position ready for turning, hold the graver as for cutting. If now the end of the rod farthest from the chuck is out of truth, hold the head in the position which brings the metal nearest the graver, loosen very slightly the back screw on the chuck nearest to you and tighten the one opposite. This will have the effect of pushing the metal away from the graver. With practice this becomes quite simple; you will know just which screw to alter and be able to make the metal run true with ease and speed. When the metal is running true enough to turn, hold the graver very firmly on the T-rest and, with its point, cut away the superfluous metal until the job runs perfectly true. We now can proceed to turn one end of the arbor nearly to size, when the metal can be removed from the screw chuck, reversed, and the turned portion placed in a split chuck, which will be quite big enough to take it, and the other end dealt with.

The chucks shown in Figs. 132 and 133 can be used for the same purpose.

Self-Centering Chuck

Fig. 137 shows a useful self-centering chuck in which the jaws can be reversed so that it can be made to hold either wheels, plates, etc., or rings, bezels, and so on.

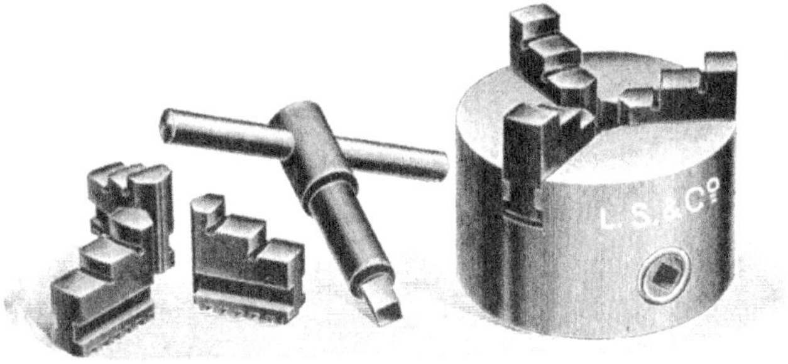

Fig. 137 – Self-Centering Box Chuck

Wax Chucks

The wax chuck (Fig. 138) is among the most useful chucks It can be used for a great number of purposes where a step or other chuck would be useless It is best to heat the chuck a little before placing it in the lathe, and to smear on to its face *a little* shellac. We will assume that it is required to turn the cover of a barrel out to free the mainspring.

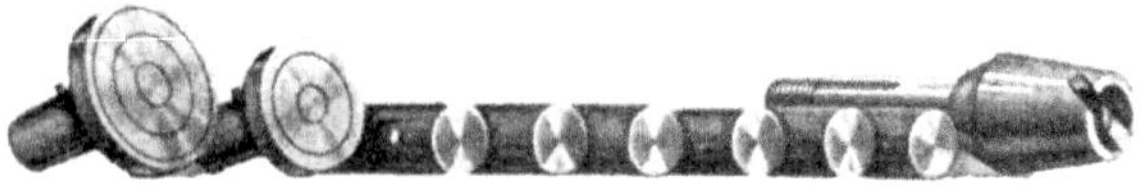

Fig. 138 – Wax Chucks

Warm the cover a little—now hold the flame under the chuck, and when the shellac is soft enough, press the barrel cover on to it. Bring the T-rest broad side round facing the work, and whilst the shellac is still soft, spin the cover true with a piece of peg wood held on the T-rest. Continue to spin until the shellac has set. It is sometimes better to turn with the graver by hand rather than to use the slide rest, especially if the cover is thin. The hand tool can be made to follow the work, where the slide rest would remain rigid and maybe take more metal than required and ruin the cover. It is advisable to use as thin a layer of shellac as possible, and to press the article hard against the chuck. This ensures a uniform thickness when the part being turned is finished.

In such circumstances the discretion of the watchmaker must be exercised.

Wax chucks are very useful for many kinds of work such as holding pieces when setting a jewel hole, holding keyless wheels when snailing, when finishing brass train wheels with a circular grain, etc.

These chucks can be purchased in all sizes, and the watchmaker is well advised to equip himself with a good supply.

Should the cover be quite substantial and it is decided to use the slide rest, proceed as follows.

Slide Rest

Figs. 139 and 140 show respectively a slide rest and cutters useful for watch work. The principal point to observe when making a cutter is to see that there is clearance on the underside. Generally speaking, cutters may be flat on top; if, however, one is required to make deep cuts—rarely needed by the watchmaker—it must be given rake to allow it to dig into the metal and wedge it off as it were. In other words, the acting part of the cutter should be thinner than for ordinary use, and to achieve this a recess must be filed on the top of the cutter about 1/4 in. back from the cutting edge. This will have the effect of turning up the cutting edge and so make the tool work more easily than if a flat top cutter were used.

Fig. 139 – Slide Rest

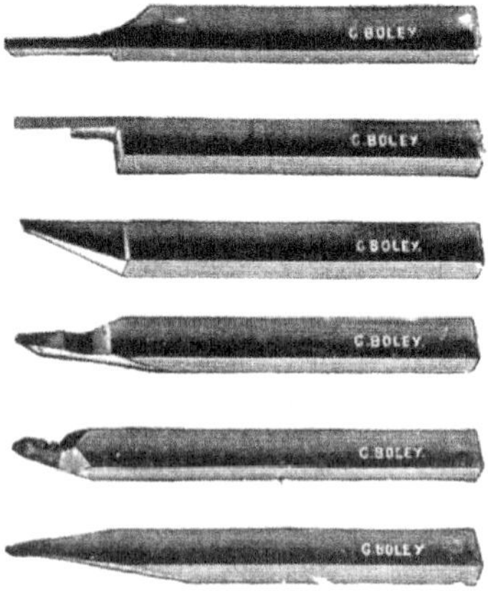

Fig. 140 – Slide Rest Cutters

Fig. 141 (*a*) and (*b*) illustrates the two types.

(*a*) Flat topped. (*b*) With rake

Fig. 141 – Cutters

The cutter must be adjusted to the height of the center of the work, and, if necessary, this can be achieved by packing with pieces of metal under the cutter before screwing down.

The cutting part of the cutter should project as little as possible from its fixing to prevent spring and subsequent chattering.

When cutting brass, a good speed should be given to the work. Steel requires a much slower speed to work well.

When turning out the barrel cover, it is better to use a tool with a finely-whetted edge, or even to polish it so that the cut surface will need no further finishing. For this purpose, the cutter of Fig. 140, marked (*a*), is placed in the slide rest so that the flat end part is presented to the work for about a quarter of its length from the point.

First cut the outer part and work on the half of the cover farthest from you. Operate the slide as far as possible towards you; then withdraw the cutter away from the work and bring it past the center and commence to cut the other half, starting from the center this time, and work the cutter towards you. It will be observed that the point of the cutter has been *drawn* across the surface of the work. Had we used the cutter with the point first there would have been a risk of digging too deep and ruining the surfaces.

If we were turning a plain disc with no projection in the center the cutter could have been brought quite across to the center.

In watch work it is not necessary, as a rule, to use any lubrication on the cutter. For work where the cutter is in use for long periods, some liquid must be used to keep the cutter cool.

The Roller Rest

In order to explain better the applications of some of the other accessories, we will proceed to finish the barrel arbor just roughed out.

Assuming the arbor is almost finished as regards size of pivots and heights, etc., and that the upper pivot needs to be squared, secure the arbor in the lathe and fix the head-stock by means of the index in one of the quarter holes to be found on the side of the head-stock pulley provided especially for this purpose—a dividing plate in miniature. Now place the roller rest (Fig. 142) in position and bring it to a height so that the top of the roller is a little above the center of the arbor.

It is advisable to file the square to a very slight taper. To effect this, pack the shoe of the roller rest on one side, nearest the head-stock, with two or three thicknesses of tissue paper; or slip in a piece of note-paper. This will slightly tilt the roller rest and give the desired result.

With a fine flat file carefully file a segment of the arbor away, but not the full amount ultimately required.

Move the head-stock round a quarter of a turn and fix with the index pin as before, now file again a similar amount and continue until four flats have been filed. This should leave four rounded corners of equal dimensions. Repeat the process until the four corners are sharp and a perfect square is the result. In this manner we can be sure not to remove too much metal and so make the square so small that the whole arbor would be useless.

Fig. 142 – Roller Rest

At the same time this simple system ensures that the square is a perfect square, since if more is filed off one side than another the contour of the round corners would differ.

Try the ratchet wheel on now. The square may need a little further reducing for it to fit, remembering that it has yet to be polished, i.e. left grey from the oilstone dust and oil.

It is always advisable to use the roller rest for jobs like this. The file will not injure it, and the surface of the T-rest is kept free from notches which the file would make on it were it used.

Sometimes when using the T-rest for turning we

may wish to run the graver along, and it is very inconvenient to find that the graver jumps and jolts because of the uneven surface of the top of the rest. These rests are not left hard by the manufacturer, because it would be difficult to hold a graver steadily on such a surface. The graver digs very slightly into the rest and in this manner it can be held firmly in one position without undue exertion; in fact one need hardly be conscious of using any pressure on the graver to keep it steady.

Another roller rest (Fig. 143) with two rollers can be used for this purpose. In this case, the file is held firmly on the two rollers only. The method is this. Place the file on the two rollers firmly and then lower the rollers by means of the knurled nut until the file comes into contact with the work. At this point, lower the rollers still a little more; it is this last movement which determines the amount of metal to be removed. It will be noticed that the file has left the roller nearest the work and is now resting on the work and the roller nearest the operator, so that if we proceed to file, holding the file firmly on the last-mentioned roller, we shall only be able to reduce the metal until the file meets the other roller, and the amount of metal so removed is controlled. If the rest is not altered and the other three sides are presented as mentioned previously, a perfect square will result.

If the ratchet is held in position by a screw cap, proceed to turn away as much of the square as is not required for the ratchet, and tap the remaining piece for the cap. If a screw only is used for the ratchet, cut the square so that it is just below the surface of the wheel. The screw will then have the effect of drawing the wheel close to its seating.

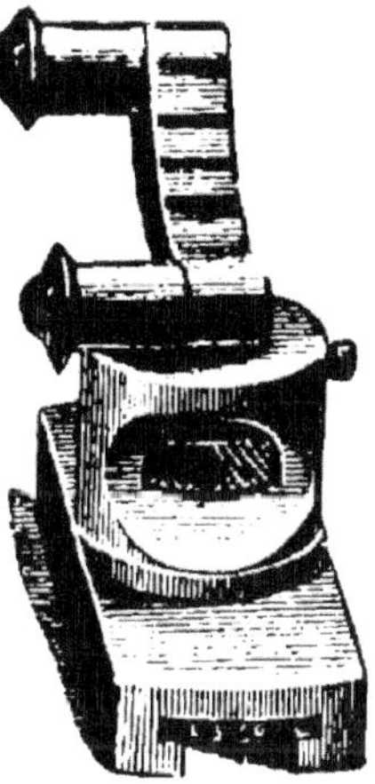

Fig. 143 – Double Roller Rest

Drilling

To drill for the screw, bring the tail-stock into position and fit to it the drilling accessories (Fig. 144). Select a drill of the correct size. (Two sizes in the screw plate *smaller* than the tap to be used for cutting the thread ensures a full thread with the minimum amount of waste cutting.) Then find a hole in the disc into which the drill just passes and make this central with the aid of the centering rod, as illustrated.

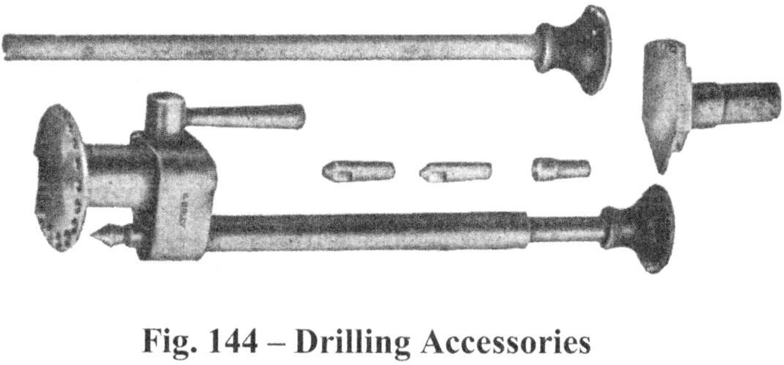

Fig. 144 – Drilling Accessories

Make the disc secure by tightening the lever. Now bring the tail-stock up to the arbor and fit the end to be drilled up to the cone-shaped hole, replace the centering piece with the drill-stock, and proceed to drill the hole. In these circumstances, drill to double the depth required. To tap the hole, do not remove the arbor from the lathe; remove the tail-stock and bring the T-rest to the work so that it faces the hole; secure the tap in the pin tongs, hold the head-stock with the left hand and, with the tap in the right, work the head-stock backwards and forwards and at the same time turn the tap a little in the opposite directions. Before tapping, make sure that the hole is free of pieces of metal that may have been left there after drilling. Apply oil during the cutting of the thread, and work very slowly. In this manner a clean thread can be cut with safety. The T-rest forms a steadying piece for the hand. If we were making a large arbor the cone plate could be dispensed with and just a point made with the centering rod to start the drill; this being replaced by the drill-stock as before.

The Milling Tool

We now proceed to cut the hook for the mainspring. The milling tool (Fig. 145) can be used. The lathe here illustrated is fitted up for wheel cutting; but for our present purpose the dividing plate will be required. Secure the arbor in the split chuck and fix the head by the index. Fix a small circular cutter in the milling tool and cut an incision on each side of the arbor as at (*a*) Fig. 146, then remove the arbor from the chuck and with a parallel file, cut as at (*b*) Fig. 146. Finally, trim the rest of the body of the arbor as at (*c*) Fig. 146.

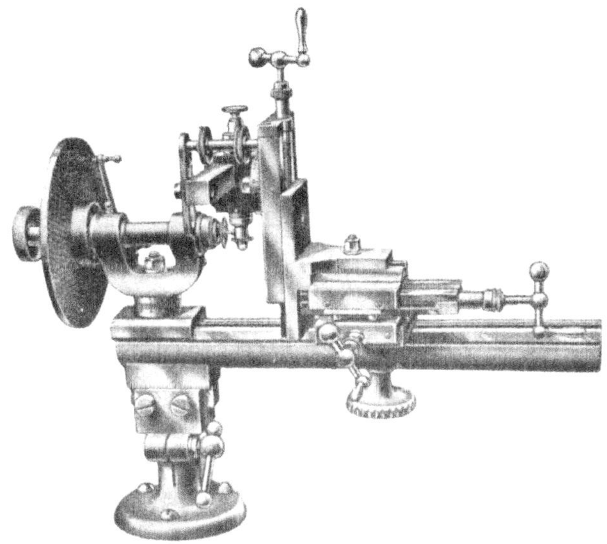

Fig. 145 – Fit-Up for Milling or Wheel Cutting

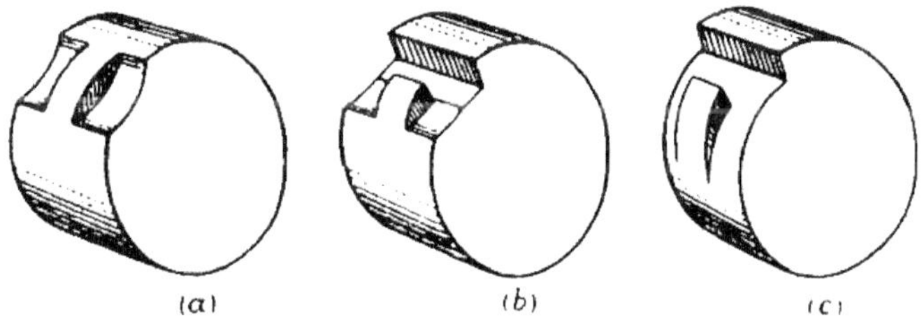

Fig. 146 – Stages in Making a Barrel Arbor

The sharp edge opposite the hook (*c*) could, with advantage, be rounded into a gentle slope. This would facilitate the removal of the arbor when the mainspring is in position, and help the eye on to the hook when replacing.

The depth the first cut made is determined by the thickness of the mainspring. The finished hook should project from the arbor a height equal to the thickness of the spring. Harden and temper the arbor, when we are ready to finish by polishing.

For this particular job the ordinary head-stock could also have been used, using the holes on the side of the pulley for the index pin but using the milling attachment as illustrated.

Polishing With the Lap

The barrel arbor is again placed in the split chuck in the lathe. Fit the polishing accessories up as Fig. 147. Two or three laps are supplied, and others can be made as required.

Fig. 147 – Fit-Up for Polishing with Lap

First of all use the iron polisher charged with oilstone dust and oil and polish the pivots which are to work in the barrel itself and also those working in the plates. This part is carried out with the hand polisher.

If, however, it is required to make many such arbors the pivots can be polished with a lap. The large shoulders can, with a little practice, be polished with the hand polisher; but, for those who prefer this method, the shoulders can be polished with the lap.

Before finishing the pivots with the diamantine, polish the shoulders with the lap. Use the iron one charged with oilstone dust. Make the tail-stock a fixture, but leave the runner with the polishing attachment free. Revolve the head-stock fairly quickly, and as the pulley on the polisher is smaller than that on the head-stock, the polisher will revolve quicker than the head-stock and so break up the grain thus avoiding circles. Bring the lap on to the shoulder and apply a gentle pressure to the runner and grind the shoulder until all turning marks are removed. Repeat on the next shoulder, and then polish the pivots with the iron polisher charged with diamantine by hand until a black polish is obtained.

Replace the oilstone dust lap with the bell metal one charged with diamantine, and proceed to polish the shoulders. Finally, with the graver finely whetted, reduce the body of the arbor a little so that the shoulder working inside the barrel is less than the full diameter of the body of the arbor. Give it also a very slight slope: not only does this achieve the object of keeping the oil at the pivots, but it also gives the work a clean sharp appearance. The arbor can now be reversed and the other half treated in the same way.

Incidentally there are many uses to which the laps can be put, and the milling tool (Fig. 145) is very useful to hold the laps when required for polishing angles, such as back slopes of balance staffs, bevels on keyless wheels, etc.; items too numerous to mention here.

The laps for the process just described are best bell-shaped, and the edge only is used. It is essential that this edge and the outside near the edge should be dead true, and they should be occasionally turned in the lathe to achieve this object.

Screw the lap in the chuck (Fig. 148) and turn the edge and the outside true. After removing from the lathe, roughen the edge with a line file, using a fairly long one for this purpose, so that it will reach across two edges at once. The object of the filing is to ensure that the metal shall retain the polishing medium.

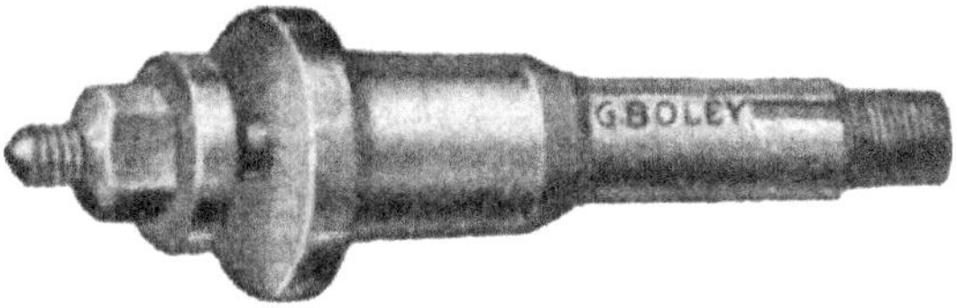

Fig. 148 – Chuck for Holding Lap

The necessity for this bell-shaped lap will be appreciated when polishing the shoulders near the arbor. The acme of perfection is for the square shoulders to meet the arbor at 90°, and the corners to be perfectly clean and sharp, without roundness; and this would not be possible with a lap out of truth or with a blunt edge.

It now only remains for the square to be cleaned up and the end of the pivot polished; and the barrel arbor is finished.

The square is polished in much the same manner as when filing it, only an iron polisher charged with oilstone dust and oil is used in place of the file. It will not be necessary to finish the square farther than the oilstone dust process.

Although the foregoing deals with a barrel arbor, it will be seen that other pieces can be polished in a similar manner. It is only a question of holding the article to be polished, and using the correct shaped laps at the right angle, and in this respect there is no hard and fast rule. It must be left to the ingenuity of the watchmaker.

Snailing

In one of the Swiss factories, keyless wheels—ratchet and transmission—are snailed and polished individually. The wheel is secured to a wax chuck, and a lap charged with oilstone dust and oil is brought on to the wheel and made to operate on half the wheel only. The lap revolves quickly and the wheel slowly and pressure is brought to bear on the apparatus carrying the lap to make contact. The sizes of the laps are about twice those of the wheels being snailed. This process gives a beautiful finish; and finally the bevels are polished with a lap charged with diamantine set at an angle.

The laps used by the Swiss factories vary. Some factories use iron for oilstone dust and oil and also for diamantine, while others use iron, bell metal, and zinc. There seems to be no set rule in this respect—it is a matter of what suits the individual best.

Another method is to use a copper lap; a worn penny answers well. The penny is mounted as the ordinary lap, and the surface is impregnated with diamond powder. The powder is lightly hammered into the surface with a round-faced steel hammer, and the lap is used with either oil or water. Once made, it will last for some time without re-dressing.

Wheel Cutting

We know that theory cannot always be carried out in practice, and this is brought home very forcibly when dealing with wheels and pinions, especially with watches, and their size is largely responsible.

We will assume that it is required to replace a fourth wheel which has been lost. The question of size immediately arises. The number of teeth can be calculated, and the size could be determined on paper, but unfortunately wheels and pinions are not always correctly proportioned, even in the watches produced by some of the best and largest Swiss factories, and so even if we deduce the size of the wheel from the escape pinion it may not be correct.

Therefore a more definite result can be arrived at in the following manner. With sharp-pointed dividers take the distance between the centers of the fourth and escape wheel holes and mark this on a piece of metal. Take the diameter of the escape pinion at the widest point with the vernier gauge and mark on the inside of the two marks we have just made a distance equal to half the diameter of the escape pinion. We now have the radius of the new fourth wheel less the amount of intersection with the pinion. We must estimate this extra for depth, double the final measurement, and we have the diameter of the wheel. If we were replanting the new fourth wheel, the sector would give us the size of the blank, as the scoring with the aid of the depth tool *after* the wheel is cut would ensure a correct depth.

It is better to adopt this very practical method, therefore, and to make sure that when the wheel has been cut our time has not been wasted. It is better to have the blank a little large than too small, because the final depth can be rectified with the topping or rounding-up tool. Now cross the blank out to match the other wheels, leaving the final crossing until after the teeth have been cut, and mount it on to its pinion before cutting the teeth, this ensures perfect truth when finished.

There are two systems of wheel-cutting tools (Figs. 145 and 149) here illustrated. In Fig. 149 the cutter is held in the lathe and the wheel in the attachment, and in Fig. 145 the cutter is held in the attachment and the wheel in the lathe. In this latter instance we select a chuck to hold the pinion and secure it in the lathe. Hold the head-stock with the index pin in the dividing plate. Select a cutter: the size can be determined as follows. (Here again, theoretically, the size of the teeth should be determined by drawing on paper as explained elsewhere in this book, but in practice when dealing with one wheel it is not necessary or advisable.)

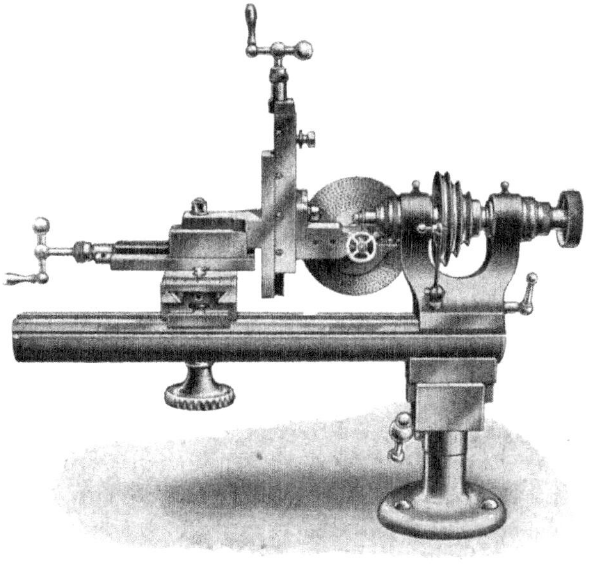

Fig. 149 – Fit-Up for Wheel Cutting

Take a piece of brass wire, flatten the end with the

hammer on a stake, make the end truly square with a file, then file parallel until it fits tightly between two leaves of the escape pinion. Finally reduce with the Arkansas slip until the wire has the amount of shake required by a tooth of the fourth wheel. Virtually we have made one tooth as regards thickness. Invariably the thickness of a tooth equals the space, so if the thickness of this single tooth is taken with a gauge and a cutter selected of the same thickness, we shall not be far wrong. Even if our fourth wheel proves to be a little out and the teeth were not equal to the spaces, the matter can be adjusted in the rounding-up tool. Incidentally, rounding-up tools are used in the Swiss factories where such instruments as the profile projector are used with the object of perfecting their tool-making department.

Now place the cutter in the tool. Make sure it is the right way round—i.e. that the cutting (wide) edge meets the metal first. It is *essential* that the cutter should be dead central with the center of the wheel, otherwise we shall have teeth cut out of upright, all slanting one way. If the wheel is to have, say, 84 teeth, place the index pin in a hole in the 84 circle of the dividing plate. Very carefully cut the first space, adjusting the depth the cutter goes into the wheel by means of the handle of the slide. See that the full cut is made and that the whole of the addendum has been formed—when we need not touch this handle again. Operate the handle at the end farthest from the head-stock, forwards, and then withdraw back again, leaving the wheel quite free; this ensures the space being fully cut. Lift the index pin out of the dividing plate and move it round one hole and refix. Now proceed to cut the next space by operating the handle last referred to on the slide and repeat in this manner until all 84 teeth are cut.

The cutter must be made to rotate anti-clockwise;

the cut will then be made towards the head-stock and there is not the possibility of buckling the wheel. Should the wheel be so thin that it will not stand up to the cutter, make a brass collar about two or three times the thickness of the wheel itself and round about the same in diameter. Open the hole in it so that the pinion will fit nicely and then, when placing the wheel in position in the split chuck, secure the collar by the wheel, pressing against it and the chuck and then tighten the hollow runner. The collar then supports the wheel and, when forming the teeth, this collar may be cut as well, but that does not matter, as the wheel will have had the support required.

It is advisable after cutting the first tooth to examine it well with an eyeglass to ensure all is in order, rather than to cut all the teeth and then find the cut has not been deep enough or otherwise.

For cutting a brass wheel the cutter must revolve very quickly.

The dividing plates are made with a series of holes allowing counts of, say, 48 up to 360 teeth, and, of course, divisions of the numbers can be taken for other counts. Thus with the 100 circle, if the index pin is placed in alternate holes we should get a wheel of 50 teeth; or if it is placed in every fourth hole, 25 teeth, and so on.

It now only remains to remove the wheel from the tool, and stone it, etc., to remove the burrs thrown up.

The fit up of Fig. 149 is the same in principle as Fig. 145, except that, as already mentioned, the cutter is held in the headstock.

It will be seen that the cutter can be used at almost any angle, which is useful for such purposes as cutting teeth of keyless wheels, the ratchet teeth of the crown and castle wheels, etc. The principle of cutting is the same as I have described, and here again the ingenuity of the watchmaker must be exercised both as regards the method of fixing the wheel and the shape of the cutter.

Fig. 150 – Dividing Plate Device Which Could Be Adapted to the Watchmaker's Lathe

A Useful Dividing Plate System

Engineers use a dividing plate in conjunction with geared wheels for cutting wheel teeth. I have seen a clever device which the watchmaker could fit to his lathe. It consists of a frame with a single worm pivoted in it, and to the extended arbor of the worm a small dividing plate is fitted. This plate has five circles of holes drilled with 7, 8, 9, 10, and 11 holes. Where the hollow runner fits in the head-stock of the lathe, provision is made for a wheel to fit friction-tight and keyed to prevent slipping. The frame is so arranged that this worm wheel gears into the worm. There are two worm wheels which can be used, one of 70 and the other 72 teeth. See Fig. 150.

With a 72 worm wheel, if we wish to cut a wheel having 72 teeth, we must rotate the worm—and with it the dividing plate—one revolution, which will rotate the worm wheel one tooth. For convenience of reckoning, let us make a fraction with numerator equal to the number of teeth of the worm wheel and denominator equal to the teeth of the wheel to be cut; so that instead of one revolution of the dividing plate, let us call it 72/72.

To cut 144 teeth, the dividing plate must be rotated half a turn and again the fraction 72/144 corresponds to this half turn. To cut 36 teeth, the plate must be rotated two turns, or 72/36.

Thus for 45 teeth, we make the fraction 72/45 which means that the plate must be rotated 72/45 turns and if we had a circle with 45 holes on our dividing plate we should count 72 of them between each cut. But we have no such circle of holes; we therefore convert the fraction into one which has a denominator equal to the number of holes in one of the circles—thus 72/45 = 8/5. Again we have no circle with 5 holes but we have one with 10, so we convert 8/5 to 16/10; we then count 16 holes on the 10 circle or one complete revolution plus 6 holes, for each cut.

Further Examples

49 teeth wanted—70/49 = 10/7 = 10 holes of the 7 circle or one complete revolution plus 3 holes.

84 teeth wanted—72/84 = 12/14 = 6/7 = 6 holes of the 7 circle.

50 teeth wanted—70/50 = 7/5 = 14/10 = 14 holes of the 10 circle or one complete revolution plus 4 holes.

When using a device such as this, provision must be made for backlash of the gears. The system I saw was primitive but most effective. Fixed to the chuck holding the wheel being cut is a cord, and this cord has a weight attached at its end, the cord is wound round the chuck at least once, and this has the effect of straining the chuck in one direction with a constant force, thus taking up any backlash or freedom there may be.

Fly Cutters

Sometimes the "fly" cutter will be used. These cutters have one tooth only and are quite simple to make. Extra speed must be used when employing this type of cutter to ensure a clean smooth cut. When making cutters, always use round steel wire of uniform thickness so that all can be used in the same carrier.

The illustration (Fig. 151) shows this carrier. The cutters are held in position by means of the grub screw. Needless to say they must fit very tightly, even before the grub screw is tightened. The diameter of the carrier should be a little less than that of a bought cutter, and the acting part of the fly cutter should not project from the carrier more than necessary for the carrier to free the teeth of the wheel; otherwise there may be trouble from springing and subsequent chattering.

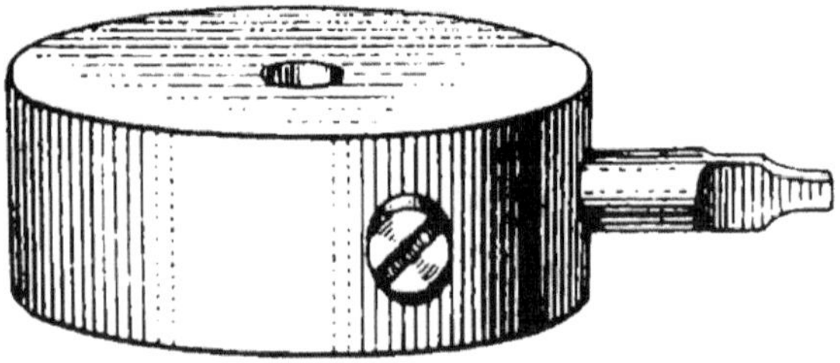

Fig. 151 – Fly Cutter and Carrier

The projecting portion of the cutter is filed as required and then hardened and tempered, and finally whetted with a fine stone. If, for instance, we want to cut a ratchet wheel, the type with cycloidal teeth, the cutter must be filed so that it just fits the space on the old wheel, if this is available, or of the transmission wheel if the ratchet is lost. Make sure clearance is left at the back of the cutter as was mentioned when dealing with the slide rest cutter. When the teeth to be cut are equal on both sides of the center, the cutter can be made by turning the steel wire in the split chuck in the lathe and turned with the graver to shape and the flats filed afterwards. The uses to which the fly cutter is adaptable are almost without limit.

Rounding-Up or Topping Tool

I mentioned that the final adjustments to our fourth wheel could be made in the rounding-up tool (Fig. 152) if necessary, and we will assume, as we anticipated, it is a little too deep.

If it were shallow, the wheel would have to be stretched and then passed through the rounding-up tool. To ascertain the depth it is better to place the wheel and pinion in the depth tool first, adjust the tool until a good depth is made, and then with the pointed runners see how this compares with the distance apart of the holes of the fourth wheel and escape wheel.

If the depth appears to be correct, place the wheel and pinion in position in the frame and try again. Should the depth be much too great, and we had tried the fourth wheel and escape wheel in the frames first, there would have been a risk of breaking an escape pivot, because there would have been undue strain to get the pivots into their holes and the escape pivot being the weaker one is almost sure to break. In any case, the wheel is too large and we proceed to reduce it as follows.

Fig. 152 – Rounding-Up or Topping Tool Fit-Up

Select a cutter (Fig. 153) that is the same thickness as the distance between two teeth; in other words, the cutter should just fit in a space. Now place the cutter selected in position. Here again the same great care must be given to ensure that the cutter is correctly aligned with the wheel both as regards the cutter being in line with the center of the wheel, and the wheel in line with the center of the cutter as regards height. Open the guide of the cutter to engage the succeeding tooth, and see that it brings the space central before the full cutting part of the cutter comes into action.

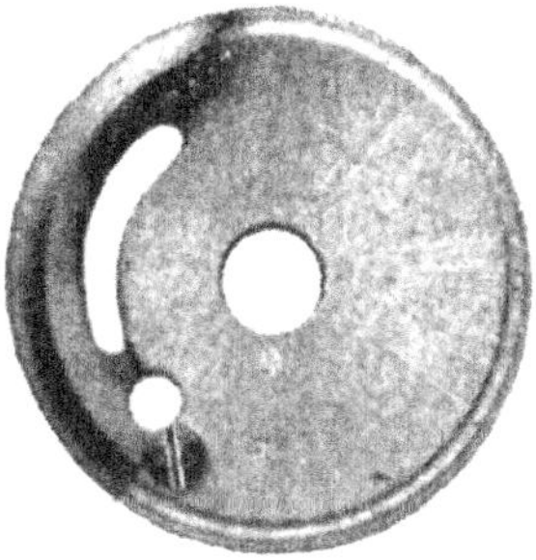

Fig. 153 – Topping Tool Cutter

Now place the wheel and pinion between the centers of the attachment: these runners are so arranged that the wheel is bound fairly tightly. We are now ready to reduce the wheel in diameter. Gradually adjust the attachment by means of the slide until a cut has been made from the bottom of a space, and proceed to cut the whole wheel.

A word here as regards the wheel will not be out of place. After cutting the new wheel, in the first place burrs will be thrown up, as already mentioned, and if these burrs during removal are partially thrown inwards, the guide will cause the wheel to rotate too far, which will result in the next tooth being cut thinner. Therefore it is of vital importance that all burrs be removed, and this is done with the wire or glass scratch brush. Remove the wheel and try the depth, and always remember that it is better to make several cuts and be successful than one cut too deep and have it a failure. On the other hand, should the teeth be too thick, by using a cutter a shade larger and adjust to enter the wheel to the bottom of a space only.

To Round Up a Thick Wheel

If it is required to pass a thick wheel such as a

barrel through the rounding-up tool, it may be necessary to make three cuts to ensure that the full thickness of the wheel has been cut.

For example, set the barrel up in the usual manner with the center of the cutter on a line with the center of the barrel teeth; cut all the teeth as required, then lower the barrel and cut again. Now raise the barrel above the first cut made and cut again.

In this manner the whole thickness of the teeth will have been cut. To avoid this cutting three times either a very large cutter would have to be used, or the whole rounding-up accessory fitted to a slide and actuated in much the same manner as when cutting wheels, as Fig. 154.

The Mandrel

The mandrel plate here illustrated (Fig. 155) is an accessory familiar as a separate tool. These attachments can be purchased to use in an existing head-stock (Fig. 156) or a special head-stock (Fig. 155) can be purchased for the mandrel plate only. The use of this accessory need hardly be described here, as it has been dealt with at some length elsewhere in this book.

Pivoting

The pivoting accessories here illustrated (Fig. 157) are used in a similar manner to the ordinary pivoting tool used by hand.

The piece to be pivoted, say a pinion, placed between centers as illustrated. The centering plate (Fig. 158) is made central by means of the centering rod, and this is replaced by the drill-stock and dull. The work is then proceeded with as explained elsewhere.

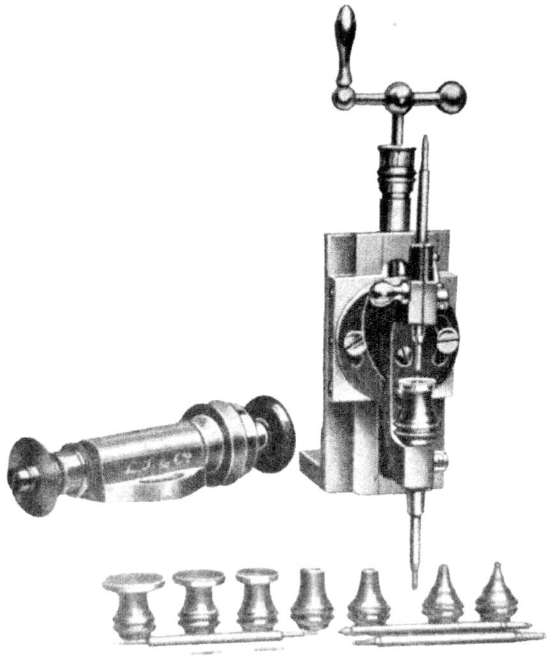

Fig. 154 – Topping or Rounding-Up Tool

Fig. 155

Fig. 156

Fig. 155 – Mandrel Head-Stock
Fig. 156 – Mandrel Accessory

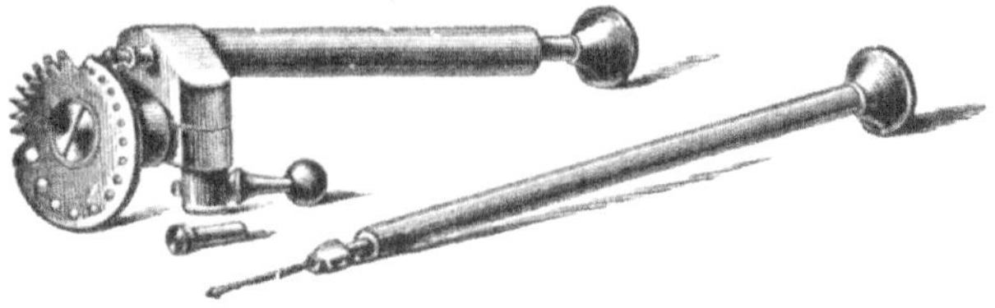

Fig. 157 – Pivoting Accessories

Fig. 158 – Fit-Up for Pivoting

Turning Between Centers

There is a diversity of opinion with respect to using the lathe for turning a balance staff, etc. I propose, therefore, to describe one or two methods using the lathe.

In the Swiss factories automatic lathes are used, and briefly this is the procedure: A piece of steel wire is fed through the head-stock. The end of this steel wire is cone-shaped and the rod is pushed through until it reaches the female runner in the tail-stock. The chuck then closes and grips the rod. Various cutters now come into operation forming the arbors, balance seating, etc., and the pivots. When these cutters have reached the end of their journey, another cutter, V-shaped, comes forward near the chuck and cuts the balance staff off, and the staff drops into a box underneath. All the cutters now recede, the chuck opens, and the wire is pushed forward for another staff to be made; and so it goes on, all automatic. Here, it will be seen, the staff has been virtually turned between centers. The pivots are polished in a jacot tool afterwards.

It is claimed by some authorities that a staff can be turned true, using the split chuck, and this is the procedure.

Use a split chuck of the *correct size* with the wire projecting from the chuck the least possible amount. Now turn the arbor for the roller, and afterwards the lower pivot and the back slope for the balance, using the tail-stock if necessary. Remove the partly made staff and select another split chuck to take the roller arbor, again of the *correct* size. Do not tighten the chuck yet, but make the head revolve, hold the projecting piece with the tip of the forefinger and, whilst still spinning, tighten the chuck. Proceed now to turn the remaining part of the staff. It is claimed that a perfectly true staff results. Obviously the lathe and the chucks must be in perfect condition to ensure this.

Another method is to use a wax chuck (Fig. 159). These chucks are quite simple to make. Turn a cone-shaped sink in the end of a piece of brass wire held in a split chuck, taking care to see there is no pip at the bottom of the cone, and also that the wax chuck is not loosened or removed from the split chuck once made.

Fill the cone with shellac, and, whilst the shellac is

warm, place a piece of steel wire into it a little longer than the finished length of the staff, hold the end with the tip of the forefinger and spin true until the shellac sets.

Now proceed to turn one end of the staff, including the pivot. Warm the chuck and remove the staff, reverse it, and with the finger as before, press it well into the cone to ensure the pivot has reached the bottom, spin until cool, and we are ready to finish the other half.

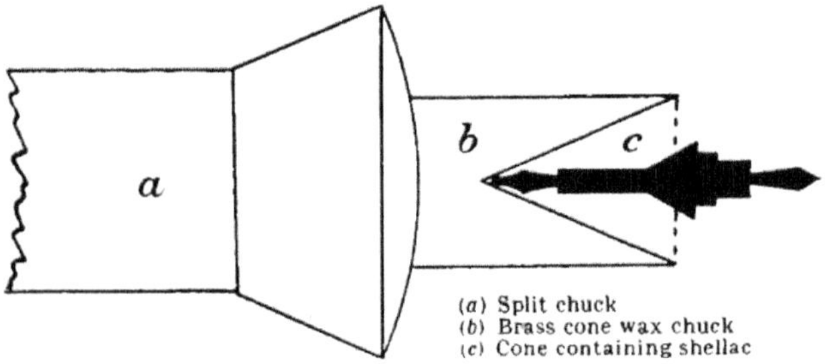

Fig. 159 – Turning a Balance Staff in a Lathe

In this instance we have virtually turned between centers, and our staff should be true.

The wax chuck must be re-turned each time it is used if it has been removed from the split chuck.

The Ideal Method

The other method is to turn between centers, and there can be no doubt that a staff so turned will run perfectly true.

This is the procedure. We have already roughed out a balance staff and left the ends with conical pivots.

Fit the lathe up with a double pulley concentric runner (Fig. 160) and attach to the staff a carrier (Fig. 161). The tail-stock is fitted up with one of the eccentric runners with dots for the conical pivot of the staff to run in. Such a runner enables the work to be brought well forward so that the pivots can be turned. The staff should fit between the centers without end shake, and just a trace of oil must be applied to each pivot.

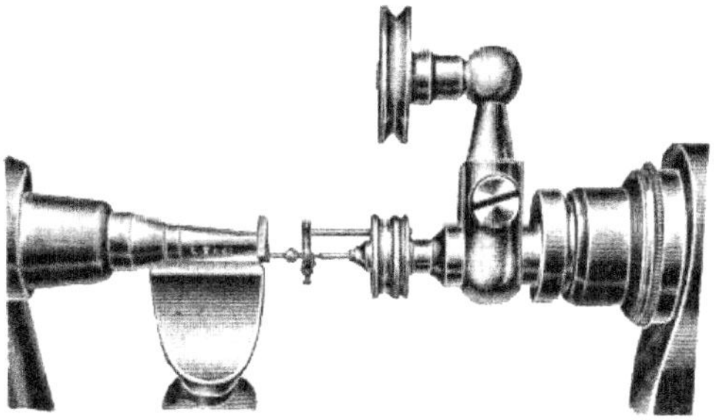

Fig. 160 – Fit-up for Light Turning Between Centers

Fig. 161 – Carriers

The line or belt passes over the top pulley and touches the under one. When starting to turn, the line can press fairly heavily on the under pulley, but as the staff progresses this pressure should be lightened. When turning a fine arbor or pivot, the graver may dig just a little too deep, and if the force used to revolve the staff is considerable there is every possibility of the staff breaking, but if this force is moderate, the pulley rotating the staff will stop, and the line will just slip over the pulley and so save the staff.

In this manner proceed to turn the back slope first, employing the method explained elsewhere when using the turns. Precisely the same method is adopted with the lathe as with the turns when turning the staff between centers, the only difference being in the motive power.

As regards the polishing, the piece should be revolved reasonably quickly to obviate the possibility of rings forming. Move the polisher as quickly as possible backwards and forwards and as much as possible, diagonally to break the grain. When the lathe has been set up for work of this description and it is found necessary to sharpen the conical pivots, a special runner is fitted to the tail-stock and the arbor is laid in the V-shaped hollow runner and the conical pivot re-made with an Arkansas slip. Conical pivots should not be made too long and pointed. An angle of 45° gives quite a good wearing pivot. The bearings should not be on the points, as these would wear too quickly and give rise to end shake of the staff and the risk of the turning becoming oval.

These cone rolling runners save time, as otherwise it would be necessary to fit the staff up in a split chuck to do this job.

Jacot Tool

The jacot tool is another accessory to the lathe with which we are familiar as a separate tool (Fig. 162). There is hardly any necessity to describe its working here. There is one point, however, which should be mentioned and that is that the double safety pulley just described should be used.

Fig. 162 – Jacot Tool Accessory

The Screw-Head Tool

The screw-head tool (Fig. 163) can be used in conjunction with the lathe, it is speedier than the hand tool and in some instances more effective, especially when used for flat work. This tool does not call for much explanation. It is usually supplied with three laps—iron, bell metal, and boxwood—for polishing heads of screws and other pieces dead flat.

Small brass split chucks to hold the thread of the screws—so as not to injure them—are supplied, and these fit into another steel chuck.

In operation the best result is obtained by making the article to be polished revolve more slowly than the polisher, whether it is the lap or hand polisher.

There is a tendency, if the article revolves the quicker, for it to take a circular, smeary, or foxy film. The method recommended cuts the grain of the polishing more, and results in a black grainless polish. This more particularly applies to the flat polishing, using the lap.

Motive Power

Now as regards motive power, there are three systems, hand wheel (Fig. 164), foot wheel (Fig. 165), and electric power (Fig. 166).

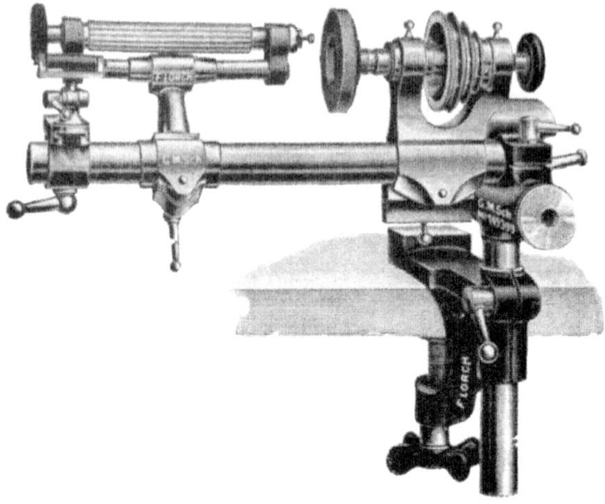

Fig. 163 – Screw-Head Tool Fit-Up

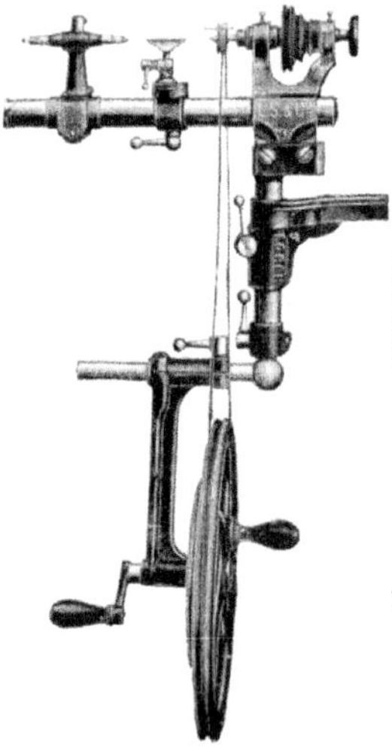

Fig. 164

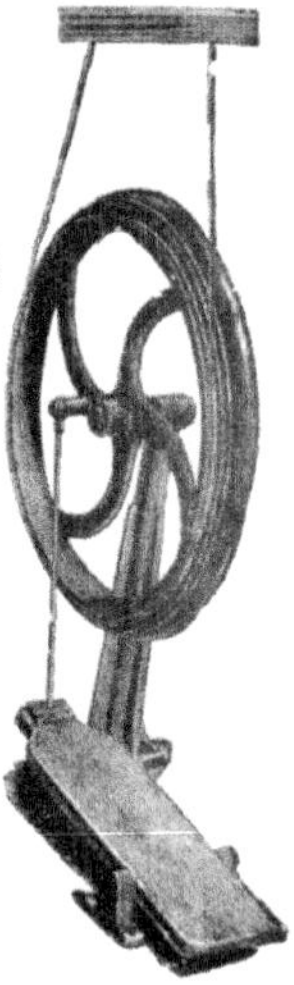

Fig. 165

Fig. 164 – Hand Wheel Fit-Up
Fig. 165 – Foot Wheel

Fig. 166 – Electric Motor Fit-Up

For most work, such as wheel cutting, lapping, etc., where the two hands are required, the hand wheel is unsuitable. The foot wheel has certain advantages over the power inasmuch as the speed can be better controlled. On the other hand, for long and continuous lathe work the power system is to be preferred. Such matters must be decided by the individual to suit his requirements.

In conclusion I will quote Alexander Cumming, 1766—"If I have anywhere misrepresented or omitted anything material, it is not intentionally."

Printed in Great Britain
by Amazon

14575229R00180